Mṛtyu

Concept of Death in Indian Traditions

Reconstructing Indian History & Culture

(ISSN 0971-3824)

1. Society in Ancient India; by Sures Chandra Banerji
2. Political Thought in Ancient India; by G.P. Singh
3. Early Indian Historical Tradition and Archaeology; by G.P. Singh
4. Vasantotsava: The Spring Festivals of India; by Leona M. Anderson
5. Ecological Readings in the Veda; by M. Vannucci
6. Vṛndāvana in Vaiṣṇava Literature; by Maura Corcoran
7. Social History of the Tamils (1707–1947); by P. Subramanian
8. Ancient Indian Coinage; by Rekha Jain
9. Buddhism and Socio-Economic Life of Eastern India; by Bimal Chandra Mohapatra
10. Chandragupta Maurya; by P.L. Bhargava
11. Mṛtyu: Concept of Death in Indian Traditions; by Gian Giuseppe Filippi
12. Yama: The Glorious Lord of the Other World; by Kusum P. Merh
13. Sacred Complex of Ujjain; by D.K. Samanta
14. Vedic View of the Earth; by S.R.N. Murthy
15. Society in the Atharvaveda; by B.S. Kharade
16. Orissan History, Culture and Archaeology; by S. Pradhan
17. Education in Ancient India; by Mitali Chatterjee
18. Surā: The Liquor and the Vedic Sacrifice; by M.B. Kolhatkar
19. Human Ecology in the Vedas; by Marta Vannucci
20. Governance in Ancient India; by Anupa Chandra Pandey
21. The Cultural Glory of Ancient India: A Literary Overview; by Sures Chandra Banerji
22. Kauṭilya's Arthaśāstra in the Light of Modern Science & Technology; by Sunil Sen Sarma
23. History of Jainism: With Special Reference to Mathurā; by V.K. Sharma
25. Ancient Indian Historiography: Sources and Interpretations; by G.P. Singh
26. Republics, Kingdoms, Towns and Cities in Ancient India; by G.P. Singh
27. Facets of Ancient Indian History and Culture: New Perception; by G.P. Singh
28. Kamakhya: A Socio-cultural Study; by Nihar Ranjan Mishra
29. History and Culture of Tamil Nadu as Gleaned from the Sanskrit Inscriptions (vol. 1: up to c. AD 1310); by Chithra Madhavan
30. Lifestyle of the Vedic People; by Pranati Ghosal
31. History and Culture of Tamil Nadu as Gleaned from the Sanskrit Inscriptions (vol. 2: up to c. AD 1310 - c. AD 1885); by Chithra Madhavan
32. Matrimonial Alliances and Ancient Indian Polity (c. 600 BCE to CE 650); by Preeti Prabhat
33. Artisans and Craftsmen of Northern India; by Kuldeep Singh Thind
34. The Evolution of Historiographical Tradition in Ancient and Medieval India; by G.P. Singh
35. Warfare in Ancient India: Theory and Practice; by Soma Basu
36. Sanskrit Education and Literature in Ancient and Medieval Tamil Nadu; by Chithra Madhavan
37. Rājadharma in Mahābhārata; by Priyanka Pandey
38. Interstate Relations in Northern India – Circa 800–1200 CE; by Shiva Gopal Bajpai

Reconstructing Indian History & Culture, no. 11

Mṛtyu

Concept of Death in Indian Traditions

— Transformation of the Body and Funeral Rites —

by

Gian Giuseppe Filippi

Translated by

Antonio Rigopoulos

DK PRINTWORLD

Publishers of Indian Traditions

Cataloging in Publication Data — DK

[Courtesy: D.K. Agencies (P) Ltd. <docinfo@dkagencies.com>]

Filippi, Gian Giuseppe, 1947- **author.**
[Il mistero della morte nell'India tradizionale. English]
Mṛtyu = Concept of death in Indian traditions : transformation of the body and funeral rites / by Gian Giuseppe Filippi ; translated by Antonio Rigopoulos.
pages cm. – (Reconstructing Indian history & culture ; no. 11)
Translated from Italian.
Translation of: Il mistero della morte nell'India tradizionale.
"Second revised edition published in 2005" – Title page verso.
Includes bibliographical references and index.
ISBN 9788124600726 (HB)
ISBN 9788124603321 (PB)

1. Death – Religious aspects – Hinduism. 2. Hindu funeral rites and ceremonies – India. I. Rigopoulos, Antonio, 1962- translator. II. Title. III. Title: Concept of death in Indian traditions. IV. Series: Reconstructing Indian history & culture ; no. 11.

LCC BL1214.72.F55 2024 | DDC 294.523 23

ISBN: 978-81-246-0072-6 (HB)
ISBN: 978-81-246-0332-1 (PB)
English translation, first published in 1996
Second revised edition published in 2005
Reprinted in 2024

Printed and published by:
D.K. Printworld (P) Ltd.
Regd. Office: "Vedaśrī", F-395, Sudarshan Park
ESI Hospital Metro Station, New Delhi – 110015
Phones: (011) 4172 2626, 98713 94815
e-mail: indology@dkprintworld.com
Website: www.dkprintworld.com

Preface

THIS study is the result of many years of research in India and Europe, in universities, museums, academies, libraries, and public and private foundations. Setting aside the impersonal, objective tone which a scientific work requires, I wish to express my gratitude to all those *saṁnyāsins*, brāhmaṇas, relatives of dead and dying persons, *ḍoms*, and to all those living around cremation grounds, whom we cannot of course mention by name. They all revealed a complex network of sentiments, beliefs, scriptural references, customs, hopes, ritual practices, and so on. They shared their intimate thoughts and feelings with great generosity, just veiled by modesty. Even the most humble, manifested great intellectual curiosity in discussing their ideas on the 'great adventure' of death. My gratitude and respect are towards all of those people who have led me to an unpretentious, sympathetic tone of exposition. This does not mean that the scholarly content of the research has not been kept under rigorous control. All sentimental contaminations, sometimes infecting scientific studies, have been avoided.

My reverent thoughts go to all those personalities of Indological studies and of the Indian cultural tradition whom it is my pleasant duty to mention here: first of all, Dr. Kapila Vatsyayan, heart and mind of the Indira Gandhi National Centre for the Arts, where, in the Delhi branch, I passed the 1992-93 academic year as visiting Professor. In my memory her personality is associated with that of the serene and erudite

Dr. Bettina Bäumer, responsible for the scientific activities of the IGNCA of Varanasi, who was always ready to offer intellectual and practical advice to all wandering Indologists in the most sublime city of the world. I am obliged to Dr. M.C. Joshi, once Director General of the Archaeological Survey of India, for generously granting me various permits and advice. Dr. R.C. Sharma, former Director General, National Museum, New Delhi and Vice-Chancellor of the Delhi University Institute, has also been extremely helpful. Dr. R.C. Sharma and my friend Prof. Pant of the same University, have kindly furnished me with research material. In the same Institute, Prof. S.P. Gupta, eminent archaeologist and generous friend, was of great help when he was the Director of the Allahabad Museum. I wish to express my appreciation to Prof. Prem Shankar of the University of Sagar, a true master who indicated the literary themes underlying my research. Moreover, it is my pleasure to extend my thanks to Pandit Prof. Satya Vrat Shastri of the Delhi University, a true spiritual guide in this tormented field of studies, as well as to Prof. Romano Lazzeroni, illustrious scholar of Indo-European studies at the University of Pisa, who furnished me with copies of texts and manuscripts which are nowadays very difficult to find. My gratitude goes to the knowledgeable Prof. M.A. Dhaky, Scientific Director of the American Institute of Indian Studies Ramnagar, at whose Library my research took definite shape, and also to the invaluable equipe of the Banaras Hindu University, composed of Profs. Kamal Giri, Maruti Nandan Tiwari and Das Gupta. In Varanasi, I have benefited from the profound insights of H.H. Dr. Vibhuti Narain Singh, Maharaja of Ramnagar and an important spiritual figure. Prof. Romano Mastromattei of the University of Perugia and President of the Inter-university Centre for the Research on Euro-Asiatic Shamanism, is also the recipient of my gratitude for the most helpful observations which he shared with me on the experience of death. In this regard, a profound thanks goes to H.H. Bhavani Singh Parmar, the ascetic Maharaja of Khajuraho and Chattarpur, a sincere friend who opened his heart to me, presenting his intimate feelings concerning the experience of death. I also wish to mention Prof. Carlo Della Casa of the University of Milan and former President of the Italy-India Association of the University of Venice, the only Italian who has dealt with this subject in the past. Good friend, Prof. Giuliano Boccali of the University of Venice, encouraged me throughout my research. I would also like to remember the honourable Prof. Lokesh Chandra, Dr. Trivedi, Director of the Lucknow Museum, Profs. Geshe Yeshe Thabkhe and Samdhong Rinpoche of the Tibetan Institute of Higher Studies of Sarnath, and H.H. Dr. Karan Singh, eminent and erudite Maharaja of Kashmir, profound knower of Kashmiri Śaivism. I also wish to express humble gratitude to Prof. B.N. Saraswati of the IGNCA, an anthropologist of great fame, who has been a counsellor and a friend, and to Om Prakash Sharma, astonishing keeper of Varanasi's secrets. In the course of my studies, I found strong encouragement from three venerable exponents of Hinduism, who kindly offered me explanations and directions, and shared their experiences with me: Pandit Vaikunthnath Upadhyaya, Pandit Prof. Visvanath Shastri Dattar of Varanasi, and Pandit Dattatreya Shastri of the Śaṁkarācārya *maṭha* of Gayā. A great share of merit for the success of my research in India also goes to the District Magistrate of Varanasi, Mr. R.K. Sinha, who granted me the possibility of taking pictures in places of Varanasi which are usually forbidden, and to Mahapandit Devi Prasad "Jayata" Pandey, a great ritual expert. A heartfelt appreciation goes to my friends Hazari Mull Banthia, K. Rai Mittal and Nikolaj Paklin, whose hospitality, generosity and attention have always encouraged and supported me; besides them I would particularly like to thank my young friend and Indologist Dr. Antonio Rigopoulos, who translated this book in English. Not last among those who have helped me with great dedication and enthusiasm, are my numerous students who, after joining me in India, helped me in all possible ways, being my secretaries, investigators, and cataloguers. I wish everybody could find such devoted disciples!

Finally, I dedicate a special thought to my wife and children who, initially puzzled by the choice of this topic, later followed the unfolding of the project with great passion, constantly stimulating and instigating my thought process. Since it's certainly not the case to dedicate a book on death to any living being, I offer my wife and children all my love.

Venice, April 1, 1996 **Gian Giuseppe Filippi**

Contents

	Preface	v
	Abbreviations	xi
	List of Illustrations	xiii
	Introduction	1
1.	The Human Being (*manuṣya*) and the Other Beings	5
2.	The Nature of Individual Beings	17
3.	The Three Evolutionary Components of Nature	31
4.	Human Life from Conception to Birth	37
5.	Human Life from Birth to Marriage	63
6.	The Structure of the Human Being	79
7.	The End of Bodily Life	99
8.	Agony and its Rites	119
9.	The Last Sacrifice: The Offering of the Body	131
10.	Transformation of the Deceased into Ancestor	149
11.	Funerals without Cremation	171

12. The New Conditions of the Living Soul 183

13. The Journey to the Kingdom of Yama 195

Glossary 209

Bibliography 243

Index 263

Plates 273

Abbreviations

AB	*Aitareya Brāhmaṇa*
AGS	*Āśvalāyana Gṛhya-Sūtra*
AiU	*Aitareya Upaniṣad*
AV	*Atharvaveda*
BG	*Bhagavad-Gītā*
BGŚBh	*Bhagavad-Gītā Śāṁkara Bhāṣya*
BhP	*Bhāgavata Purāṇa*
BPS	*Baudhāyana Pitṛmedha Sūtra*
BṛU	*Bṛhadāraṇyaka Upaniṣad*
BṛUŚBh	*Bṛhadāraṇyaka Upaniṣad Śāṁkara Bhāṣya*
BS	*Brahma Sūtra*
BSOAS	*Bulletin of the School of Oriental and African Studies*
ChU	*Chāndogya Upaniṣad*
ChUŚBh	*Chāndogya Upaniṣad Śāṁkara Bhāṣya*
CS	*Caraka Saṁhitā*
ERE	*Encyclopaedia of Religions and Ethics*
GauḍK	*Gauḍapāda Kārikā*
GP	*Garuḍa Purāṇa*

JAOS	*Journal of American Oriental Society*
JRAS	*Journal of the Royal Asiatic Society*
KU	*Kauṣītakī Upaniṣad*
MāUŚBh	*Māṇḍūkya Upaniṣad Śāṁkara Bhāṣya*
Mbh	*Mahābhārata*
MDhŚ	*Mānava Dharmaśāstra*
MS	*Maitrāyaṇī Saṁhitā*
PB	*Pañcaviṁśa Brāhmaṇa*
PU	*Praśna Upaniṣad*
ṚV	*Ṛgveda*
SGS	*Śaṁkhyāyana Gṛhya-Sūtra*
ŚU	*Śvetāsvatara Upaniṣad*
TA	*Taittirīya Āraṇyaka*
TS	*Taittirīya Saṁhitā*
TU	*Taittirīya Upaniṣad*
TUŚBh	*Taittirīya Upaniṣad Śāṁkara Bhāṣya*
VP	*Viṣṇu Purāṇa*
YV	*Yajurveda*

List of Illustrations

1. Vārāṇasī, Maṇikārṇikā Ghāṭ, one among the five *śmaśāna* of Kāśī.
2. Vārāṇasī, the preparation of the *piṇḍa*s.
3. Vārāṇasī, the eldest son shaves his hair before his father's cremation.
4. Vārāṇasī, the corpse is lifted from the stretcher and put on the pyre.
5. Vārāṇasī, the *piṇḍa*s are offered to the ground *Gnius*.
6. Gayā, collective *piṇḍadāna* on the shore of Phalgu.
7. Vārāṇasī, the eternal fire of the Ḍoms.
8. Vārāṇasī, Ṭiku, an *aghorī*, shows its *kapāla*.

Introduction

YAMA is a diety who inspires dread. In India, talking about him or simply pronouncing his name is avoided even today. Paradoxically, the phenomenon of death doesn't cause a similar fear in the soul of Indians. Accepted with what Westerners would define an attitude of 'fatalism,' it is considered a natural event, a part of life, just like poverty, sickness, and old age. On the contrary, the god of death is the mysterious principle of transformation, not to be taken lightly, especially when the physical and metaphysical laws which he governs are unknown. This is probably one of the reasons why the traditional authors and Indian scholars have carefully avoided a study of Yama and the deities of his retinue; whereas, on the contrary, they have devoted themselves to a detailed description of various posthumous destinies.

In the Western world the opposite tendency has prevailed. Death is an abstract, philosophical subject of study, which is tackled from a speculative point of view, and to which no immediate efficacy is attributed. Actually, the curious illusion underlying this intellectualistic approach, originates from a morbid desire of bodily immortality. If death is undeniably a universal phenomenon, then why is it constantly exorcized and shunned in our daily experience. Various interesting studies have been written on death in the West, and quite revealingly they are all focused on sociological, ethnological, and psychological analyses. These studies confirm what we ascertain in everyday life, in which hospitals are viewed as 'warehouses' of the dying. This approach spares Westerners from experiencing death in their own homes. Such an aseptic death brings with it the simplification of funeral rites and the abolition of mourning. Of great importance is the unlimited trust which Westerners place in medicine. Medicine is perceived as the instrument of achieving an indefinite prolongation of life, in the irrational hope for the discovery of an elixir of eternal youth. This attitute is symptom of the fear of death, not to be disjoined from the horror — even of an aesthetic kind — that the West manifests towards poverty, sickness, and old age.

We thought it would be interesting to present this study, intending to expound and analyse the phenomenon of death from the Indian point of view. In this regard, we must make clear on the outset that what has been examined is contemporary Hinduism, studied on the basis of its living rituals and beliefs. The brief references to the Buddhism or Jainism have been utilized only as useful explanatory devices. After all, both Buddhism and Jainism have such great relevance in and of themselves, that to study their specific outlook on the subject would have required a separate treatment. The material gathered — both written and oral — has been read in the light of the plurimillennial living tradition of the Hindus, having their roots in the oldest times of Indus valley civilization and in the Vedic Texts. It must thus be clear that the interpretation of the old texts confided to us by our informants is a contemporary one. In other words, the methodology of research incorporated thorough and inquisitive examination of the phenomenon of death in today's India, registering its influences on the social environment, and then searching, when possible, for its oldest cultural roots. For this reason, we have verified the texts and our informations from their original Sanskrit. On the other hand, we have utilized historical translations of works which were doctrinally less relevant. Our research has been carried out primarily as an Indological enterprise rather than an ethnological one, although to be sure, ethnological considerations have often been employed. This has been done precisely in order to study the origins of the speculations about death. The result of this study has been gratifying and surprising: in fact, the thought of modern Hindus appears to be very close to that of their ancestors of proto-historic times. Indeed, although in today's India Western mentality sometimes has affirmed itself, especially in urban centres, in rural areas traditional life — with its rhythms, rituals, and beliefs going back to time immemorial — has been maintained.

Mṛtyu: Concept of Death cannot of course end here. Our research has taken into consideration not only the moments from conception to the death of the body, passing through the phases of birth, growth and ageing; we have also shortly examined the journey which the soul makes as soon as it leaves the body. It is however evident that the speculations and beliefs concerning the posthumous destinies, and the issues of and liberation require further exploration. A lot of work awaits us in the future.

In our research we have referred to all those studies on the subject which have appeared both in India and the West. We have utilized these sources, adapting them to the perspective of our enquiry, going back in time and comparing present beliefs with the literature and the artistic documents of the past. It did not appeared appropriate to us to take into account, in this very first inquiry, those studies that followed a purely philosophical perspective: we would perhaps utilize these materials for our future research. We have also avoided any reference to those popular texts dealing with 'apparent death,' 'reincarnation,' and 'talking with the dead.'

The Sanskrit texts that have been referred to during the research have been mentioned in a separate section in the Bibliography. Besides these the historical translations that have been taken into account have been enlisted in the second list of Bibliography. Worldwide accepted transliteration marks have been used in India works so as to aid in the formulation of exact pronunciation. Through the use of English alphabet 's', the non-english words have been brought in plural form.

We hope that this study on death in Hindu civilization stimulates a comparative reflection even among non-specialist Western readers. For this reason, we have reduced technical language to a minimum, avoiding the flexion of Sanskrit terms and minimizing the use of Indological parlance. The aim has been to maintain maximum scientific rigour with readability.

1

The Human Being (manuṣya) and the Other Beings

IT has been said that in India death (*mṛtyu*) is not opposed, as is in the West, to idea of life (*jīvan*) but rather to birth (*jāti*).[1] This statement is indeed intriguing and contributes in presenting, with indelible colours, the picture of the beliefs that have been shared on this topic — and today still are — by the people of the subcontinent. Nevertheless, such a statement, due to an excessive schematism, appears too generic, since the

1. The idea of a death-life opposition is really derived from the attitude described in the *Vedas*, and particularly in the *Ṛg* and *Atharva Saṁhitās*, in which life is celebrated and death exorcized. *See* J. Varenne, "Le jugement des morts dans l'Inde," In *Le jugement des morts* (Paris : Seuil, 1961), pp. 211-12. On death-life opposition, *see* A. Hillebrandt, "Death and Disposal of the Dead (Hindu)," In *Encyclopaedia of Religion and Ethics*, IV, 475 a.

   However, to a more careful observation it appears clear that the horror of death and the consequent opposition with the joy of life, concerns only premature death: ". . . really destined to you, old age, may this person grow, none other of the hundreds death may harm him." *See* R. Lazzeroni, "Il nettare e l'ambrosia: su alcune rappresentazioni indoeuropee della morte," In *Studi e saggi linguistici* (Pisa, 1988; suppl. of *L'Italia dialettale*, vol. LI, n.s. XXVIII), pp. 181-83. In this context, I prefer *jāti* to *janman*, this latter term being particularly used for referring to bodily birth. On the other hand, *jāti* has taken a wider set of meanings in the course of time and might signify the birth into a particular caste or with an already defined *karman*, etc.

points of view which have developed over the centuries are many and complex.

Rather than opposing or relating to each other, death and life tend to superimpose in pan-Indian thought, appearing as two aspects of a single phenomenon considered from two different viewpoints. Thus, it can be said that whenever someone or something changes in state, the death takes place with respect to the preceding condition and birth with respect to the new condition.[2] The most common scriptural example to illustrate this belief is that of water changing into steam when thrown on fire. This change shows the death of water at its liquid state and shows the rebirth at its aerial state. We shall later see how this conception is central in the ritual of the corpse's cremation.[3]

The change of state is ritually connected with what is known as the theme of 'passage,'[4] the 'door' through which it is effectuated being viewed as both an entrance and an exit. As

2. ". . . . then he succumbs to death and is reborn: thus he is made to rotate like a water vessel on the wheel of existence;" *Garuḍa Purāṇa*, II.32.71. The second *kāṇḍa* of this *Purāṇa* (*GP*), known as *Preta Mañjarī*, had constituted one of the principal scriptural sources for this study. "'Birth' and 'death' were never considered as very distant phenomena by ancients. These two are inseparable aspects of one and the same cycle of regeneration. Death is the precursor of future creation. This attitude is manifested in many religious symbols;" Sh. Atre, "Many Seeds Apple: The Fruit of Fertility," In *Bulletin of the Deccan College*, XLV (1986): 1.

3. "Then, when he dies, they bring him in oblation to the fire; the fire becomes his fire; the fuel, his fuel; the smoke, his smoke; the flame, his flame; the ash, his ash; the sparks, his sparks. In this fire the gods offer man. From this sacrifice man comes out covered in light;" *Bṛhadāraṇyaka Upaniṣad* (*BṛU*), VI.II.13-14.

4. Although ethnology is nowadays structured in a less schematic way, it is A. van Gennep's merit to have given prominence to this issue in his classic *Les rites de passage* (Paris, 1909).

the descent and the ascent, the entrance and the exit are determined by the understanding of the movement operated. The door in and of itself is but an opening which permits passage through the border or *limen* which separates two environments. It's the consciousness of the person performing the passage through the door which establishes when and what is the phase of entry and the phase of exit.[5] In general, in the different religious and philosophic conceptions of India, the womb is considered as the tomb of the preceding state. Analogously, the tomb ritually used for deceased children is considered a womb in which the dead person is collocated as an embryo in view of a successive rebirth. The burial of a corpse is really a *regressus ad uterum*, an idea widely attested to even among the ancient Western civilizations.

An immediate consequence of what has just been said is the following. If the passage death-birth is one and the same phenomenon simply considered from two different perspectives and in temporal succession, not the same thing can be said of the reverse pair birth-death. These two terms in fact do not coincide, since between them is interposed a duration, namely life, in the course of which an existence develops.

The entry of a person into a Hindu temple passing through the entrance door under the signs of death and rebirth (*kāla-kīrti mukha*), it symbolizes his death to the external world and rebirth to a more sacred condition.[6] One thus finds himself in

5. With his usual acumen, R. Lazzeroni upholds the hypothesis of Thieme, namely that the term 'nectar' etymologically means 'crossing death.' To comfort this thesis, he quotes and analyses various Vedic passages from which one also deduces that the verb *tarati* 'to cross' means "passing through the bottleneck." *See* R. Lazzeroni, *op. cit.*, p. 180. Cf. also A.K. Coomaraswamy, "Swayamatṛnna: Janua Coeli," In *Zalmoxis*, II, 1939.

6. G.G. Filippi, *Tantrismo e Arte* (Milano: Arché, 1978), p. 45.

a vestibule (*maṇḍapa*) which must be walked through in all its length in order to pass, through another door, into an even more interior and sacred hall. This continues for two, three, or even five halls or rooms in a row, until one reaches the *sanctum sanctorum* (*garbha-gṛha*). As said, all doors show on the architrave and on their posts the sculptured signs of death and rebirth; it is thus evident that the visitor is introduced to the supreme mystery by passing through a sequence of halls representing different and successive existences. It is here that for the first time the doctrine of transmigration is manifested, that is, the doctrine of purification through subsequent births. From this example we derive one more element of the theorem we are analysing, namely action (*karman*), in the absence of which no movement or change can take place.[7]

Becoming (*kāla*) is the moving principle of action, which forces all things and beings to go through all the innumerable rooms which make up the temple of the universe.[8] Beings who have obtained birth in a determined existence and in a well-defined world — a definite room of the temple — develop a multiplicity of actions which will lead them step-by-step and fatally to the extreme limit of their existence in that particular world. So doing, they shall develop their own special characteristics or, at least, those potentials which are best suited to be cultivated in that special environment. The passage from potency to action inevitably leads to the exhaustion of this becoming. Thus, the development and manifestation of all

7. "The action which springs out of mind, speech and body;" *Manu-Smṛti,* XII. 5; ***see*** *Yājñavalkya-Smṛti,* III.134.
8. "Kāla creates all things, Kāla destroys them all; Kāla burns all beings, Kāla then extinguishes the fire; all good and bad things in the three worlds are created by Kāla; Kāla destroys them, Kāla remanifests them; Kāla is the only one watching when everyone and everything sleeps, Kāla can be won by nobody; Kāla proceeds without being stopped;" *Mahābhārata* (*Mbh*) I.1.245-47.

the potencies of a body[9] necessarily lead to their exhaustion, that is, to death.[10]

Thus, just like a bud that manifests all its beautiful potentials of form, colour and smell and, finally, having come to the exhaustion of its phantasmagoric blooming withers, we may think of a being as developing its special characteristics during the time of its contingent existence. Having expressed and exhausted all his potentials he has no need to remain enclosed in that same condition. Thus he frees himself out of it, so as to elevate to a less limiting plane of existence. To use another example, it is like a snake which frees itself from its old skin representing all its already exploited potentials.[11] European idealism might see in the example of the blooming flower and of the snake's skin two opposite judgements, pessimistic the former, optimistic the latter. Indian thought, however, following different categories, considers that even if the two examples are different the intrinsic significance of the phenomenon remains the same. Taking the last comparison, we may say that as the change of skin is negative for the skin itself which falls lifeless to the ground, the same happening is

9. The potencies which dwell in the body are the individual psychic faculties. These are considered as deities since, in keeping with a macrocosm-microcosm correspondence, the gods who dwell in all the fourteen *loka*s must also be present in the body. *See GP*, II.31.40.

10. "When the actions caused by previous births exhaust themselves, then a man dies;" *GP*, II.24.31.

11. "In this way they freed themselves from their old skin, continued to ascend, avoided death and conquered it;" *Pañcaviṁśa Brāhmaṇa* (*PB*), XXV.15.4. The symbolism of the bud which opens and then withers, follows the description of the opening of the lotuses during the ascent of the *kuṇḍalinī* in Tāntrik meditative practices. *See* A. Mookerjee, *Kuṇḍalinī: The Arousal of the Inner Energy* (London: Thames and Hudson, 1982), p. 39.

positive for the snake. The same may be said for the flower which, after death, transforms itself into a fruit.

Going beyond the metaphor, the being which abandons a particular existence is forced to tranfer[12] itself to a different domain in which it will have to unfold different potentialities in this new life condition, characteristics which it could never have developed in its previous existence. It's in this way that the potentiality to fly can be developed in a butterfly but not in a caterpillar. By the same token, the butterfly can no longer walk around collecting and extending the segments of its own body, since in its new condition this possibility has been exhausted and lost forever. This is an illuminating example of a single being passing through two different states and life conditions.

Thus, every being possesses a multiplicity of capacities which it needs to develop in the course of a determinate existence. Moreover, between an existence and the following, there appears to be a relation of succession or, at least, of causality. The entrance into a plane of existence constitutes a manifestation or birth, and simultaneously the corresponding exit — or death — from the preceding state.

The reader must have noticed the carefulness with which the term 'being' has been used so far. The word translates the Sanskrit *sat*, present participle of the verbal root *as*, 'to be.' Perhaps, I could have translated *sat* more appropriately with a term such as '*ens.*' This, however, might prove misleading by reaching conceptions of Western philosophy.[13]

---

12. The *jīva*, together with the negative and positive results of its actions and the five *tanmātras*, enters into a new body as a houseowner moves after the fire of his old abode;" *GP*, II.3.95.

13. *Sat* is a term of erudite origin which, with the irradiation of Vedānta philosophy in nineteenth century Hinduism, has

→

Beings are manifested in all the indefinite worlds which make up the universe, or, if one wants to use a different term, the manifested existence. All beings as manifested creatures are limited by birth and death, even though these terms assume different valences according to the plane of existence to which they belong.[14] If we take into consideration the plane of existence characterized by the manifestation of human life, this world of humans (*manuṣya loka*),[15] the other and the different possibilities must none the less be kept in mind, i.e., the inferior worlds (*pātāla*)[16] — abode of the titans or anti-gods (*asura*) — and the superior worlds (*svarga*),[17] abode of the gods (*devas*). We shall shortly see how, conceptually, the *pātāla*

→ nowadays come to be used at all levels. In the Vedic period, on the other hand, the term *asu* was used. ***See*** Carlo Della Casa and Pier Angelo Carozzi, *L'aldil a nella fede dei popoli* (Milano: Unicopli, 1985), p. 35. ***See also*** Arthur Berriedale Keith, *The Religion and Philosophy of the Veda and Upanishads.* 2 vols. (Delhi : MLBD, 1989;[3] 1st edn. 1925), vol. 2, pp. 403-5.

14. "As death has been ordained for humans, so it has been for the gods . . . ;" *ṚV*, X.13.4.

15. For the identification of the world of human beings with "this world," ***see*** Jan Gonda, *Loka. World and Heaven in the Veda* (Amsterdam: Noord-Hollandsche Vitgevers Maatschappij, 1966), p. 84.

16. The *pātāla* or *asura lokas*, are seven inferior regions which extend below the world of human beings. Sometimes, in the Purāṇas, they are variously classified as *atala, vitala, sutala, talātala, mahātala, rasātala*, and finally the *pātāla*, the deepest of abysses. The titans or dragons of the abysses are also distinguished in various classes such as the *asuras* themselves, the *daityas*, the *dānavas*, the *nāgas*, etc., according to different traditions.

17. *Svarga* is a term which must be accurately distinguished from *deva loka*. Indeed, this latter term — as well as its related or, sometimes, opposed term *pitṛ loka* — designates a region of the same *manuṣya loka*, in which the souls of the departed go and stay before being reborn. In some middle and recent Purāṇas, however, *svarga* and *deva loka* are used as synonyms and this has caused some confusion.

worlds might be viewed as antecedent to our world and the *svarga* worlds as subsequent. The world of humans represents the hinge between the āsuric and divine manifestations, on analogy with the present time which functions as a hinge between past and future.

Setting aside, for the moment, the beings inhabiting the *manuṣya loka*, the inhabitants of the *svarga* and *pātāla loka*s appear as if endowed with greater possibilities and with a longer life-span.[18] This is due to the fact that both the gods and the titans are not subjected to the limits of individuality. The length of their existence is coextensive with the whole cycle (*kalpa*) during which their worlds develop.[19] To use a modern terminology, the existence of the *asura*s is comparable to that of certain kinds of monocellular bacteria of the human world, whose individuality is not clearly defined and that appear endowed with a longevity co-extensive with that of the environment in which they live.[20] Truly, the texts of Hinduism present us with a much more solemn and terrifying portrait of these inhabitants of the underworld oceans (this being the meaning of *pātāla*). Analogously, even the *deva*s populating the superior skies (*svarga*) are said to be endowed with prodigious attributes and gifted with an apparent immortality. As in the

18. The length of the *deva*s' and *asura*s' existence is symbolized by their eternal struggle for the possession of the *amṛta*, the drink of immortality; *see Viṣṇu Purāṇa* (*VP*), II.12. ". . . and the length of Manu (of humanity); of the gods and others, is equivalent to 852,000 divine years of 306,720,000 years of the mortals . . . ." *see VP* , I. 3.

19. H.H. Wilson, *The Vishnu Purana* (Calcutta: Punthi Pustak, 1972[4]), p. 24 n. 9 (1st edn. 1840).

20. "Il créa les Dieux en partant des plus hautes formes de l'énergie vitale, c'est pourquoi ils sont des Dieux (*Sura-s*) et avec les formes inférieures de la vie il a formé les Anti-dieux, c'est pour cél a qu'ils sont des Anti-dieux;" Alain Daniélou, *Le Polythéisme Hindou* (Paris: Buchet-Chastel, 1960), p. 217.

mythologies of many different cultures, even the Hindu gods and titans are in constant conflict among themselves, involving and upsetting the fragile world of mortals, which finds itself 'suspended' between the armies of the two opposing contenders.

I have deliberately evidenced how the human being, if compared to the angels and demons, is often defined as mortal. None the less, it must be noticed how neither the superior beings nor the inferior ones are immortal or eternal. Each of them is manifested in his respective world, from the time of its formation, and will be swept away by the catastrophe, which will destroy it. All mythologies know of the fall of the giants, their destruction, and the mineralization of their monstrous bodies. All peoples hand down the feared prophecy of the twilight of the gods, when all the celestial beings will die in the final battle against disorder, after which a new sky and a new earth will appear in a renewed creation.[21]

Thus one might ask why only men are considered mortals. The answer is implicit in what has been just described: *asura*s and *deva*s are born at the dawn of their worlds and die with their destruction. Their life, as already stated, is co-extensive with the life-span of their plane of existence. Instead human beings, and not only them, have only a short life at their disposal, within the limits of a birth which is analogous but not coincident with the origin of the *manuṣya loka*, and a death which is analogous but not coincident with the end of this human world. The point is that the human species is made up of an indefinite multiplicity of individuals who takes birth and meet death in succession, developing in this fragmentary way all the potentials of the genius of the species. At the same time, each individual realizes his own potentials, which belong to

21. *VP*, VI.1. On this topic, *see* J. Fonterose, *Python* (Berkeley and Los Angeles: University of California Press, 1980).

him or her as a being (*sat*), independently from the species of which he or she is only a fraction. We could say that the human species — or, better, the genius of the species, the true Man — is comparable to an *asura* or a *deva*. This could've been so, of course, if it were possible to altogether avoid the objective reality of individuality.

The problem is solved in the light of the doctrine which affirms that certain worlds, such as that of humans, is subject to two particular conditions of existence: the name (*nāman*) and the form (*rūpa*). This pair represents the principle of individuation and separation, which proceeds through duality (*dvaita*), generates the two sexes and, as a consequence, gives place to reproduction.[22] Indeed, it is not casual that the gods of different mythologies are considered sterile; in fact, they either generate by themselves in wonderful ways, or unite with beings of opposite sex but belonging to different species.

In general, the term life (*jīvan*) is used to denote an individual existence. If it is used in the context of god or gods, it is improper or is used in virtue of analogy. Instead, the terms birth (*jāti*) and death (*mṛtyu*) are commonly used not only to define the beginning or end of an individual being, but even of an entire world or plane of existence.

From this we deduce that birth and death are far more universal terms than life. And to this clarification one must add another morphologic definition. An individual being which manifests in a world characterized by the conditions of name and form, is necessarily endowed with life.[23] This does not

---

22. ". . . he remembers the composition of the world immediately preceding the *pralaya*, and expresses the wish: 'May I become manifold!';" *see Brahma Sūtra (BS), Bāladeva Bhāṣya,* I, III, VII, 30.

23. *See* G. Mukhopadhyaya, *Studies in the Upaniṣad* (Calcutta : Sanskrit College, 1960), pp. 79-80 (Calcutta Sanskrit College Research Series, no. IX).

necessarily mean bodily life. All individuals remain in a state of latency in their respective species from the beginning of the cycle in which they are bound to manifest, until that special time (*ṛtukāla*) in which they enter a matrix (*yoni*), so as to develop a body made up of the five elements (*pañcabhūta*).

After the analytical development of their bodily life, the individuals, having left the body, will have to wait for a variable time-period in order to abandon this world.[24] In other words, an individual will remain in a subtle dimension of this world waiting for another suitable bodily existence. After the short earthly cycle, he goes back to the same subtle dimension where he will remain until conditions permit him to leave the world of men manifest. This occurs at the end of the temporal length granted to this world, when, together with all the other living and dead individuals, he will be allowed to exit from the *manuṣya loka*.[25] If one considers this same issue from a synthetic viewpoint, it may be recognized how the human species behaves like the *deva* or *asura* 'species,' the only difference being that it manifests in succession in the world through individuals who are reabsorbed at the end of the cycle.

We shall not concern ourselves now on these two states of inactivity which precede and follow the bodily life of an individual, since these are related to the beliefs regarding the *post mortem*, a subject with which we shall deal later on. This anticipation is necessary in order to underline that the term life has for a Hindu a more restricted and, at the same time, a wider extension than that which the Western mind commonly

---

24. "It's certainly more difficult to get out of this condition;" *Chāndogya Upaniṣad (ChU)*, V.10.6.

25. "The deceased will remain in heaven (*svarga*) until the coming of the *mahāpralaya*, when all living beings will be destroyed;" *GP*, II.34. 89. Here the term *svarga* is used as a synonym of *deva loka*; *see* n. 17.

attributes to it. In restricted sense *jīvan* implies only individual existence; and in wider sense this term comprises the whole length of an individual existence, not just the short life-span of the gross body.

Given these indispensable premises, it is precisely from the body that our investigation must start. Indeed, the body is the part of one's own individuality which ordinary man knows best and recognizes as real.[26] After the examination of the problems relating with birth, bodily life in its development, and death, it will be easier to peneterate the complex set of Indian doctrines concerning the fate of the deceased.

---

26. After all, it's precisely from the body that the self-awareness of an individual arises. Without the human body, not even a wise *yogin* can reap the pleasurable effects of his actions; *see* *GP*, II.24.30.

2

The Nature of Individual Beings

ACCORDING to Sāṁkhya, every being is endowed with an intellect (*buddhi*) which represents in some way his archetypal essence. When *buddhi* falls into an environment subject to conditions of *nāmarūpa*, it produces *ahaṁkāra*, individual consciousness. Exactly in the same way, Brahmā, in the form of the supreme swan, descends on the surface of the primordial ocean, to place the divine egg, *brahmāṇḍa*.[1] *Ahaṁkāra* is the seed (*piṇḍa*) from which the entire individual composite of a human being will develop. Analogously, *brahmāṇḍa* is the cosmic egg, which, upon opening, will give birth to the world and its becoming.

On the basis of this precise similarity between the manifestation and the development of the microcosm and the macrocosm, one can affirm that as the seed (or *kṣudra-brahmāṇḍa*), so the divine egg — *yathā piṇḍa tathā brahmāṇḍa*.

Individual consciousness contains *in nuce* a certain number of possibilities, manifested at the moment of the production of the individual when he assumes a body.[2] These possibilities are

1. *See Maitrāyaṇī Saṁhitā* (*MS*) I.9. For a comparison with different versions of the Purāṇas on the subject, *see* S.S. Dange (ed.), *Myths of Creation* (Bombay : University of Bombay, 1987).
2. *See* chapter 1, n. 10, "Although the new-born child is thus unaware of his accumulated *karman*, it is there nevertheless, together with other predetermined factors: 'A creature in the mortal world is born because of his own *karmans*; his life-span, *karman*, wealth, →

the *tanmātras*, subtle principles of bodily elements, such as sound (*śabda*), touch (*sparśa*), vision (*rūpa*), taste (*rasa*), and smell (*gandha*).[3] These principles are manifested in a gross way through manifestation in the five elements (*pañcabhūta*).

Ether (*ākāśa*) is the element filling space, an environment permitting the vibration of sound.[4] It is present in all solid space, but particularly in places commonly considered empty such as in ravines, large caves, ear and heart cavities, in which sound is able to spread and re-echoe better. Architects and artisans study ways to contain more ether in high rooms and in the acoustic causes of percussions and stringed instruments.

Air (*vāyu*) or better, wind, perceived only by means of the skin, through touch is the element that whips and caresses. In continuous movement, *vāyu* moves planets, chases clouds away, raises sea-waves. This element surrounds bodies, enveloping them, and penetrating them with violence, putting liquids into motion and circulation. In this way, *prāṇa* (*vyāna*, to be precise), or the air breathed in, activates the blood circulation, the heartbeat, and the movements of the digestive tract. Air is particularly present in places producing current,[5] where there are temperature changes, and in tropical zones.

→ learning, and death are born with the embodied creature in the womb. Head down and feet up, the embryo gives forth a breath, and from birth the illusion of Viṣṇu deludes the creature'" (*GP*, II.22.18-21); Wendy Doniger O'Flaherty, "Karma and Rebirth in the Vedas and Purāṇas," In Wendy Doniger O'Flaherty (ed.), *Karma and Rebirth in Classical Indian Traditions* (Delhi: Motilal Banarsidass, 1963[1]) p. 21.

3. *See* Īśvarakṛṣna's *Sāṁkhyakārikās*, chapter XXVI.
4. ". . . ether has the quality of the echo, of the hollow, of the position in space, of being audible and of support;" *GP*, II.32.41.
5. For this reason, the layout of a construction plan is called *vāyu*. *See* Stella Kramrisch, *The Hindu Temple* (Delhi: Motilal Banarsidass, 1976;[2] 1st edn. Calcutta, 1946), pp. 51-52.

Fire (*tejas*) is intended here as a luminous element, rather than a heat producer.[6] By illuminating, *tejas* permits the visibility of things both in form and colour. It is really as colour that *tejas* is present in all objects, given that every colour is only a fraction of light. Fire lives intensely in things producing intense light, be it natural phenomena such as the stars, the sun, the eye, or in the domestic things like fireplace, altars, lamps lit by man.

Water (*āpas*) is the element transmitting taste, dissolving solids, and building organic composition. Water, as the oceanic mass, is the inexhaustible reservoir of life and nutriment. All bodies are composed in great part of water, from human body to the simplest crystal. Saliva is watery, and has the property of capturing the taste of food, and of dissolving it, nourishing the body of vital elements. Along with blood, lymph, phlegm, bile, mucus, semen, and tears, saliva is a modification of that water circulate in the body.[7] Water is present in every place, taking the form of the container in which it is put, be it the ocean or a glass.

Earth (*pṛthivī*) is the thickest *bhūta*, that which most grossly transmits the various sensitive vibrations. The earth is the vehicle of odours, but this sensation is perceived only when air lifts up its tiny particles and puts them in contact with nose, through mucus and other liquids. More often the earth is related to unpleasant odours, produced by dirt, excrements, and decomposition. Perfumes are often attributed to water and to taste (*rasa*), almost as a kind of nutriment.[8]

6. *See* D.M. Knipe, *In the Image of Fire, The Vedic Experience of Heat* (Delhi: Motilal Banarsidass, 1975), pp. 52-53.

7. *See BS*, III.1.2. In particular, *see* Śaṅkara's *Bhāṣya* on this verse of the *Brahma Sūtras*; *BSŚBh*, III.1.2.

8. *See* Padma Sudhi, *Aesthetic Theories of India* (New Delhi: Intellectual Publ. House, n.d. vol. III), p. 52. In fact, the *gandharvas* feed →

Every solid body is composed of the five elements in an inextricable way. We can distinguish a predominance of one *bhūta* over the others in the parts of the body, only in a relative sense. From this we can deduce that one *bhūta* alone, without blending with the others, cannot manifest itself. For example, a flame, even though it is composed of the fire element, makes noise, so it is also made of ether; if touched, it burns, so it is also composed of air; it smokes, meaning that the flame has water in it; it has a burning smell, being mixed with earth. An analogous demonstration is possible for the other four elements also. I have described this in detail in order to make the following more understandable. We must not forget that at the present point of this treatise, the *bhūta*s have not yet manifested to form a body, remaining undifferentiated in their principles. The gross elements at this stage are contained in their subtle causes, the *tanmātra*s, which are latent in the individual consciousness, *ahaṁkāra,* in its seminal state of *piṇḍa.*[9]

Furthermore, *ahaṁkāra* contains other potentialities called *indriya*s, or faculties. These are eleven in number, and the first is *manas*, the rational faculty co-ordinating the other ten *indriya*s, divided into two series of five. The first series is represented by the *jñānendriya*s, faculty of sensations, through which *manas* becomes acquainted with the outside world. The second series is made up of *karmendriya*s, faculty of actions, through which *manas* can actively intervene in the external

→ themselves on scents: it's interesting to note that Indian cuisine prefers the scent of spices to the taste of the food itself.

9. "Consciousness is present in the *piṇḍa* in its seminal form;" *GP,* II.32.21. In this study, the term *piṇḍa* is used — as the Sanskrit requires — with two different meanings. In the first the subtle seed (λόγοζ σπερματικόζ) is defined, preceding the *jīva*'s descent in the bodily frame. In the second, *piṇḍa* denotes a round sweet, made of various cereals, offered during numerous Hindu rites. The reader should always distinguish the two meanings according to the context.

environment. Both the *jñānendriyas* and the *karmendriyas* are closely connected with the five elements. Most particularly, in the case of the *jñānendriyas*, the five *bhūtas* are the object of their sensory inquiry.

The first faculty of sensation is hearing (*śrotra*), sonorous vibrations transmitted through ether. Second is touch (*tvac*), which receives tangibility from the air. Next comes sight (*cakṣus*), which investigates luminous objects. Taste (*rasana*) is obtained by tasting water. Odour (*ghrāṇa*) perceives the fragrance of the earth.[10]

In principle, we must imagine that when a sensory faculty investigates the external world, it receives a message that it transmits immediately to *manas*. The mind confronts the news it has received with others sent by the remaining sense faculties, thus drawing a global meaning. The concept of this meaning is then transferred from the mind to the individual consciousness, where it is permanently memorized. In this way we can explain that, if a man burns himself by touching fire, he does not need to repeat the experience again to avoid burning himself in the future. *Manas*, having analysed the information received by the sense-organs, orders the *karmendriyas* to react in an appropriate way to the stimuli. Going back to the experience of burning oneself, *manas*, informed by touch of the pain it has experienced, quickly orders the legs to move the body away from the source of heat.[11]

---

10. "Whoever depends on the Self is happy; instead, whoever depends on the objects through his senses may lose himself, just like the deer, victim of hearing (being attracted to music); or like the elephant, victim of touch (being attracted to female elephants); or like the moth, victim of sight (attracted of fire); or like the bee, victim of smell (attracted to the lotus scent); or like the fish, victim of taste (attracted to the bait)," *GP*, II.12.17-18.

11. *See* Īśvarakr̥ṣṇa, *Le strofe del Sāṁkhya*, a *Le stzofe del Sāṁkhya*, a cura di C. Pensa (Torino: Boringhieri, 1960), ch. 33. This translation, →

The first faculty of action is speech (*vāk*), which acts directly on the ether. Walking (*pāda*) is the second, closely associated with the wind, which is always in movement. The third *karmendriya* is reproduction (*upastha*), because this faculty, as we shall soon see, is in relationship with fire, intended as erotic ardour. Grasping (*pāṇi*) is the faculty in harmony with the plasticity of water. As this element surrounds and holds on to the objects immersed in it, so the hand takes on the form of the object it clutches. The last faculty of action is excretion (*pāyu*), correlated with precipitation, which is one of the characteristic of the earth element.

Because this complex series of elements and faculties are synthetically contained in the *ahaṁkāra* latent in the subtle seed, we must now consider its process of differentiation and of manifestation, leading to the formation and development of the body and, as a consequence, to its birth.[12]

Generally we think that a being is born when it appears on this earth (*bhū*) with a solid body (*sthūla śarīra*) composed of the five gross elements. This body must, at some moment, be considered separate and autonomous from its mother and of the matrix that produced and incubated it. However, this is a simplification of the complex process of birth. Analogously to the 'moment of death,' the 'moment of birth' is far from being instantaneous. On the contrary, these processes are eloborated over a period of time, rarely brief. This development is determined with a parabolic course and only the climax or critical apex, appears to the witness as the awaited 'moment.'

The "moment of birth" does not represent a definite detachment of the infant from the mother's body, because a

→ clear and precise, affords a thorough examination of the content of the *kārikās*, without the lexical contortions of many versions of Sanskrit philosophical works in European languges.

12. *See ibid.*, p. 99.

bodily continuity is protracted for an indefinite time even after this striking 'moment.' For example, an infant already expelled from his mother, continues for a brief time to exchange his blood with hers until the umbilical cord is cut. But even after this separation, the baby will continue to grow, fed only by his mother's milk. The symbiotic continuity is therefore maintained at a nutritive level. Even when this last bodily continuity is interrupted, the relationship of dependency on the mother continues. Psychic ties are even more cohesive and durable than bodily ones, to the point where, in certain pathological cases, they are not interrupted at all, conditioning the son to a perpetual state of infancy, and impeding him from reaching a state of individual fullness or maturity.

As we go down the scale of other beings, above all of inferior animals and vegetominerals, the separation from the matrix becomes still more dubious and problematic. For example, crystals never separate from the matrix that produced them.[13] So it must be admitted that the 'moment of birth' is extremely difficult to establish, and certainly not in absolute terms.

We have used the term 'individual beings' for the world of man (*manuṣya loka*). This is motivated by the fact that many categories of the living correspond to Western definitions of animals, vegetables, and minerals, besides that of man, who is a case by himself. None the less, this is a simplification of the complex birth process. Moreover, in this same human world live other beings, who may be considered intermediary between man and the god, or man and the *asuras*: *yakṣas*, *rākṣasas*, *gaṇas*,

13. The jeweller operates as 'midwife' for the birth of gems, as the miner for the birth of metals. Precious stones are placed under the moon's influence, together with all things and beings subject to fluxes of growth and decay; *see* Varāhamihira, *Bṛhat Saṁhitā*, XVI.9-12.

gandharvas, *apsaras*es, and others. These beings must be considered apart, having no solid and complete body. As fairies, nymphs, elves, gnomes, and *jinn*s of other cultural areas, these beings enjoy an ambiguous and mythically complex existence, which obliges us to drop the subject for the moment.[14]

Returning to the diverse categories of beings living in our world, having name and form (*nāmarūpa*), there is a three-fold classification in India, determined by the different modality of birth.[15] The first category is of viviparous (*yonija*), man and mammals, considered as superior animals in this context.[16]

---

14. The study of A.K. Coomaraswamy, *Yakṣas* (Washington, 1928-31), must still be viewed as an indispensable guide to the understanding of these subtle beings.

15. According to the authority of *Aitareya Upaniṣad* (*AiU*) V.3, within Purāṇic tradition the classification of earthly living beings is prevalently four-fold: besides the ones already cited, a fourth category is mentioned: those who are born from moist heat or perspiration, *svedaja*. The major invertebrates, trees, and plants are differentiated from those beings which are born from putrefaction and fermentation, such as worms and moulds (*GP*, II.12.2-4). Interestingly, in various mythological accounts gods like Gaṇapati, the sacred grass *dūrvā*, and human beings themselves, are viewed as born from the perspiration of some other deity. A first allusion to the four-fold division of living beings is found in *ṚV*, X.54.4.

16. The subtle beings populating the human world seem to belong to still another category associating them to the gods, of which however there is no textual mention. First of all, as noted, unions between males and females of the same species result barren. When a being remains impregnated, the delivery takes place from the most diverse openings: ear, side, nose, etc. In this regard, it is useful to remember the birth of Athena from the head, and that of Dionysus from the thigh. In India, even *ṛṣi*s and *muni*s, due to their superhuman nature, enjoy the privileges of *yakṣa*s and deities: mention should here be made of Gautama the Buddha, Ayyāpam, and of Gorakh Nāth, born from a cow's dung. On these issues, an indispensable instrument of comparative mythology is →

These individuals are incubated in the same womb in which they are conceived. During the prenatal period, they breath and are nourished through the mother's blood; they are born still attached to the mother through the umbilical cord, the sign of which they will carry until death. Lastly, they depend upon mother's milk for nourishment and survival.

Man, among the *yonijas*, is the most dependent and defenceless at the moment of birth. Therefore, we can affirm that a major independence at birth corresponds to a minor importance on the hierarchical scale of the viviparous.

The second category consists of the oviparous (*aṇḍaja*), including birds, reptiles, amphibians, and fish.[17] These animals live in two environments that are respectively over and under the earth, which is the domain of the *yonijas*. Birds live in the sky and are figures of Uranic deities for this reason. Reptiles, amphibians, fish, and abyssal creatures represent the titans. The egg, in which the tiny *aṇḍajas* pass their gestation period, has a reserve of food and an air chamber which puts the circulation of all substances of the embryo into motion, along with respiration.

The third category is comprised of germinparous (*udbhija*), and is lowest in order, besides being the most composite and

→ the work of U.P. Arora, *Motifs in Indian Mythology: Their Greek and Other Parallels* (New Delhi: Munshiram Manoharlal, 1981), in which the entire second chapter is dedicated to the theme of miraculous births. For an illustration of more recent Indian beliefs, ***see*** the lengthy introduction of Sadal Misra in D. Dolcini (ed.), *Un mito indiano: Nasiketa ovvero la storia del nato dal naso* (Treviso: Pagus, 1988).

17. Reptiles and fish are often unified in a single category of beings which, by moving in water, symbolize the water's flux. One must never forget the great quantity of river and sea reptiles infesting India. On this issue, ***see*** Jean Przyluski, "La Princesse a l'odeur de poisson et la Nāgī dans les traditions de l'Asie Orientale", In *Études Asiatiques* (1925): pp. 322 f.

numerous. The invertebrates, vegetables, and sometimes minerals make up this group. The first seem to be born from the putrefaction of more complex organic composites or by fermentation.

The form of life of minerals is crystals, born from a matrix under the combined effect of heat and water. They grow, assuming individual characteristics in respect to the structure of their 'species,' and after a generally lengthy period, they flake away or die, returning to the amorphous matter that produced them.[18] It is interesting to note that in the West, the jewellers call an uncut stone 'dead,' when it loses its luminescence and tends to flake away.

Before continuing, we must make a clarification. In the light of the Sāṁkhya doctrine, all beings in this world are endowed with *ahaṁkāra*, individual consciousness. We have seen that *ahaṁkāra* produces the *tanmātras*, the five gross elements, the mind, and the ten faculties of sensation and action. At first glance, it would not seem that all individual beings are endowed with these twenty-two components. For example, snakes have no legs, and neither do vegetables, that remain in the same place for all their earthly existence.

Minerals, if we wish to enumerate them among these beings, don't seem to have any individual faculties. Many animals seem to lack vision. In the case of man, some are born deformed or disabled. To these we must add mutilations occurring during life, accidentally or not, which deprive man of a sense or action organ.[19]

---

18. For the hypothesis on the gems' 'birth,' *see* Varāhamihira, *Bṛhat Saṁhitā*, LXXX.3.

19. "Without voice it is possible to exist, since one sees mute people. Without eyes it is possible to exist, since one sees blind people. Without hearing it is possible to exist, since one sees deaf people.

→

To clear up these problems, we must analyse these latter cases. Earlier we made the distinction between faculties of sensation and action, and of their corresponding organs. If, for example, the speech faculty has the tongue as its organ, the absence or removal of this organ does not effect the faculty in itself. A mute man will always be able to express himself by means of sign languages. The faculty of speech (*vāk*), in this case, uses another organ to express itself. Thus, the man who is blind since birth, or due to illness or accident, will use his sense of touch as his sight organ. Whoever is deprived of feet will move around helped by his arms, or, without these, would creep like snakes, or would make vertical movements as caterpillars. Birds and many insects have feet as well as wings, which serve as added locomotive organs, so that the faculty of *pāda* may be affirmed also in the air. To a superficial glance, vegetables seem blind and immobile. In reality, their sensitivity to light is well-known, and this is due to their sense of sight, even in absence of a specialized organ such as the eye. This form of action of *cakṣus* makes the plant move its leaves, following the sun's course, using the vegetable faculty of *pāda*. Thus we must not fall into the error of confounding the faculty with the corresponding organ. This error of evaluation would be comparable to a bird; considering all beings, not having wings as, immobile.

The example illustrating the existence of *cakṣus* and of *pāda* in vegetables is illuminating. In fact, when a sense faculty furnishes information, and this information puts a corresponding action faculty into motion, we deduce that even in the vegetable there is a *manas*. Therefore, there is a mind capable of interpreting messages and of giving orders. In this case, it

→ Without the mind it is possible to exist, since one sees foolish people. Without arms and legs it is possible to exist, since one sees people like this," *Kauṣitakī Upaniṣad* (*KU*), III.3.

is evident that the *manas* of a plant does not act by means of a complex organ such as the brain of man and animals. However, if there is mental activity, there must necessarily be a vegetable organ that carries out mental functions characteristic of the specific *manas*.

As we go down the scale of beings, the possibility of identifying organs corresponding to the *indriya*s are always minor, reaching the extreme limit of the crystal. Its growth exhausts all its potentialities of movement, vision is limited to its colour, and *manas* is reduced to a simple geometric structure, indistinct from *ahaṁkāra,* the principle of individuation.

All these considerations are important for our treatise, because they demonstrate that all beings act and develop in a differentiated way, according to their species and category. At the same time, every conscious being (*cit*), or unconscious (*acit*), has a unique essence acting as a structure for single individuals, that is *ahaṁkāra*.

If all beings have in common all the components of *ahaṁkāra,*[20] these will develop more or less in conformity with the hierarchical importance of the species they belong to. This is fundamental for understanding the destiny of every single being and its possibility of posthumous evolution. In any case, the individual born from a mother, or hatched from an egg, or germinated, belongs to the same category of living beings (*jīva*s). Some schools of speculation distinguish the *cit* beings from the *acit,* denying to the latter a possibility of exchange with the environment, because of their crystallized psychic life.[21]

---

20. "The body of the four types of living beings — corresponding to the four types of birth mentioned above — has the same nature and the same constituents;" *GP,* II.31.41.

21. This is the usually adduced reason for not considering rebirth →

Independent of these speculative considerations, every being brings to completion its programme of individual development, in established stages, according to the order (*ṛta*) that was codified in it since conception, and which collocates it in a class, species, caste, family, and in a precise place and moment of historical development of these categories. This guarantees a natural continuation of line (*paramparā*) to the individual, fixed by biological heredity (*gotra, jāti*).

Thus, a being developed in the uterus of an elephant will be born after two years of gestation, will walk after a certain number of hours, will be weaned at a certain age, can reproduce when it has reached maturity, and will hopefully live for sixty years. The same holds true for the larva, which, after an established number of days, closes itself into a cocoon, then passing from the state of chrysalis, to be transformed into a perfect insect.[22]

Amidst a great number of characteristics of the species to which it belongs, the individual also manifests its own unique characteristics. An individual is always distinguished from all others belonging to the same species. To use the examples just given, an elephant develops its life according to the biological sequence characteristic of its species. It would thus be impossible for it to pass through the phases of larva, chrysalis, and insect. If the elephant belongs to its species, it will also be distinguished

→ under mineral forms. Not so, however, in the *GP*, II.49.11, where it is stated that: "The souls of the dead enter in unconscious objects, minerals, worms, birds, animals, humans, and gods: however, after liberation, they do not enter anymore in objects or in bodies." Even *Padma Purāṇa* (*PP*), II.94.12 states: "Due to his *karman* a being may become a god, a man, an animal, a bird, an inanimate object."

22. ". . . thus the foetus cannot be produced from a cause which is not its own, as the plant which one desires will not grow from a seed which is not its own;" *Caraka Saṁhitā* (*CS*), IV.3.9.

from evey other elephant, due to its physical and psychic chracteristics.

So we can affirm that the natural order (*ṛta*) that guarantees development according to the inherited code, also furnishes the elements to manifest the possibilities of a single being. When an individual fulfils its biological code to perfection, we can say that it plays its role (*svadharma*) within the metacosmic order regulating the universe (*dharma*).

3

The Three Evolutionary Components of Nature

BEFORE continuing with the subject of this study, it is opportune to give our attention to a very old doctrine, which finds its expresssion in the *Bhagavad-Gītā*, even before becoming the foundation of Sāṁkhya cosmology. This is the doctrine of the three attributes (*guṇa*s) of *prakṛti*, the universal substance that manifests the cosmos. *Guṇa* is a difficult term to translate, given that etymologically, it calls to mind the idea of potentiality, of dynamics, of tensions that tend to break an equilibrium. *Guṇa* is the situation of a taut rope, of the force of bow before the shooting of the arrow. *Prakṛti,* before manifesting the universe, was in a precarious balance between three opposing tendencies. It takes nothing, a trifle, and the equilibrium breaks, causing the *guṇa*s to scatter in the directions to which they are inclined, and projecting the productions of the substance in the manifestation.

The three *guṇa*s are: *sattva,* the attraction towards being truth, described as a tendency towards purity; *rajas,* the desire of expansion and development, which we imagine as a horizontal movement in rapid expansion; and *tamas,* the repulsion for truth, a falling into ignorance, described as an inert precipitation towards low levels. The description of *triguṇa* does not necessarily have moral connotations. For instance, even though the force of gravity is viewed as one of the actions of *tamas*, nothing negative or sinful is ever attributed to it.[1]

All beings, all worlds, all actions participate in the *triguṇa*. At the beginning of this study we described the *trilokas*, the triple division of the Universe, composed of *pātāla, pṛthivī,* and *svarga,* thus applying the doctrine of the *guṇas*, according to the *Bhagavad-Gītā*. In fact, in the world of titans, the abysmal ignorance and inertia of *tamas* prevails. In the human world, the activity and expansive energy of *rajas* prevails; while in the world of gods, contemplation and the peace of *sattva* dominates. But even in one being alone it is possible to find the presence of all three *guṇas*. In man, a contemplative intellect (*buddhi*) corresponds to *sattva*. The psyche composed of the principle of individuation (*ahaṁkāra*) — the mind that analyses, receives, and catalogues all data — the senses, and the faculties of action, represent *rajas* in its dynamic tendency towards expansion. The body is composed of the five gross elements, the outer limit of human manifestation: it is inert, weak, vulnerable to illnesses and fatigue, which represent *tamas*. If we consider the human body to the exclusion of the other individual faculties, we note that it is also tripartite: fat and nerves, which are governing activities, are *sāttvika*, organic liquids in continuous circulation are *rājasika*, while muscles and bones, heavy and inert masses, are *tāmasika*.

---

1. On the contrary, gravity is believed to act through ether, the highest among the five elements, since it makes the position of bodies in space steady; *see* chapter 1, n. 26. According to Hindu astrology, all bodies are attracted to Agastya, that is, the southern constellation of Canopus; *see* G. de Santillana — H. von Dechend, *Il mulino di Amleto* (1st Italian edn. Milano: Adelphi, 1983, ch. 20). In Indian mythology, Agastya is an anomalous *anārya ṛṣi*, who has the capacity of both keeping mountains anchored to the earth and changing their position; *see* Varāhamihira, *op.cit.*, XII.7-22. Agastya is thus the personification of the force of gravity.

Among the animals inhabiting the earth, the bipeds called *dvipāda* since Vedic times, are more *sāttvika* because of their vertical position, in respect to quadrupeds (*catuṣpāda*), that are *rājasika*. Birds are the most *sāttvika* of creatures, while slithering snakes and fish, living in the abyss, are *tāmasika*. In this subtle play of relationships, it is noteworthy that the cobra (*nāga*), known for his capacity to hold himself erect by a third of his length, is the most *sāttvika* of serpents, and therefore worthy of being king (*nāgarāja*).

It is easy to see that the applications of the *triguṇa* theory are innumerable. What is important to us here is that the three *guṇas* are at the base of the conception of the *trimūrti*, the triple divine personality, formed by the gods Viṣṇu, Brahmā, and Śiva.[2] Viṣṇu is the god manifesting *sattva*, who leads the worlds towards their just goal, in harmony with cosmic order. Brahmā, who spreads the process of manifestation in the world, in an expansive sense, corresponds to *rajas*. Śiva, the god of destruction and death, represents *tamas*. This god is very complex, and I will come back to him later. Śiva is also identified with the principle of transformation. In fact, everything happening under Śiva's dominion turns to ash; but from this same ash, like the phoenix, all rises again to new life. According to the cosmogonic doctrine of *Maitrāyaṇī Upaniṣad* (*MU*), V.2, the first *guṇa* to be manifested was *tamas*, representing the dark root of the universal manifestation (*mūla*). As soon as *tamas* was differentiated from the substance of *prakṛti*, the process of development of successive worlds and beings began.[3] From *tamas* evolved *rajas* through expansion, and from *rajas*, *sattva*, through exaltation.

2. *See* L. Renou-J. Filliozat, *L'Inde classique* (Paris, 1947), I, 518.

3. For an 'evolutive' interpretation of theogony and of its sacrificial meaning *see* G.G. Filippi, "Sacrificial Meaning of the *Mahiṣamardinī*," In *Annali di Ca Foscari*, S.O., XXXII, 1993.

Thus, from the doctrine of the *Maitrāyaṇī Upaniṣad* we see that the subterranean worlds are the obscure root of all others. Darkness preceded the light in the sense that the amorphous material became the substantial cause of the objects that proceeded from it. In the same sense, the *asuras* are the oldest generation of beings, as in Greek-Roman mythology. The deities of the night and the titans are more ancient that the Olympic gods.[4]

Thus, the manifestation of all worlds and of all beings came about in the Beginning, thanks to a temporal fiat. But in this first phase, the manifestation is only a seed. It must form a root to appear on the surface of the earth, growing to reach the highest heavens, eventually. In other terms, the manifestation (*sṛṣṭi*) happens instantly due to the precipitation of *tamas* and the consequent withdrawal of the Beginning.

Up to this point, the cosmos was considered as a whole, composed of an unlimited number of worlds (*lokas*) in simultaneous coexistence. From the doctrine contained in the *Maitrāyaṇī Upaniṣad*, the cosmos may be observed as an evolving whole. In simpler terms, if in the simultaneous perspective the subterranean worlds are low, and the heavens are on high, in respect to the human world, the lower worlds came first and the heavens came after. To make a comparison, in three-fold time (*trikāla*), the present is the moment separating the past from the potential future. In the same way, the *manuṣya loka* is intended as the only effective world, separating a long series of past worlds, populated by the deceased, from another series of worlds to come, inhabited by still unborn beings. This is why mythology describes the titans and giants as nightmares of a shadowy past, or as huge corpses upon which the living

4. This constitutes the subject of the judgement of the Athenian Areopagus in Aeschylus' *Eumenides*.

world leans like a blanket, or better yet, as beings fallen into the viscera of the earth, fossilized, and transformed into rocks, mountains, bones of the earth.

Analogously, gods and angels are described as good and naïve genies, forced in their choices and indefinite in their characteristics, inconsistent and capricious, but nevertheless full of future potentials.[5]

We must not fall into the error of considering these diverse aspects as being opposed in an irreducible way. There is an ulterior perspective that is interposed between the simultaneous and the evolutionary visions of the cosmos. Accordingly, one must consider that, if the *asura*s and their worlds are dead for ever, the beings that populated them have passed into the human world by transformation and transmigration. Snakes have passed into the *manuṣya loka*, leaving only their skins in their old world.[6] At the same time, with the exhaustion of this present world, the beings inhabiting it will pass into divine worlds, giving them life and actuality. In this manner, the *asura*s are gods, and the gods, *asura*s. Or, rather, they are men (*puruṣa*), because man is the only present being in development.[7]

When a being has realized and exhausted the potentialities that he was given to develop in a particular world, he no longer has any need to remain in that same environment. The same world that hosted him will cease to exist at some point. The being, taken into consideration, will have to migrate to another world, to take actions and develop possibilities incompatible

5. *See* A.K. Coomaraswamy, "Angel and Titan: An Essay in Vedic Ontology," In *JAOS*, LV.

6. "Taṇūnapāt (Agni), being an asuric embryo, when born is the glory of men," *R̥V*, III.29.11.

7. "Then, indeed, after having fixed himself (to the zenith), he will never rise or fall anymore; alone, he will remain the only one," *ChU*, III.11.1.

with the conditions of the preceding world. As an absurd example, a horse that had the potentiality of having a horn on his head cannot actualise such a possibility in the conditions of this world, which, instead, guarantees this possibility to animals of other species, such as the rhinoceros. The horse must necessarily transmigrate, after death, to another world, where conditions permit the existence of the species of unicorns, to be able to actuate his potentiality, and thus evolve.

We can derive that if a man is born into the world that we call *manuṣya loka*, it is because he was forced by the necessity of putting into act potentialities and actions that he can realize only with the characteristics of human individuality. As noted, development is the means for exhausting possibilities, and it follows that every actuation or realisation signs an inexorable step towards bodily death, the end of human life.[8]

In India, the development of a man's whole psychosomatic complex is marked in its main stages by rites called *saṁskāras*. These are passage rites, following different phases of actuation of individual potentialities that have their common cause in *ahaṁkāra*. Of course, all beings living in the world of men have an analogous, though certainly not indentical, development, in view of their specific differences and they also perform rituals. Only certain acts, such as the education that old animals impart to their young, the acceptance of the young into the herd, courtship, and special moving customs towards the dying, have been observed and recognized by man. These have given rise in the Indian soul to an indelible respect towards other living creatures.

8. On the basis of this conception, it is stated that death awaits man from the very moment of conception; *see GP*, II.24.29.

4

Human Life from Conception to Birth

As we have seen in the preceding Chapter, the human being appears in this *manuṣya loka* in the seminal form, as *piṇḍa*,[1] since the beginning of the present world of man. Every being, human or not, is necessarily a present component since the beginning, because he represents a determined aspect in the evolution of the cosmic cycle (*kalpa*), corresponding to *manuṣya loka*. The concept of *piṇḍas*, all manifesting simultaneously into their corresponding worlds, is the furthest possible from the Western creational conceptions. Man, who manifests bodily in a determined moment of a *kalpa*, is not the object of a creation

1. *See* Chapter 2, n. 5. All beings were contained in seminal form within the *brahmāṇḍa*, before its shell opened: ". . . from this egg Brahmā came out, the sole Prajāpati; and then Manu, Ka, and Parameṣṭhin; then Pracetas and Dakṣa; then also Dakṣa's seven sons; then the Viśvedevas, the Ādityas, the Vasus, the two Aśvins, the *yakṣas*, the *sādhyas*, the *piśācas*, the *guhyakas*, the *pitṛs*; and then the sage *brahmarṣis* apperaed, and the numerous *rājarṣis* possessed of all virtues; and thus were manifested the water, the sky, the earth, the air, the ether, the cardinal points, the years, the seasons, the months, the fortnights called *pakṣas*, with day and night alternated; and thus were manifested all things which are well-known to humanity;" *Mbh*, I.27-37. In this passage, the term *pitṛ* does not indicate those who have become ancestors after their life on earth, since these *pitṛs* manifested when nobody had yet died. Instead, these are the *piṇḍas* of humanity, generations of beings who lived in previous worlds. On these issues, ***see also*** *Bhāgavata Purāṇa* (*BhP*), I.5.3.

ad hoc, but is already latently present in the 'genius' of the species, in the same way in which a hair, a tooth, or a fingernail are part of the genetic makeup of an individual even before growth. And exactly as a hair, a tooth, and a nail, the single man appears on earth with a body at an established time in the historical development of humanity.

The human being, therefore, may even wait for this moment for an extremely long time. During this period, his existence is comparable to that of vegetable seeds, that pass long seasons inert, stored in barns. Only when the seed is sown into the earth, the germ (*bīja*), develops into a plant.

During the period of latency, the *piṇḍa* has the individual consciousness enveloped within itself. *Ahaṁkāra*, which has not yet unfolded its powers, finds itself in the situation indentical to that of a man sleeping without dreaming (*suṣupta sthāna*), inert, immersed in a state of pure potency.[2] At this point, one may object that individual consciousness cannot remain closed in a situation in which it has no awareness of itself. Can consciousness be unconscious? This is only an apparent contradiction. In reality, *ahaṁkāra* must be understood here as inactive. Its consciouness can be activated towards the external world exclusively by means of the *indriyas*.[3] Consciousness, when abiding in itself, remains inactive like a sole acrobat, with no one's shoulders to jump on, without ceasing to be an acrobat, because of the lack of a partner however.

Ahaṁkāra, in this stage, has effective contact only with its immediate cause, *buddhi*. To go back to the analogy based on

2. On the unconscious state of the *piṇḍa*, from the moment of its descent on earth until its conception, *see ChUŚBh*, V.10.6.
3. "When Shakti is plunged into the last and most gross of *tattvas*, solid matter ('earth'), nothing more remains for Her to do. Her creative activity then ceases and She rests;" *see* Arthur Avalon, *Il potere del serpente* (Roma: Mediterranee, 1968), p. 39.

the *Māṇḍūkya Upaniṣad*, even during sleep without dreams (*suṣupta sthāna*), consciousness is temporarily suspended.[4] This does not mean that it ceases to exist, but that for a time, *ahaṁkāra* is turned inwards towards its root, instead of towards the exterior. At the same time, we can deduce that the individual consciousness affirms and realizes itself by developing its components. *Ahaṁkāra* manifests its powers in all their extensions, realising not only the completeness of a single individual, but the manifestation of the entire surrounding *loka*. In this sense, we can say that the world is manifested through consciousness.

The *piṇḍa*, in this state of envelopment, does not have the possibility of developing the powers with which it will become conscious of the outside world in detail. However, in it a tension is displayed towards bodily manifestation, expressed through a search for a matrix in which to take abode, so as to develop as a complete individual.

When the husband deposits his semen in his wife's body, the *piṇḍa* enters into the phase of fulfilment.[5] The rite consecrating this event is the *saṁskāra* called *garbhādhāna*, the gift of the embryo.[6] Even if codified in the Gṛhya-Sūtras, this ritual is of Vedic origin, and is still in use among young Hindu

4. On the doctrine of the three states of consciousness, *see* *Māṇḍūkya Upaniṣad* (*MāU*), 3-5. This doctrine has its oldest origin in *BṛU*, II.1.17-20; IV.3.7-34.

5. "The husband who put his semen into his wife, is indeed a farmer sowing his ground;" *GP*, II.32.17. The father is the *guru* of all things; he is a visible deity, superior to the gods since he produces the body and the body may bestow damnation, salvation or *mokṣa*. *See* *GP*, II.21.29-31.

6. "The *saṁskāras*, improperly translated sacraments, are the rituals which follow and lead the correct development of man, beginning from conception up to death;" *see* Raj Bali Pandney, *Hindu Saṁskāras* (Delhi: Motilal Banarsidass, 1969;[2] 1948[1]), pp. 48-59.

couples. The only difference is that nowadays, the ritual is effected only once, after the wedding-ceremony, and consecrates all possible future conceptions of the couple.

The rite in itself is of a simplicity that only archaic rituals conserve. The husband, once purified, recites the following *mantra*:

> May Viṣṇu prepare your womb. May Tvaṣṭṛ ably model the forms. May Prajāpati move the current, and may Dhātar depose the seed. May Sinīvālī get the seed ready; may you prepare it, Sarasvatī. May the divine Aśvin twins, crowned with lotus flowers, bless the seed. The seed that they produced by the rubbing of the two golden sticks together, the seed that you will carry until the tenth month; this we invoke.[7]

In this *mantra* the god Viṣṇu represents the principle guaranteeing the correct development of the embryo, preparing the uterus to receive it, according to the laws of cosmic order (*ṛta*). Tvaṣṭṛ, artisan of the gods, projects the forms that individuals will develop during the course of their entire earthly existence. Prajāpati, demiurge of the macrocosm, vehicles the spermatic flow into the mother. Dhātar, often considered identical to Brahmā, installs the seed in the uterus. Sinīvālī and Sarasvatī represent two divinities who act upon the waters.[8] Finally the Aśvins, gods of medicine, are configured here as

7. *ṚV*, X.184; *Atharva Veda* (*AV*), V.25.5.

8. "Sinīvālī denotes the day of new moon and its presiding spirit, which, in accordance with widespread ideas concerning the connection of the moon and vegetation, is one of fertility and growth;" A.A. Macdonell-A.B. Keith, *Vedic Index of Names and Subjects* (Delhi: Motilal Banarsidass, 1982, 2 vols.; London, 1912[1]), p. 449. Sarasvatī, as the most sacred river of Vedic India, represents the flux of celestial waters on earth; *see* David Frawley, *Gods, Sages and Kings : Vedic Secrets of Ancient Civilization* (Delhi: Motilal Banarsidass, 1993), pp. 93-96.

the *genii* who have presided over the intercourse of the parents, as we deduce from the allusion of sticks being rubbed together, symbolizing the drill producing fire.

The bride, also purified, eats rice balls cooked in milk, called *piṇḍa*: these sweets, in fact, symbolize the infant who is about to be conceived. Rice is the cereal most frequently representing the male seed, both because of its whiteness, and because of the water in which it is cultivated. The same watery semen is represented by clarified butter which amalgamates the rice. The milk in the *piṇḍa* is an anticipation of the mother's milk which will nourish the infant.[9] Rice has two other characteristics that relate it to human beings: rice needs to be transplanted in order to grow, as human sperm waits to be placed in the right matrix. Also, rice can be cultivated any time during the year. Therefore, it can be 'generated' in any season, just as man, whereas animals and plants are born at fixed times, after the annual mating season.

Other cereals symbolize the variety of other individual beings at the latent state, with the exception of the sesame which represents the souls of the deceased, as *jīva*s who have gone back to a state of latency. This may be because of the black colour of its seeds.

The bride eats the rice *piṇḍa*s, thus performing a rite similar to the *śrāddha*, offered in honour of the dead. In fact, similar *piṇḍa*s are offered daily to the deceased, during the first ten days of mourning, representing the ten lunar months of gestation.[10] "It is stated in the Gṛhya-Sūtras that during the ancestor propitiation rituals the *piṇḍa* offered by the grandfather

9. *See* Wendy Doniger O'Flaherty (ed.), *Karma, op.cit.*, p. 6.

10. The deceased, after ten days of *piṇḍa* offerings, acquires the body of a *pitṛ*, just as the growing child in the mother's womb, after ten lunar months, acquires a human body; *see GP*, II.34.44.

of the householder should be eaten by his (householder's) wife if she is desirous of a son."[11]

In the above case, the *piṇḍa* eaten by the bride is considered as a real offering (*caru*) to the deceased. This is the reason why the bride always eats the remains[12] (*ucchiṣṭa*) of the funeral offering (*śrāddha*) because if they were dispersed, the dead would weaken. Anyhow, both in the case of the deceased as well as of the unborn child, the ritual of eating food means that the body which is about to be manifested, will be made up of food (*annamaya*).[13]

The *Taittirīya Saṁhitā*[14] tells us that if, in place of the remains of the offering to the deceased, the future mother swallows the remains of the rice offering dedicated to the gods (*prasāda*), she might become pregnant without the intervention of her human husband. Leaving aside cases of miraculous conceptions, which I have already mentioned,[15] we can now offer a more complete analysis of natural procreation. The following question arises: What relationship is there between the *piṇḍa* or the individual who is about to be conceived, and the father's seed? And what continuity is there between the *piṇḍa*, lacking a gross body, and the human being in his wholeness, that is, having a body?

11. Veena Das, *Structure and Cognition: Aspects of Hindu Caste and Ritual* (Delhi, 1977), pp. 101-02.
12. According to the Vedas, this remnant, called *iḍā*, was used at the conclusion of various rites, thus enacting a communal meal. The eating of this sacrificial blessing acquired such importance that it was personified by the goddess Iḍā; ***see*** Jan Gonda, *Le religioni dell'India* (Milano: Jaca Book, 1978, 2 vols.; Stuttgart, 1960[1]), vol. 1, p. 151.
13. *See Taittirīya Saṁhitā* (*TS*), II.2.
14. *See TS*, VI. 5.1. ***Also see*** *MS*, I.6.2 and IV.6.9.
15. On this issue, ***see*** the comparative study of U.P. Arora, *op.cit.*, pp. 45-80.

From certain texts we come to the conclusion that the *piṇḍa* is the same paternal seed that is deposited into the uterus, its refuge, shelter, crucible. Other texts indicate that the future being is a combination, a mixture of male seed and female blood.[16] In both cases, it seems that conception, the beginning of life in this world in the gross form, depends on the formation of a simple bodily composite in rapid development, and in which is installed, from the first moment, an abstract individual principle or soul. This, however, is a hasty reading of Indian texts, and would be conditioned and prejudiced by the Semitic conception of the creation *ad hoc* of the soul in this precise instant.

As I have repeatedly affirmed, the *piṇḍa* is complete with all the productions of *prakṛti*, comprising the subtle principles of the *bhūtas*, all in latent form. The *piṇḍa* remains in wait — to be able to develop its powers — until the right moment and environment present themselves. As the vegetable seed, taken from the granary, sowed in the soil, watered, and warmed by the sun, only then can manifest its powers, in the same way, the human seed is projected into the uterus, bathed by the paternal seed, and warmed by the mother's blood.

The synthesis of sperm and blood is made by the *piṇḍa,* which nourishes itself on it, taking its abode in this fusion of substances (*dhātus*).[17] To go into greater detail, the *jīva* chooses

16. "The semen, mixing itself with the blood, produces the embryo", *GP,* II.32.20. "Uniting the semen and the blood the embryo arises;" *Garbha Upaniṣad* (*GU*), 2. ***See*** G.G. Filippi, "The Secret of the Embryo according to the *Garbha Upaniṣad,*" In *Annali di Ca' Foscari,* S.O. 31, 3 (1992): 304.

17. "When the conscious and vital principle (*jīva, cetanadhātu, ātman*) enters in the clot of semen and blood, conception takes place. Of course the *ātman*, being omnipresent, doesn't enter anywhere, since it is already everywhere: the mind, with which the *ātman* is →

the seed of a certain man and the ovule of a certain woman, which it recognizes as favourable to its future development.[18] The *jīva* unites them, and from this moment on begins to grossly multiply its *bhūta*s. The five *tanmātra*s had manifested the five elements of the external environment at the beginning of the *kalpa*. Now the *jīva* recovers them through nutrition, so as to be able to develop and grow in the bodily domain.[19] If it

→ conjoined, penetrates the inert elements of sperm and blood thus starting their development;" ***see*** Antonella Comba, *La medicina indiana* (*āyurveda*) (Torino: Promolibri, 1990), p. 197.

18. "The mixture of semen (*śukra*) and blood (*śonita*) in the matrix, which comprises *prakṛti* and his *vikāra*s, controlled by the *ātman*, is called foetus: in the foetus there is consciousness;" *Suśruta Saṁhitā* (*SS*), II.5.2. "Thus, being pushed by the Self under the guise of orgasm, the sperm, which has the potentiality of semen, is projected out of the male body and, through natural ways, enters the uterus and mixes itself to the blood;" *CS*, IV.1.7. We shall later see which developments characterize the Self when it takes the form of orgasm. All this may be usefully compared with the testimony of a contemporary *guru*: " '*Gahana karmaṇo gatiḥ*' : the ways of *karman* are profoundly deep. Sometimes even when there are plenty of sperm they [the spermatozoa] run into a 'No Vacancy' sign when they try to meet the egg. If there is no *jīva* with sufficient *ṛṇānubandhana*, or if the horoscope which would result will not fit the requirements of the *jīva*, or if there is some curse, you pour in liters of semen and still conception will not occur," R.E. Svoboda, *Aghora: At the Left Hand of God* (Albuquerque: Brotherhood of Life, Inc., 1986), p. 258.

19. The internal *vāyu* elevates and augments the heat generated from the friction of the sexual organs during intercourse. *Vāyu* and heat cause the semen to be ejected from the sac or deposit which is in a man: it enters in the female uterus through the vaginal duct and here it mixes with the blood (*artavan*), which is emanated and produced in an analogous way. The mixture of blood and semen later installs itself in the uterus (*garbhāśaya*). "Finally, the one known as the self-conscious, the sentient, who touches, smells, sees, hears, tastes, the Self, the creator, the conjurer, the witness, →

were not so, the situation of *piṇḍa*s would be like that of the seed in a barn, which, after having been stored for a long time, is sown on a stone. If the humid germ of this seed is planted in the fertile earth, instead and watered and heated by the sun, the plant will grow.[20]

→ the arranger, the word — who, though eternal, is unmanifested and unattainable in its true nature — takes possession of the five *tanmātra*s, acquires a subtle form made up of the three *guṇa*s: *sattva, rajas*, and *tamas*, and, carried by *vāyu*, is locked in the uterus where he will evolve as a god, an animal or a demon, depending on actions performed in his previous life;" *SS*, II.3.3. "The phases derived from nutrition are body making, growth, continuity of breathing, satisfaction, swelling, and energy;" *CS*, IV.3.12. On the production of *bhūta*s by *tanmātra*s at the dawn of the world of humans, ***see*** G.G. Filippi, "Alcune considerazioni sui *bhūta* come composti corporei," In *Atti del Settimo Convegno Nazionale di Studi Sanscriti* (in press).

20. From this it follows that a given *jīva* will start picking up the *bhūta*s from the outer environment subsequent to the fusion of semen and blood, which are *dhātu*s made up of the five elements produced by the parents' bodies. The *jīva*, as the quotation from the *CS* n. 75 says, adds the feeding capacity to his corporal individuality. This allows him to nourish himself with the food offered by the maternal organism, and to transform it in one of his own *dhātus*, thus beginning the growth process or, as it has been said previously, of passing on to the phase of *morula*; ***see*** G.G. Filippi, "On Some Aspects of *Bhūta*s in the Birth-Death Passages," In K. Vatsyayan (ed.), *Prakṛti*: *The Integral Vision*, New Delhi, D.K. Printworld (P) Ltd., 1995, 5th vol. Also interesting is the following translation of *Mbh*, I.90.10f., accompanied by a note: "Yayāti spoke: 'The wind at the time of the *ritu* carries the seed up to the womb, mingled with the menstrual fluid; there it makes the embryo gradually grow, wielding sway over the atoms. When the human being has now taken the material to himself, and is born, then he takes his place in his consciousness,* and so hears sound with his ear, see shapes with his eye, smells with his nose, and tastes with his tongue, feels touch with his skin, and perceives his condition with the *manas*.

Life is possible because of an alternate exchange between the interior of an individual and the external environment. Breathing in, a man is nourished by the air and ether which are external to him; breathing out, he frees himself from aerial and ethereal toxins, expulsed from his lungs.[21] The same exchange takes place in the acts of drinking and eating, actions that permit the assimilation of fire, water, and earth, while the refuse of these same *bhūtas* are expelled as excrements, urine, perspiration.

The *piṇḍa*, then, together with its individual characteristics, enters into a nutritional relationship with the mass caused by the fusion of the paternal seed and the maternal blood. Through nourishment, it assimilates the characteristics of its parents, of the family, of the caste, of the environment in which it will be born.[22] In this way the individual inserts himself into

---

→ * Makes use of his consciousness (*samjñām adhiṣṭhāya*); *see* Johann Jacob Meyer, *Sexual Life in Ancient India* (Delhi: Motilal Banarsidass, 1989²), 363.

21. "The five breaths are life or its pre-requisite and instrument. Deglution, the digestive transit, excretion, the movement of limbs are the results of different breaths as are speech and digestion. This last is a kind of 'cooking' that occurs by the action of breath on the fire whose presence in the body is known by the heat therein. Through the external respiration there is an interaction of the breaths of the body with the wind in the cosmos," Jean Filliozat, *Religion Philosophy Yoga* (Delhi: Motilal Banarsidass, 1991), p. 381.

22. "When a man endowed of sound semen has intercourse at the right moment (*ṛtukāla*) with a woman endowed of genitals and normal blood and uterus, the Self, pushed by the mind, descends in the compound semen-blood which finds itself in the uterus: then the embryo is formed. . . . The embryo is produced by the mother, the father, the Self, the right moment, to which are to be added food and consciousness," *see CS*, IV.3.3. ". . . The components which are particularly maternal and which are produced by the mother are: skin, blood, muscles, fat, navel, lungs, liver, spleen, →

a biological chain and inherits a specific genetic code. Naturally the impulse pushing the *piṇḍa* to choose one matrix rather than another to be conceived in guarantees that only that environment will be the one in which he will manifest himself.

In other words, a calf will choose a cow as the matrix in which to develop, excluding every other female of other species.[23] This is a rule which is never infringed upon apart from miraculous exceptions. A fraudulent exception is the case of the cuckoo. The female, noted for her sloth, lays her egg in the nest of other species, generally smaller, saving herself the toil of breeding. As soon as the baby cuckoo breaks through the egg, the mother hurries to throw the legitimate birds and eggs from the nest. The owner of the nest, to whom destiny has saddled with this ungrateful parasite, feeds and weans it as her own, out of material instinct. But the cuckoo doesn't change;

→ kidneys, bladder, colon, stomach, intestines, rectum, anus, small intestines, large intestines, omentus and the mesentery: these are produced by the mother," *CS*, IV.3.6. ". . . The components which are particularly paternal and which are produced by the father are: hair, hair on the face, nails, hair of the body, teeth, bones, veins, ligaments and the seed: these are produced by the father;" *CS*, IV.3.7. "The components which are produced autonomously by the Self are: birth in a given species, the length of life, the consciousness, the mind, the faculty of sensation, the breath, the movement, the nutrition, the physiognomy, the voice, the appearance, the fine qualities and the bad qualities, the [capacity of] attraction and repulsion, the awareness, the rightousness, the intellect, the memory, the ego and the will: these are produced by the Self;" *CS*, IV.3.10.

23. ". . . That which is called semen comes from the energy of all the limbs' (*AiU*, II.1.1). It is for this reason that he assumes his father's form: that is, from a human being is born another human being, as only from a cow can a calf be born. The body does not take the form of a species at random. Thus, it is correct to say that he is born with a definite form, in the most general sense of the term;" *ChUŚBh*, V.10.6.

he will always be a cuckoo, son of this unnatural and crafty mother cuckoo.[24]

There are well protected frauds hidden by legal codes, such as the adoption of an abandoned child, or to save the child from persecution, as in the case of Kṛṣṇa. The *avatāra* of Viṣṇu was saved from a death sentence decreed by his uncle, King Kaṁsa, and was hidden with a family of shepherds.[25] Nevertheless, Kṛṣṇa never ceased being a prince by birthright; in fact, according to myth, he succeeded in winning the throne of Dvārakā.

Therefore, the parents are very important because they infuse the genetic characteristics to the *piṇḍa* through prenatal nourishment and respiration. These continue by way of the umbilical cord for ten lunar months or nine solar months, as is well-known.[26] Ritually, then, it is important that the couple,

24. In the *śruti,* the cuckoo is called *anyavāpa,* that is, 'transplanted nearby others,' precisely for its habit of laying its eggs in the nests of other birds; *see MS,* III.14.18; *Vājasaneyī Saṁhitā,* XXIV.37. Cf. G.G. Filippi (ed.), *Salute Malattia Morte: India ed Europa a confronto* (Milano: I.p.L., 1991), p. 294. Thus, the reason why the adopted son is not allowed to officiate at the funeral rites of his parents, has to be found in the ancestors' cult, which requires a bloodline; *see GP,* II.25.36.

25. "Having arrived at Nanda's Vraja, Vasudeva found all shepherds plunged in deep sleep. After placing his Son on Yaśodā's bed and taking her daughter in his arms, Vasudeva returned home;" *BhP,* X.3.51.

26. In two passages, *GP* refers to the umbilical cord utilising different terminologies. In one, it refers to it as *vāpyāyaṇī* (II.32.61), that is, "that which carries water from a reservoir," in accordance with *Mārkaṇḍeya Purāṇa* (*MP*), XI.11-12, which more aptly defines it as *āpyāyaṇī,* "that which makes grow." In another passage, *GP* defines the umbilical cord utilising the yogic term *suṣumnā* (II.32.33): clearly an allusion to the passage of *prāṇa* from the mother to the son. In *GU,* 3, the term *nāḍīsūtra* is employed, cord in the form of vein; *see* G.G. Filippi, *The Secret of the Embryo, op.cit.,* p. 302.

before uniting (*garbhādhāna*) eat and drink pure food and beverage, full of positive influences, and with the consecration of sacred Vedic *mantras*. One may also try to influence the formation of the individual composite by choosing selected foods, considered catalysts of beneficial influences.[27]

A last point to clear up is the relationship between *piṇḍa* or *jīva*, and the paternal seed. What was said above does not contradict the fact that in practice, there is not a close association between the seed and the *piṇḍa* that has chosen it as its vehicle. Semen is an organic liquid that together with blood, lymph, bile, and others, belongs to the body of the individual that produces it.[28] In short, it is an organic component of the father. The *piṇḍa* in some way joins with the semen to be deposited in the womb in which it will develop.

Therefore, it is necessary to distinguish between two associated beings. The *yakṣa*s, that live in trees, for example, sometimes are confused with the essence of the tree itself.[29] The tree, however, is a complete and independent being. If it grows, it is because it is a living being. Sometimes under its

27. "As the object of thought at the time of death determines one's rebirth in a certain body or in a certain condition, so the maternal mind can impress on the son the form of her object [of thought]," *see* A. Comba, *op.cit.*, p. 202. *BṛU*, VI.4.1 20, has a whole section devoted to methods for positively influencing the characteristics of the son about to be conceived.

28. "As we have already seen, sperm is a corporeal constituent (*dhātu*) which results from the transformation of all other *dhātus* . . .;" *see ibid.*, p. 196. "That which stays in the sperm, which is other than the sperm, which the sperm does not know, of which the sperm is a covering, that is the *ātman*, the internal immortal ruler, which sees but is not perceivable, which hears but is not audible, which thinks but is not thinkable, which knows but is not knowable . . .;" *BṛU*, III.7.23.

29. *See* Odette Viennot, *Le culte de l'arbre dans l'Inde ancienne* (Paris: P.U.F., 1954), pp. 104-11.

branches you can find a traveller who has mysteriously died. The responsibility for the misdeed or crime is wrongly attributed to the tree, when the real culprit is the *yakṣa* vampire inhabiting it.[30] Cutting down the tree strikes the innocent victim, even if such action forces the demon to move out. Exorcisms would be fairer to the tree and more efficient by punishing the guilty and preserving the tree.[31] The confusion between *yakṣa* and the tree itself is comparable to the confusion of considering *piṇḍa* identical to the paternal seed.

The male seed has the power to fecundate only because it carries individual *piṇḍa*s to the maternal womb. The proof of this reality is the fact that there are physically fit men who can emit seminal liquid, but who are not able to impregnate their wives.[32] This means that they have no *piṇḍa* that can associate with their semen; the reason must lie in a preceding existence, which condemns them to sterility.

From the moment of conception, the *jīva* begins its development,[33] manifesting the external components. Development during life in the womb goes through different stages that synthesize the expansion of earthly beings, from minerals to

30. Well-known throughout India is the case of the *akṣaya vaṭa*, the immortal banyan tree of Allahabad, thought to be the home of a cannibal *yakṣa*. Even today, this tree is fearfully worshipped within the subterranean temple hosting it.

31. Whoever cuts down a tree without valid reasons, is said to go to the *asipattra* hell; ***see*** *BhP*, V.26.7-15.

32. And, by analogy: "If these factors (sperm, blood, *piṇḍa*) are not in their best condition, even a fertile woman cannot conceive;" ***see*** A. Comba, *op. cit.*, p. 199. ***See also*** note 12 of this chapter.

33. "The embryo develops in the uterus as the moon in the sky;" *GP*, II.32.20. This principle justifies the use of the lunar month for measuring the length of pregnancy and, by analogy, for measuring the various periods of transition from one state of manifestation to another.

vegetables to animals. The *piṇḍa*, now bodily, grows in volume and subdivides into an aggregate of equal sections, arranged geometrically. Modern medicine defines this stage of the embryo *morula*, while the Sanskrit term is *kalila*.[34] The *piṇḍa* is now composed of the five gross elements, but there is not yet any specialized subdivision on which the activity of the *indriya*s may base itself. After a week the embryo begins to grow like a ball of foam (*budbuda*). After fifteen days the 'ball of flesh' (*peśī*) begins manifesting the first differentiation of organs.[35] A miscarriage from this moment on is considered with regret, as a lost occasion. But certainly there is less pain for the death of the embryo than when it is more developed, since the *peśī* is viewed as similar to a vegetable.[36] Thus a provoked abortion,

34. *GU*, 3 presents this stage as follows: "One night after the union in a fertile period, arises a nodule (*kalila*); after seven nights it changes into a bubble (*budbuda*) . . .;" ***see*** G.G. Filippi, *The Secret of the Embryo, op. cit.*, p. 304.

35. According to *GP*, the primitive nucleus of the *piṇḍa* is formed during the first day. After five days, the embryo grows becoming a bubble of foam. By the end of the second week, the embryo is like a ball of flesh kept alive by the lymph. After twenty days, the embryo becomes soild; after twenty-five days, the process of differentiation begins. Only at the end of the first month is the embryo formed by the five elements; ***see*** *GP*, II.32.23-25. For a comparison between the various Purāṇic accounts and the *GU*, ***see*** G.G. Filippi, *ibid.*, pp. 300-02. Curious is the myth of Gāndhārī, who, having had an abortion, produced a ball of flesh. This was cut in a hundred parts and placed within a jar of *ghṛta*. After two years ninety-nine sons and one daughter were born from this flesh; ***see*** *Mbh*, I.115-16.

36. As observed in the above note, the embryo at this stage carries on a lymphatic existence. This is why the mourning for the abortion is quite mild. Mourning is observed by the family for as many days as the months of pregnancy have been; ***see*** *GP*, II.24.36. The *peśī* of Purāṇic terminology, is in *GU*, 3 once again called *piṇḍa*; ***see*** G.G. Filippi, *ibid.*, p. 304.

a crime impeding ancestors to have a descendency, in this phase is sometimes tolerated.

During the period from the third to the fourth month of pregnancy the embryo (*peśī*) passes into the stage of foetus (*garbha*). The body is sufficiently outlined and the organs differentiated in a way permitting life at an animal level.[37] In this period the foetus begins to move, showing that the *indriya*s have begun to take possession over the corresponding organs. Respiration and blood circulation take place through the umbilical cord. Even *manas* and the individual consciousness

37. "According to Suśruta, in the third month five masses develop, that is, the two hands, the two feet, and the head, while there remains a subtle division, imperceptible, among the principal limbs (*aṅga*s: arms and legs, head, thorax, abdomen) and the secondary ones (*pratyaṅga*s: chin, nose, lips, ears, fingers, heels, etc.). Caraka maintains that during the third month all organs and limbs of the foetus appear simultaneously;" ***see*** A. Comba, *op.cit.*, pp. 204-05. The Āyurvedic perspective thus appears more scientific, viewing the harmonious growth of the foetus in its entirety. On the contrary, sacred scriptures affirm that the organs in charge of nobler functions develop prior to the other organs. This phase is popularly known as the time in which the "descent of the soul in the foetus" takes place. "Up to this point it appears to be regarded as pure matter, as body, without soul. The soul or 'vital breath' (*prāṇa*) — my informants do not discriminate — which will now enter it has meanwhile been wandering in the atmosphere (*vāyu-maṇḍala*) in search of a new 'house,' having left its previous one month before. But it is only at this point that its quest can succeed. Entry is gained through the suture at the top of the skull;" Jonathan Parry, "The End of the Body," In M. Femer (ed.), *Fragments to a History of the Human Body* (New York: Urzone Inc.), II Part, pp. 497-98. "The Jiva enters the zygote at the moment of conception, to be sure; otherwise growth and movement would never occur. We say, though, that life really begins in the fourth month, and after the seventh month the Jiva has firm grip on the foetus because it is then that the foetus becomes viable if premature labour occurs . . .;" R.E. Svoboda, *op.cit.*, p. 258.

(*ahaṁkāra*) have by now taken abode in the *garbha*'s heart. But they are in that special dream condition called *svapna sthāna*.[38] It is possible for the foetus to return to deep sleep as he does after birth, but the normal consciousness of the foetus is characterised by *svapna sthāna*.

From this moment on he is considered a human being, and his presence provokes tender loving care and delicate attention to the prospective mother, who nourishes him with her blood and cradles him by her careful movements. The foetus dreams, enjoying this peace, but is ready to violently protest with kicks and brusque movements if the mother assumes uncomfortable positions.[39]

Psychologists of classical India knew that dreams are states when the mind projects a drama in which the sleeper is both actor and spectator.[40] In this drama, the forms, costumes, and the script are borrowed from the outside world, stored in the memory bank. During the waking state (*jāgarta sthāna*) the senses refer news of the external world to *manas*, and *manas*,

38. "Even though they go to another body with their sensory faculties still undeveloped, in reality, they go endowed with consciousness. As in a dream state, they proceed together with consciousness in a condition of latency, loaded with the potentials of their accumulated *karman*, as it is said by the *Upaniṣads*;" *ChUŚBh*, V.10.6.

39. The Tāntric outlook differs enormously on this particular aspect of the embryo's life. The uterus is viewed as a veritable hell: herein the foetus suffers for faults committed in a previous existence and, from this suffering, it frees himself only at birth; *see* Jonathan Parry, *The End*, *op.cit.*, p. 498.

40. "There are no carts, nor animals yoked to them, nor are there streets, but he himself manifests carts, animals yoked to them and streets; there are no enjoyments, nor pleasures, nor amusements, but he himself manifests enjoyments, pleasures, amusements; there are no swimming pools, nor tanks, nor rivers; but he himself manifests swimming pools, tanks, rivers; this because he himself is the actor;" *BṛU*, IV.3.10.

after having catalogued it, jealously stores it in its archives. The mind, in *jāgarṭa sthāna,* continually draws the elements it needs from the memory deposit with the scope of forming new ideas. But in the dream state, the mind enters that deposit as a plaything, without a conditioning logic. Therefore, some combinations not possible in the objective world can occur. As an example, we have the concept of horns, from the real objects we have seen on animals such as deer, goats, gazelles, etc. The concept of 'horse' lies in the memory storehouse of everyone who has ever seen the animal. In the dream state, the mind has the freedom of composing and decomposing the immense puzzle of recollections, without being constrained by the laws of the bodily world. *Manas* can then compose the idea of horn with that of horse, and dream of a unicorn, which is real in *svapna sthāna* and unreal in the waking state.[41]

Given this premise, psychology scholars in classical India asked themselves the following question: if the foetus dreams, and has had no experience of the outer world, with what memories can he eloborate his dream experience? The only acceptable answer is that the foetus still conserves some residual memories from his preceding existence.[42] This

41. "Where does this capacity of having a cart appear in an instant come from? For the most part, these carts, etc., seen in the dream state have their origin in the waking state. They are also made to disappear in the course of the same dream, and there is no incongruity between their beginning and their end, since that which in a dream appears as a cart may transform itself all of a sudden into a man, and that which appears as a man may abruptly transform itself into a tree;" *BSŚBh,* III.2.3.

42. "When the body is destroyed, the memories of past lives remain associated to the *ātman*, although inactive. Only when the *ātman* re-enters in a matrix and takes up a new body, the momories resume life;" *GP,* II.48.23. This is evidently the passage to a dream state from a previous condition of deep sleep, which takes place during the life of the embryo.

conception implies the doctrine of *karman*, to which we shall return later.

With the foetus's first movements, the second *saṁskāra* of its manifestation in this world is celebrated. This rite is called *puṁsavana*, or animation, and it creates a sacred barrier around the pregnant woman, impeding the demons of abortion from casting their spell.[43] The foetus is already considered a human

43. A still existent belief, which goes back to archaic origins. The *rākṣasa* causing abortions appears in *Ṛgveda*, X.162 with the name of Durnaman, flux of blood; *see* R.T.H. Griffith, *Hymns of the Ṛgveda* (2 vols.; Delhi: Munshiram Manoharlal, 1987;[2] 1889[1]), vol. 2, p. 665. J. Filliozat notes: "Many of their misdeeds do not directly interest us, but the *rākṣas* already encountered by us and who specialise in provoking abortion seems, according to a hymn of the *Ṛgveda*, to be considered capable of causing the death of the child during the different stages of confinement. This hymn is interesting to study as it seems to attest that the different stages of confinement as also the risk run by the child during this period, had been noted.

    1. That with the help of the incantation, Agni, killer of *rākṣas*, push away from here one who, being ill, having a sinister name, sits in thy foetus, in thy womb.
    2. That, which being disease, having a sinister name, sits in thy foetus, in thy womb, (he) the eater of flesh,* with incantation Agni has expelled it.
    3. The one, who kills thy (foetus), which is about to descend, which is seated, one who (kills it) when it slips fast, who wants to kill it when born, we suppress it from here.
    4. The one who separates thy things, who lies down between husband and wife, who licks the womb inside, we suppress it from here.
    5. The one, who having become a brother, a husband, having become a lover, lies down with you, the one who desires to kill thy progeny, we suppress it from here.
    6. The one who lies down with you, having misled you by means of sleep, of obscurity, he who desires to kill thy progeny, we suppress it from here."

→

being who will, when grown, make the rites to redeem his ancestors (*pitr̥*) and provide further descendants. The foetus represents a promise and hope for the family, both past and future. The *puṁsavana* is considered to be a rite propitiating the birth of a male child.[44]

---

* *kravydam* in the accusative refers to a demon, causing abortion and this is not the only example of a similar use. But frequently Agni itself receives the epithet of "eater of flesh," *kravyd*. In this case, it refers specially to the fire of the funeral pyre (cf. V. Henry, *Magie . . .*, p. 217). This is another example of antagonistic forms, assumed by the same entities. Here, Agni, Fire, chases the *kravyd*; elsewhere he himself is the *kravyd* (cf. Oldenberg, *R̥gveda . . . Noten*, Berlin, 1912 on X, 16-9-11).

J. Filliozat, *The Classical Doctrine of Indian Medicine* (Delhi: Munshiram Manoharlal, 1964), p. 129. I have included the translation of this Vedic text (together with the footnote appended to it) by the eminent French Indologist, in consideration of the fact that Prof. Filliozat was also a doctor. It's interesting to note that the *rākṣasa* of abortion represent, the demonic counterpart of the *gandharva* Viśvavasu, about whom more will be said later. Fom the passage "who lies down between husband and wife," one might argue that if the *gandharva* is not duly sent away during the wedding rites, he may transform himself in a *rākṣasa*. *Arayī* is the name of those *rākṣasī* who threaten the life of embryos; *see R̥V*, X.155.1.4. Even *kaṇvas* are viewed as a category of demons causing abortion. In contemporary India, pregnant women are exhorted to not to keep inappropriate, postures, in order to avoid the easy entrance of demons in their wombs. According to *BhP*, VI.18.23-77, Indra penetrated the uterus of Diti, who had fallen asleep in an incongruous 'open' posture, with the aim of cutting her foetus to pieces. Subsequently, these pieces became the *maruts*. The instance of a natural miscarriage, on the other hand, is mythically represented by the case of Mārtaṇḍa, Aditi's son; *see RV*, X.72.8-9.

44. "The purpose of this rite, as its name indicates, is to secure the birth of a male child;" Ram Gopal, *India of Vedic Kalpasūtras* (Delhi: Motilal Banarsidass, 1983[2]), p. 257.

After *puṁsavana*, the mother becomes the object of great regard in the family. She is spared from hard toil, and the purest food and drink are given to her, as well as the cleanest and most beautiful saris to wear. It is believed that the foetus, from this moment on, has all the components of *ahaṁkāra*, which start their development, beginning with the descent of the corresponding bodily organs. The foetus already has eyes, but they do not yet serve as instruments of vision; it also has a tongue, although it does not yet have the faculty of speech.

In the following months, the foetus perfects its organs in such a way as to be functional for the *indriyas*. The ancient Indians knew that, at least theoretically, from the sixth month birth is a possibility, even though with few chances of survival for the premature. Thus, around the sixth month, the third *saṁskāra* is celebrated, *sīmantonnayana*, meaning 'parting of the hair.' The husband parts his wife's hair in the middle, using a comb formed by three porcupine prickles.[45] In the part, he rubs red powder, and this gesture will be repeated everyday of her life. This ritual alludes to the fact that the wife is ready to

45. "The *Puruṣa*, going to the point where the hairs part, passes out piercing the skull;" *TU*, 1.6. ***See also*** R.B. Pandey, *op.cit.*, pp. 64-69. A porcupine's prickle, which must bear a white coloured end, is required in the performance of the *sīmantonnayana* rite — ***see*** *Pāraskara Gṛhya Sūtra*, I.15.4 and *Śāṁkhyāyana Gṛhya-Sūtra*, I.22.8 — as well as in the performance of wedding rites, according to *SGS*, I.12.6. Before beginning the *dīkṣanīyeṣṭi* rite, the *adhvaryu* performs the parting of the hair and beard of the patron of the rite using a porcupine's prickle divided in three coloured segments: the first is white, the second is black, and the third is white; ***see*** *Bhāradvāja Śrauta-Sūtra*, X.3.10.5. From this latter text, we learn that the porcupine's prickle is believed to be a weapon of defence against evil influences. In witchcraft, widespread in rural areas, the prickle bearing a white end is used for harmful purposes as an 'evil pin,' ***see*** R.N. Saletore, *Indian Witchcraft* (Delhi: Abhinav Publications, 1981), pp. 68-69.

deliver her child, and from this moment, uterine dilation begins. However, even though the mother is prepared to deliver, and the foetus is completely developed so as to survive at least theoretically, numerous rites are performed in order for birth to be delayed to the most propitious moment, at the end of nine solar months. One might ask: which signs determine the celebration of the *sīmantonnayana*? These are the prospective mother's sudden desire for special foods, different from her usual eating habits. In this phenomenon, we can see the first manifestation of an autonomous desire of the foetus, who subliminally transmits its wish to the mother. The desires (*dohada*s) in such an undeveloped being concern food, given that the grossest consciousness of its own individuality consists in the awareness of a body made of food (*annamaya kośa*). These *dohada*s are no longer those reactive movements which manifested earlier.[46] These 'desires' demonstrate the foetus' interest towards the outside world, a desire for contact and exchange with the environment. Thus *ahaṁkāra* shows its availability to come out from its dreamy isolation. Therefore, it is opportune for the mother to be ritually prepared for the

---

46. "In the fourth month, the division between principal and secondary limbs becomes clear, and since even the heart — which is the seat of consciousness — differentiates itself, the consciousness of the foetus begins to manifest with the arousal to desires;" *see* A Comba, *op. cit.*, p. 206. These 'desires' appear when the foetus begins sucking through the umbilical cord, manifesting its actual nutritional needs; *see CS*, III.4.15. Subsequently, these 'desires' assume the characteristic of childish whims, involving even the mother with requests which are at times exhilarating and, at other times, exasperating; *see CS*, III.4.19, IV.4.24. "The mother's desire during this period of pregnancy is for the most part, merely a reflection of the desire of the child;" Vaidya Bhagwan Dash, *Ayurveda for Mother & Child* (New Delhi: Delhi Diary Publications, 1975), p. 29.

separation from her unborn child. While awaiting birth, the foetus undergoes a physical and psychic evolution, permitting it to have a normal extrauterine existence. It spends time in a state of semi-awareness, opening and closing its eyes, and sucking its thumb, indicating that it is ready to put the *indriyas* into action.

Once born, the baby enters into a new phase of development. The ancient *saṁskāra* that is celebrated, the *jātakarma* (*janman*),[47] signifies 'the birth ritual.' Divided into three parts, it consecrates the infant's three components of *ātman, jīva,* and *śarīra*. The first phase, called *medhājanana,* directs attention to the infant's intellect. His individual consciousness, through the mind, is invited to explore and take possession of the outside

47. *See* R.B. Pandey, *op. cit.*, pp. 70-77. "O Pūṣan, we trust in you! May you Aryaman, who manifest the world, bestower of goods, be favourable to this birth. That this woman may cautiously stay relaxed; that her organs may expand so as to give birth. The four directions of the sky and the four regions of the earth, while have formed the foetus, may have it come out easily from the hiding-place of the matrix. O woman, maintain your organs soft and relaxed, let us make it so that the *yoni* may expand; woman, remain traquil for the delivery; courageous and patient, give birth. That the placenta may not remain adherent to the flesh, nor to the fat, nor to the marrow; as a smooth leaf may it come down and may the dog eat it; may you make the placenta come down. I widen to you the genitals, the *yoni,* the groin, I separate the mother from the child, I separate the child from the placenta; may you make the placenta come down. As the breath, the mind, the flight of birds, you, who are born on the tenth month, may you come down with equal facility with the placenta; may you make the placenta come down;" *AV,* 1.11. "The same foetus, with the passing of time, becomes child, mature and old: beginning from its conception it is said to be born, whereas in its previous condition it is said to be not-born. Thus, it is at the same time born to one state (the present) and not-born to another state (the successive one);" *CS,* IV.3.8.

environment.[48] The second phase, *āyuṣya,* is an invocation for vital force and longevity. The third phase is a 'spell' to render his or her body robust and strong. These three invocations are uttered by the father as soon as the baby is expulsed from the mother, while the umbilical cord still unites their two bodies. When this rite is completed, the cord is cut;[49] this brief and simple ritual, dense with emotion, does not last more than a minute.

Jātakarma is preceded by a rapid offer to the family ancestors (*nāndī śrāddha*); if the baby is a boy, the father — with this rapid sacrifice — frees himself from his own debts towards his ancestors by delegating them his son. This series of brief rites is concluded when the father whispers the child's name in his ear.[50] This whisper is based on the belief that the infant has a developed sense of hearing (*śrotra*) from the moment of his birth. It's curious to note that the development of the faculty of sensation begins with the most elevated *indriya,* corresponding to ether (*ākāśa*), while the first faculty of action to be in movement is excretion (*pāyu*), corresponding to earth (*pṛthivī*). In fact, one of the first things the infant does is; urinate, followed by an evacuation of the intestines. It follows

---

48. "The *Vyhrtis* uttered on this occasion were symbolical of intelligence; they were recited with the great Gayatri *mantram* which contains prayer for stimulating talent;" R.B. Pandey, *op. cit.*, p. 74.

49. In Gutierre Tibon's peculiar and interesting book — *La triade prenatal* (*cordon, placenta, amnios*) (Mexico: FCE, 1981) — it is observed that the act of throwing the placenta and umbilical cord to dogs has profound ritual significance. In fact the dog is a psychopomp animal, as demonstrated by the cases of Anubi; Cerberus, Yama's dogs Śyāma and Śabala, and Garmr in the Edda poem.

50. "A male will be born, his name will be . . . — and he pronounces the name, which will be kept secret;" *Gobhila Gṛhya-Sūtra,* II.7.15-16.

that the tendencies of development of *jñānendriyas* and *karmendriyas* will be in a relation of mutual opposition.[51]

During the celebration of *jātakarma,* another relevant event takes place in the infant's life. When the pulsations of the umbilical cord become weaker, the baby feels a sense of suffocation, forcing him to free his lungs from the state of decompression in which they were during pregnancy. As one who has stayed too long under water, holding his breath, so the baby avidly breathes air in from the environment with all his might.[52] *Vāyu,* entering with violence, gives impetus to his blood which begins to circulate actively and autonomously.

Inspiration (*apāna*) puts other bodily liquids into motion, including mucus and tears, during his first cry. His screams are not yet the manifestation of speech, of course; it will take years to complete that development. However, the noises emitted by the infant are the beginning of his sonorous evolution.

---

51. And, correspondingly, " . . . Going forward through the same path which is followed backwards at the time of death, the *ātman* unites itself first with *ākāśa* and then with all the other elements, on analogy with what takes place at the time of the creation of the cosmos;" A. Comba, *op. cit.*, p. 197.

52. The contact with air gives relief to the intrauterine distress and, at the same time, determines the oblivion of past actions; ***see*** *GP*, II.32.68-69. "Finally, when offspring of a long series of matrices arrives at the door of the uterus, and pushed by spasms, is born with great pain, then, encompassed by Viṣṇu's wind, it forgets the previous births and deaths, and favourable and unfavourable *karman;*" *GU*, 4. ***See also*** G.G. Filippi, *The Secret of the Embryo, op. cit.*, p. 305. Here, the deity supporting life is Viṣṇu, whereas Brahmā presides over birth and Śiva over death.

5

Human Life from Birth to Marriage

THE first inspiration gives new impulse to the blood supply of the brain, leading the infant out of his torpor. For the first time he discovers that state of consciousness already described as the waking state, *jāgarṭa sthāna*. During his infancy the baby sleeps for long time in a day, but with the passing of months and years there occurs an inversion of this tendency until he reaches the so-called insomnia of the elderly.[1]

During the second day after birth the infant begins to examine and amplify his contacts with the external world. He begins to breast-feed; as previously noted, this alimentation is less dependent on the mother than the prenatal one. However, the baby maintains a strong bodily and psychic dependency on the mother. During this period of breast-feeding, the mouth of the infant serves as a prehensile organ, considering the force with which he attaches himself to the mother's breast. His mouth, used as an organ of the *pāṇi* faculty, corresponds to the water element. At the same time, the infant's mouth is concentrated on his sense of touch, because he recognizes the form of the nipple; certainly he grabs at it confusedly, because

1. "Sleep of short duration [denotes] a very slight amount of sleep. For it has been said in the Suśruta [Saṁhitā]: 'Insomnia [arises] from wind and bile' (sa. 4. 42a);" G. J. Meulenbeld, *The Mādhavanidāna and its Chief Commentary* (Leiden: E. J. Brill, 1974), p. 94. The situation described is exactly opposite to that of infancy, in which lymphatism prevails.

he is eager to suck anything that is offered to him. From his first days of life the sense of touch is diffused all over his body, he is sensitive to warmth and cold, and reacts by crying. This means that the second *jñānendriya* manifested is *tvac*, touch, of which the corresponding element is air.

To celebrate his son's development and his adaptation to life, the father on the tenth or twelfth day gives him a name before a brāhmaṇa and the family relatives with the *nāmakaraṇa saṁskāra*.[2] As already stated, the infant's eyes are open since birth or even before. It's certain that the baby in his brief periods of wakefulness, keeps his eyes open but doesn't see. Only at the end of the first month is he able to focus his pupils. The baby cannot co-ordinate his vision with his ability to grasp objects until the third or fourth month. At the fourth month his vision becomes co-ordinated but it will take several more months before he reaches optical maturity.

Another phenomenon begins in this period. The infant manifests an appreciation for whatever pleases him and he smiles and laughs. His presence in the world is no longer negative as it was in his first weeks when he cried continually. By the third month the little man, when tickled and amused, demonstrates pleasure (*kāma*).[3] This phenomenon is considered the beginning of libido at its earliest stage.

---

2. R.B. Pandey, *op. cit.*, pp. 78-85. I shall not dwell on implications of astrological order, on whether the imposed name is auspicious or not. On this issue, *see* the cited work of Pandey.

3. "Where joys and happiness dwell, where enjoyments and pleasures dwell, where satisfaction is born with *kāma*, there make me immortal;" *ṚV*, IX.113.11. To this mysterious conception of infant libido refer the myths and iconographies of Kṛṣṇa, Kāmadeva, Eros and Amor, all represented as child-lovers. In keeping with our theme, one could say that the play-word between Amor and Mors (*amṛta, mṛtyu*), corresponds to the pair of Greek deities Eros →

Between the third and fourth month, the *saṁskāra* called *niṣkarmaṇa* is celebrated.[4] It's a very important rite in the life of an individual, the beginning of a more direct contact with the earthly plane, determined by the element fire (*tejas*). Vision (*cakṣus*) and erotic pleasure in a reproductive sense (*upastha*) both depend on the fire element. It's important to stress that the psychic life itself is considered luminous (*sūkṣma, taijasa*) and that fire and heat give the idea of expansion, therefore of *rajas*.[5] Not by chance *niṣkarmaṇa* is a *saṁskāra* pivoting on the cult of light. The father with the baby in his arms goes outdoors to see the sun for the first time. As already pointed out, *niṣkarmaṇa saṁskāra* is dedicated to vision rather than to reproduction. A relationship is established between the eye, particularly the right eye, considered propitious, and the sun. The right eye is inhabited by the god Indha, he who inflames, he who animates the incandescent sun in the microcosm.[6] The relationship

→ and Thanatos, iconographically represented by a child and an old man. On Kṛṣṇa's duplicity as child-lover, ***see*** W.D. O'Flaherty's interpretation in *Women, Androgynes and Other Mythical Beasts* (Chicago: University of Chicago Press, 1980), pp. 101-04.

4. "The answer for the choice of the third or fourth month is given by Yama who affirms: 'The rite of looking at the sun must be performed on the third month, whereas that of looking at the moon on the fourth (*Vīramitrodaya Saṁskāra Prakāśa*, I. 250)." The sun and moon obviously refer to the right and left eyes.

5. "Agni is alive in plants and trees (*ṚV*, 2.10.3; *TS*, 4.1.4; *AV*, 3.21.1) and even in stones as well (*AV*, 3.21.1), so it is not unnatural that he is connected with the passionate heat of the feminine genitals, the fiery semen of the male and the desire that unites the two;" D. M. Knipe, *op. cit.*, p. 103. For a study of the term *rajas* in the sense of 'passion' or even as female semen, ***see*** W. D. O'Flaherty, *Women . . .*, pp. 35-37.

6. "The *puruṣa* who dwells in the right eye is called Indha (that who inflames): though he is Indha, he is also known as Indra, (using) a metaphoric and mysterious form. This because the gods, thus →

between macrocosm and microcosm (*adhydaiva-adhyātma*) permits us to consider the following important fact. The *indriyas*, both of sensation and of action, led by *manas*, their governor and substitute of *ahaṁkāra*, are identified with the gods. *Ahaṁkāra* itself corresponds to Prajāpati, the "Lord of submitted beings," who manifests the human world in all its components. Prajāpati, a form of Brahmā, installs the ruling gods in all his domains and delegates to the great regent Virāj the government of this world and of all the gods. Similarly in the microcosm, *ahaṁkāra* manifests the gross physical body composed of five elements (*pañcakṛta*), installs in it the divine regents (*indriyas*), and names *manas* as his vicario. As we can easily understand from the preceding, the gods that reside in the human body, senses or activities, tend to move towards the external world in order to know it or to intervene in it.[7] The development of bodily organs during infancy and youth and their reciprocal co-ordination are considered as the effects of

---

→ veiled, may be free from that which is ordinary and obvious." (*BṛU*, IV.2.2).

7. The *Kauṣitakī Upaniṣad* (II.12-14) describes in a masterly manner this process of the deities entering the bodily organs, vehicled by *prāṇa*, so as to activate it in relation to the external world. In order to establish who among them may be the regent of individual life, the following play is set up: "Now then, who possesses supremacy? The deities themselves, when disputing for supremacy, left this body. Thus it laid inert, as a piece of wood. Then word entered it, but the body, though it could speak, continued to lie inert. Then sight entered it, but the body, though it could speak through word and see through sight, continued to lie inert. Then hearing entered it, but the body, though it could speak through word, see through sight and hear through hearing, continued to lie inert. Then mind entered it, but the body, though it could speak through word, see through sight, hear through hearing and think through mind, continued to lie inert. Then *prāṇa* entered it, and immediately it rose . . . ."

the efforts of these deities to develop their functions in the earthly environment. This belief is supported by observing the development of vision. The newly born infant is born blind, his eye is vacuous, the pupil is unfocused and his contact with external objects are delegated to his hearing and to his sense of touch. But during the first month one notices change: the baby's eye begins to identify lights and darks, he begins to follow the movements of shadows around him. His pupil contracts in a disorganized fashion in an attempt to focus, often with comical results of strabismus. By the end of the third month, his eye becomes lively, focusing requires no effort on his part, and his iris assumes a definite colour. After having examined this process by which the god Indha forces the instrument of vision in order to have outlets in the human environment, the ancient Indians used by analogy the same experience with regard to other sensory and action organs and of the gods supporting them. Man thus makes contact with the world around him, manifesting his divine powers on the outside, much like a turtle asleep in its shell, which extends its limbs towards the outside upon awakening.

Between the seventh and eighth month the child takes his first solid food (*annaprāśana*).[8] This *saṁskāra* coincides with the beginning of teething and marks the first development of his sense of smell (*rasana*). With the nutrition of solid foods his dependency upon the mother's body weakens and the alimentation is assimilated directly from the environment. According to pan-Indian thought, food is not only nutriment but becomes an organic component of the body. Therefore the

---

8. For this first solid meal, a mixture of pure elements such as yoghurt, milk, boiled rice, clarified butter and honey is used in differing proportions, according to region and family traditions. Some Gṛhya-Sūtras even prescribe bird and fish meat, a custom which is no longer followed; *see* R.B. Pandey, *op.cit.*, pp. 91-92.

food must be pure, *sāttvika*, noble, solar, sweet, in such manner that these characteristics fix themselves in the body and psyche of the individual. Instead, spicy and energetic foods, *rājasika*, form a robust body and a choleric temperament. One avoids eating impure food, *tāmasika*, spoiled or sour, in order not to have a devilish temperament and a repellent body.[9] These are the reasons for which rice and honey are the preferred foods during *annaprāśana*. In this same period the mouth becomes specialized as the seat of taste, and the child reaches maturity in his ability to grasp objects, using his thumb and fingers in juxtaposition. In early infancy his hands remained closed in a fist, but by the age of *annaprāśana* he is able to grasp objects with one hand only.

In this important period the baby begins to crawl around, stands up for lengthy periods and tries to take his first steps at about his first birthday. In this way he uses the *karmendriya* of deambulation, *pāda*. The syllables he emits asking for food and calling his mother will soon become a rudimentary language.

The *saṁskāra* that follows signs the end of infancy; that is, the adaptation of the organs to their functions. This is *cūḍākaraṇa*, literally 'purification,' a rite during which the child has his first haircut.[10] This Vedic rite is performed in *uttarāyaṇa*, when the sun is to the north, in the semester between the summer

9. "The kind of food which prolongs life (strengthens), one's energy, force, health, well-being and appetite, which is tasty, digestible, nutritious and agreeable, is preferred by *sāttvika* beings. The kind of food which is sour, acid, salty, spicy, pungent, which is burning and causes suffering, pain and indisposition, is preferred by *rājasika* beings. The kind of food which is cold, tasteless, bad-smelling, stale, impure, putrefied, is preferred by *tāmasika* beings. . . .;" *BhG*, XVII.7-10.

10. Even the *Āyurveda* considers hair cutting, beard shaving and nail cutting as producing well-being and removing impurities; *SS*, XXIV.72.

solstice and the winter one. The barber himself personifies the sun (Savitar).[11] The child's hair is cut, almost as if a second umbilical cord, and this act sanctions another grade of independence from the mother. The child's body is now complete, except for the reproductory capacity that is retarded to puberty, because of its eschatological implications and the fact that it involves other persons. The completeness sanctioned by the *cūḍākaraṇa* is sealed by the closing of the fontanel,[12]

11. "Savitar has come here with the razor; come, O Vāyu, with hot water; may the Ādityas, Rudras and Vasus altogether moisten it; may he shave king Soma with wisdom. May Aditi shave his beard; may the waters moisten him with splendour; may Prajāpati raise him so as to lengthen his life and sight. With the same razor with which Savitar shaved king Soma and Varuṇa, may the priests now shave this man; may he be rich in cows, horses, descendents." (*AV*, VI.68) The sun, with its warmth, gives life to all beings. At he same time "the sun is Death since it measures and limits the world by means of time, nights and days, etc." (*ChUŚBh*, II.10.1) In this way it's possible to understand why Yama and Manu, the god of death and the genius of human species, are both sons of Vivasvat, the sun. After all, even in Greek-Roman mythology Cronos-Saturn, the solar god of the golden age, makes plants grow, which he then harvests with his scythe. The boy, who in the *cūḍākaraṇa* rite succeeds in passing the test of the solar razor, evidently succeeds in passing a first encounter with death. All references to the prolonging of life derive from this.
12. From the ancient tradition which goes back to the *ChU* (VIII.6.6), the sacred literature of India has developed through the centuries a rich thematic material concerning the opening of the head (*brahmarandhra*); even today *yogīs*, particularly those belonging to Tantric schools, perform severe ascetic feats in order to obtain the reopening of this 'solar door,' through which one communicates with the supraindividual worlds. During cremation, in case the skull of the deceased does not open naturally despite the heat, the officiating priest must break the cranial cap with a strike of bamboo cane, precisely in order to allow all *prāṇas* to leave the body. This rite is known as *kapāla kriyā* (passim).

about which every race has created interesting legends. With this healing all the animic powers that constitute the *antaḥkaraṇa*[13] are established in the heart and head of the young individual. Usually the *cūḍākaraṇa* takes place when the child is a year and a half and is walking and talking. With the acquisition of these two latter abilities he can move around where he pleases, without being carried like a parcel by his mother. He can also express his will and ask questions to satisfy his curiosity, inquiring continually 'why,' to the joy and torment of all young parents. This development of *vāc* indicates the frenetic activity of *manas* and of a definite consciousness of his own individuality impressed by *ahaṁkāra*. The desire for affirmation of his own individuality is externalized by the overbearing words 'it's mine' with which the child creates his own dominion within the family during the 'terrible twos.' In this same period his sense of smell (*ghrāṇa*), almost lacking until he is a year and a half, develops.

There is an important connection that is established during the ritual of *cūḍākaraṇa* between the child and the sun moving to the north; it is an allusion to the way of the gods which we shall deal with presently. It almost means that the child, having completed the development of his *indriya*s, may start having powers on a more elevated level.

The child now begins perfecting the faculties just inaugurated, corresponding to his educational period. Thus, the *karṇavedha*,[14] the *saṁskāra* during which his earlobes are

---

13. "The collective name for intellect (*buddhi*), egoity (*ahaṁkāra*) and mind (*manas*). *Tantrāloka*, IX.236, *Śāradātilaka*, I.36. The Advaita treats *antaḥkaraṇa* as being composed of four divisions while the Mīmāṁsā treats it as composed of only one entity, namely, *manas*;" N.N. Bhattacharyya, *A Glossary of Indian Religious Terms and Concepts* (Delhi : Manohar, 1990), p. 17.

14. There is no authoritative reference to this *saṁskāra* in the sacred →

pierced, represents the first invitation to hear well, meaning listening to sacred words, and to be deaf to blameworthy things. Even the *saṁskāra vidyārambha*,[15] the learning of the alphabet, is part of this series of rites with educative scope. This *saṁskāra* occurs between the ages of five and seven, the years universally recognized as those when the child's mind is able to function autonomously. The boy is entrusted to a teacher at the village temple. He learns to read and write, and learns the most recurrent invocations by heart, and basic arithmetic. These last two rites have been inserted among the *saṁskāras* only in recent times, since the weight of the transformation that they operate is evidently reduced.

The most important *saṁskāra* is undoubtedly *upanayana*.[16] This marks the youth's entrance into the age of adolescence

→ scriptures of India. It could have a tribal origin, or be an Āyurvedic practice which — for its common usage — was elevated to the dignity of a *saṁskāra*. *See* R.B. Pandey, *op. cit.*, pp. 102-05.

15. Although no ritual definition is given to this *saṁskāra* by the sacred texts, the literary references lead us to think that the *vidyārambha* was already in use around the seventh century AD. Probably, in more ancient times, oral learning did not contemplate the study of the written alphabet. In this way, oral instruction coincided with the learning of Vedic *mantras*, as also nowadays during the fulfilment of the *upanayana saṁskāra*. *See* A.S. Altekar, *Education in Ancient India* (Benares, 1934), pp. 3-5.

16. The great antiquity of this *saṁskāra* is proved by *ṚV* (III.8.4-5; X.109.5) and *AV* (VI.138; XI.5). This rite should not be defined with the anthropological term of initiation, since the 'rebirth' it produces is the aggregation to the caste. Initiation as spiritual rebirth may occur promptly after the *upanayana*, if the youth immediately performs the *vedārambha*. Otherwise, one is free to look for a teacher (*guru*) from whom to receive initiation (*dīkṣā*) later on, in the course of life. In fact, on the basis of authorities such as Mitramiśra, we can say that, beginning from at least the seventeenth century, in the great majority of cases, one's own →

and takes place between the ages of eight and thirteen, according to the family caste. This rite or ritual concludes his childhood with the acquisition of the ability to reproduce. The child, up to this moment, even though much beloved, is considered to be the larva of a man, a spoiled and pretty 'creature.' Now he 'dies' at this preparatory stage, to be reborn as a man, with full rights to belong to a caste, to approach holy things, both texts and rites, that previously were forbidden to him. He has the consciousness of assuming his own responsibilities. The adolescent, through *upanayana* is reborn as *ārya*, assuming the teacher as a new father-mother figure who will conduct him into the successive stage of life.[17]

Only the three higher *ārya* castes, through this rite, become twice born, *dvija*.[18] Whoever does not belong to these castes, or who, although born into a noble caste but who does not perform *upanayana*, remains a child for all his life, with no

→ father and not a *guru* is chosen as guide after the *upanayana*, thus postponing the *vedārambha*, which may or may not be performed, to a later period. *See* A.S. Altekar, *op. cit.*, p. 9.

17. The teacher transforms the disciple into an embryo, and, through formulas of reanimation, calls him back to life as a *dvija*. "The *ācārya*, having welcomed the new disciple, lets him enter into the dwelling-place of the embryo [the *āśrama*]. He instructs him for three nights and then, having bestowed on him the sacred thread, presents him to the holy assembly." (*AV*, XI.5.3).

18. After the *brahmacārin* has been dressed with an animal skin garment — of a black antelope in the case of a brāhmaṇa — the *guru* makes him perform a *pradakṣiṇā* around the sacred fire and gives him a new name. The teacher then unites his right hand with the pupil's right hand, with their thumbs fitting together, and gives him initiation in Bṛhaspati's name. Finally, with an emblematic gesture, he touches his heart and navel, pronouncing the formula: 'In my heart may your heart dwell. . . .' The initiatic teaching of the *gāyatrī* (*ṚV*, III.62.10) then follows;" *see* J. Gonda, *Le Religioni . . .*, vol. I (3.3), pp. 171-72.

possibility of assuming social functions or celebrating holy acts. This is the condition of the *śūdras*, condemned to servile work, destined to passively enjoy the benefits derived from the rites of the twice born.[19]

Probably in the Vedic epoch the *upanayana* also comprised the study of the Vedas and of ritual, but after the compilation of the *Vyāsa-Smṛti* and of the *Paddhatis*, another *saṁskāra* came into being. For this reason, at least in principle, it is possible that the adolescent, once introduced into the caste, may remain in society to do any sort of work he can find. This is what occurs today, above all in the big cities in which modern life has imposed its rhythms.

In normal times, and today in villages and in the provinces, *vedārambha*[20] follows *upanayana*; that is, the study of the Vedas. The correct pronunciation of *mantras* signals the complete maturation of the youth's faculty of speech: *vāc* is the last *indriya* to wholly develop. The youth is accepted by a *guru*[21] who will teach him the sacred texts, the sciences on which these texts are based, the correct pronunciation,[22] and the fulfilment

19. "The castes of brāhmaṇas, kṣatriyas and vaiśyas are of the twice-born (*dvija*), whereas the fourth caste has one birth only. There is no fifth caste;" *Mānava Dharmaśāstra* (*MDhŚ*), X.4. "No instruction should be given to a śūdra, nor food remnants, nor food offered to the gods, nor should *dharma* be explained to him, nor should any vow be imposed upon him;" *MDhŚ*, IV.80.

20. In origin, the *vedārambha* was part and parcel of the *upanayana*. It is mentioned for the first time as a separate *saṁskāra* in the *Vyāsa-Smṛti* (I.14). The disciple learns either the *mantras* of a single Vedic Saṁhitā or the four Saṁhitās altogether.

21. With the passing of centuries, this custom has bit declined among members of the kṣatriya and vaiśya castes, though it is still alive among members of the priestly caste.

22. Learning the correct pronunciation begins in all cases with the learning of the most sacred *mantras* of all, the Gāyatrī. One can →

of rites. Object of careful study are the commentaries, the hidden meanings, the mysteries (*rahasya*).[23]

After having been initiated by a *guru*, the youth goes to live in his house,[24] repaying the tution with *sevā*, service which also comprehends taking care of the fire, if it is maintained, and the collection of alms. The boy becomes *brahmacārin*, student of holy things, observing severe control over his chastity during this period. Now he is like the larva, closed within its cocoon, concentrating all his potency unexpressed within himself. Later he will break through the cocoon like a snake shedding its skin, as the new-born infant lacerates the placenta during the birth process.[25] The period of *brahmacārin* lasts a long time

→ understand the importance which this didactic *saṁskāra* has achieved in modern times, with the diminished diffusion of the Sanskrit language. On this issue, ***see*** R.B. Pandey, *op. cit.*, p. 142.

23. This means that the approach to texts is not exclusively rational and bookish, but first of all meditative. At the same time, the young man is also instructed in the ritual application of the learned *mantras*. It's evident that, already in this phase, the thorough study of the texts inclines either towards ritual or towards knowledge, directing the *brahmacārin* into the analysis of the *karma-kāṇḍa* or the *jñāna-kāṇḍa*.

24. From several centuries now there is the habit of spending one's *brahmacarya* period at a *maṭha*, a term which is improperly translated as monastery. It conveys however the correct idea of a collective instruction given by a spiritual guide (*ācārya*), generally a *saṁnyāsin*. On these issues, ***see*** William Cenkner, *A Tradition of Teachers : Śaṅkara and the Jagadgurus Today* (Delhi : Motilal Banarsidass, 1983), pp. 154-61.

25. "**Jarāyu** is found once in the *Atharvaveda* in the sense of a 'serpent's skin.' Usually it denotes the outer covering (chorion) of the embryo, as opposed to ulva, the inner covering (amnion);" A.A. Macdonell and A.B. Keith, *op. cit.*, vol. I, p. 278. "They transform in an embryo the one to whom they bestow the *dīkṣā*: they sprinkle him with water, and the water is the semen. . . . They take him to →

and the boy spends his time in the hermitage studying, meditating, and serving the master.

The successive stage in the life of an *ārya* is that of *gṛhastha*, when the boy, now a full grown man, goes back to society to form his own family, to procreate, and to perform the daily sacrifices. When his children are old enough to be independent, every upper class Hindu becomes *vānaprasthin*; at this point he cedes the reins of the family to his eldest son, such as the domestic rites and his work, and he goes to live in a hermitage,[26] preparing to renounce the well-being of this world. When he reaches the supreme stage in the life of an *ārya* he becomes *saṁnyāsin*. Now he is free of all constrictions, free of all possessions, alone and naked as at birth.[27] These *āśrama*s are still followed by a large percentage of orthodox Hindus with the exception of *vānaprastha*, which is currently in decline.

Vedārambha is a ritual based on the most elevated component of the individual, the intellect (*buddhi*). The *brahmacārin*'s studies are not restricted to books but are rather a real

---

→ a sacred hut, and the sacred hut is the sacred womb. They take him in his mother's womb. . . . They cover him with a garment and the garment is the sacred amnio, thus they cover him with the amnio. Above this there is the skin of a black antelope, and this is the placenta above the amnio, thus they cover him with the placenta. He clenches his fists, and with closed fists the embryo stays inside; with closed fists the baby is born . . . ;" *AB*, I.3.

26. Nowadays *vānaprasthin*s have almost become a rarity. In fact, there is the custom of dedicating oneself to a life of renunciation by becoming *sādhu*s or *sant*s within some order or *sampradāya*, so as to obtain initiation to *saṁnyāsa* quickly. Presently, *vanaprasthin*s very rarely live in forests, as according to tradition, but rather in institutes situated in sacred centres, such as the Momokṣa Bhavan in Varanasi.

27. *See* W. Cenkner, *op. cit.*, pp. 38-41.

meditation course.[28] Up to this age, the man's development appears as an affirmation of the principle of individuality, almost as if it were not possible to reach the end of the joyous *rājasika* expansion of *ahaṁkāra*.

The *guru*, the new parent of the *dvija*, curbs this egocentric tendency of the adolescent, activating the disciple's intellect with his *dīkṣā*. For the first time in his life the youth is induced into considering the limits of his individual condition. We must remember that *buddhi* is the root of *ahaṁkāra*, and once activated, it is able to determine the limits of its own production. While meditating the *brahmacārin* is able to thoroughly understand the limitation of his mind, of his individual powers, and of the brevity of his life.[29]

Therefore, the period of *brahmacārin* represents a *regressus ad uterum*. As already stated, the *Atharvaveda* calls the *guru*'s abode in this manner. The individual is reborn to knowledge, this is his spiritual rebirth, and only after which can he reach the state of the twice-born. This is why in ancient times *upanayana* and *vedārambha* were not distinct: in fact, the rebirth that *upanayana* alone procures is effective in a social sense, with the aggregation in a caste but not in an intellectual sense. The Upaniṣads distinguish the brāhmaṇa of the brāhmaṇa caste

28. "In the intellect of the learned one there are two treasures, one is close (the Veda), the other [the *Brahman*] is high in heavens. The *brahmacārin* preserves them through asceticism, and becomes a knower of *Brahman* which bestows liberation." (*AV*, XI.5.10) "Bookish knowledge is petty as magic." (*GP*, II.49.73) "Of all the scriptures, only the word of the *guru* is vivifying." (*GP*, II.49.89)
29. This is the goal of vows (*vrata*) which the teacher periodically imposes to the disciple through the performance of fasting, silence, isolation, night watch. *See* Ram Gopal, *op. cit.*, pp. 306-10.

from the real brāhmaṇa who is recognized as one who possesses the Truth, the *Brahman*.[30]

Also the two *saṁskāras* that follow are concomitant: one is *keśānta*, the first shaving of the beard, and *samāvartana*, taking leave of the teacher. The *keśānta*, which is ritually expressed by the gift of a cow (*godāna*) to the *guru*, signals the end of life in the forest. The *samāvartana* is a simple complete ablution of the body, symbolizing the youth's rebirth to life in society:[31] the *guru*'s matrix is expanded, and emerging from the waters the infant appears under the semblance of the dwarf (*vāmana*).[32] These two *saṁskāras* take place between the ages of sixteen and

30. ". . . thus the *brahman* who has profited from the teaching (*pāṇḍityam*), from the effort (*bālya*), has become a *muni* (a silent one; here it indicates the state of spiritual isolation). Having known everything with and without meditation, he knows *Brahman*." (*BṛU*, III. 5.1) ". . . being a *brahman*, he plunges into *Brahman*" (*BṛU*, IV.4.6)

31. The youth, from this moment, is called *snātaka*, "he who has taken the bath." His skin garments and stick are thrown in the same pool where he has bathed. He then dresses with new garments, wears a pair of sandals, covers himself with an umbrella and holds a mirror. *See* J. Gonda, *Le Religioni . . .*, vol. I (3.3), p. 173. Thus, isolated from atmosphere, earth and sky, and able through the mirror to recall within himself the power which his face emits, he can re-enter society. Today *brahmacārins* wear white garments, symbolizing through this mournful colour the period of their initiatic death.

32. The iconography of the dwarf as an image both of the embryo as well as of the infant, has found a pioneer in Coomaraswamy. Unfortunately, the iconologic study of Viṣṇu's *Vāmanāvatāra* has not yet been undertaken along these lines, which could lead to very interesting developments. "The god Vāmana should be represented with short arms and legs; should be fleshy, bearing a rod in his hand, and in the attitude of one who is about to read. He should have green skin as the *dūrvā* grass and wear an antelope skin;" *Viṣṇudharmottara Purāṇa*, III.4.85.54.

twenty. The young man, back in his village, marries, forms a new family nucleus, finds a job, and takes his place in society. But above all, he performs rites in favour of his ancestors and guarantees the continuation of his lineage. Marriage (*vivāha*) is ritually celebrated with great simplicity. Already in the *Ṛgveda*[33] a wedding procession is described in which the bridegroom goes to the bride's home to pick her up. Together they go to the place where the wedding banquet will be held. After having eaten sacrificial foods, the groom takes the bride's hand and together they make a ritual deambulation (*pradakṣiṇā*)[34] around the holy fire. Even today, after so many centuries, these are the salient moments of marriage, although with diverse ceremonial additions over the course of time. Even for Hindu marriages the seal that sanctions the union is consummation. The physical union of the couple is simultaneously the *garbhādhāna*, the first *saṁskāra* for a new life.

---

33. The celebrated hymn *ṚV*, X.85 is even today the principal source of wedding *mantras*. I shall later come back to some verses of this hymn which are of difficult interpretation.

34. *Pradakṣiṇā* is the walking around a sacred centre keeping the cult-object to one's right (*dakṣiṇā*), and, as a consequence, one is left towards the outside. This is the walking which is performed for auspicious rites or in honour of the gods. On the contrary, *prasavya*, walking in the opposite direction, is performed in rituals in honour of the dead. It's evident that the direction of the *pradakṣiṇā* derives its positive force from the observation of the movement of planets, sun, moon and stars, representing the gods.

6

The Structure of the Human Being

MANU[1] enumerates eight different types of marriages. The first, called *brāhma*, takes place when the father gives his daughter to a man celebrated for his virtue and his illustrious ancestors. The second, *prājāpatya*, takes place when the bridegroom desires his bride with such ardour that he renounces the dowry and any other financial gain. *Ārṣa* is the marriage when a wife is obtained by the offering of a cow. The *daiva* marriage occurs when a father concedes his daughter to a sacrificer (*ṛtvij*) who, in his honour, celebrates a rite in the *śrauta* tradition. All these are considered auspicious marriages, blessed and full of promise; certainly the *brāhma vivāha* is considered the most fortunate.

The following four types of marriage are considered unbecoming in different ways, and are tolerated, or undergone, or avoided. The first is *gāndharva*, in which the two passionate lovers meet secretly and consume their love. Dumézil affirms that this is called *gāndharva*, for the characteristic passion distinguishing this union.[2]

The *āsura* marriage, today much more diffused than one would like to admit, is that in which the father sells his daughter to a suitor. The *rākṣasa* marriage takes place following kidnapping and rape. The least desirable of all is the *paiśāca*,

1. *MDhŚ*, III.27f.
2. G. Dumézil, *Mariages indo-européens* (Paris: Payot, 1979), ch. 2.

the worst because it involves violence upon the woman who is in an altered state of consciousness, either having fainted, been drugged, in coma, drunk, or likewise.[3]

The importance of full awareness for the effectiveness of the rites must be remembered. No matter how auspicious or blameworthy, all the above types are considered true marriages, since from them a new human being may be conceived.

Marriage therefore presents two aspects: the first regards the couple who love one another, the second regards the individual who is about to be conceived by the couple. Reassuming, for the couple this *saṁskāra* is *vivāha*, while for the future entity it is *garbhādhāna*. Desire or attraction (*kāma eṣaṇā*)

3. He who performs this kind of marriage behaves exactly as in a nightmare: indeed, the *piśāca*s, as the *graha*s, possess women during sleep. Taking advantage of the woman's weakness, the *piśāca* can take firm abode in the victim's body even during the waking state. In this case, the possessed one must be taken to sanctuaries or to persons specialized in the *piśācamocana* exorcism, that is, "the liberation from the *piśāca.*" Even worse is the *piśāca*'s attack upon pregnant women, since it provokes abortion: the most efficacious defence is, as we have seen, the performance of *sīmmantonayana*. Concerning men, through the *samāvartana* rite they obtain the gift of a rod for protection, during their *gṛhastha* stage, from the snares of female *piśācī* or *grahī*. On these issues, *see* R.B. Pandey, *op. cit.*, p. 27. I may add that the nightmare appears in dream as a demon who weighs upon the sleeping one (see the Spanish *pesadilla*) lying upon (*incubans*) her, causing erotic and suffocating sensations at the same time. Often the nightmare is with a horse's head (*see* the English word *nightmare;* mare also means ghost, from which derives the French *cauchemar*, oppressing demon), bringing us back to the iconography of many intermediary beings of Indo-European mythology. *See* Pilar Pedraza, La Bella, *Enigma y pesadilla* (*Esfinge, Medusa, Pantera . . .*) (Valencia: Almudin, 1983). *Keśin* are called those nightmares having horse form, which oppress pregnant women and force them to abort. (*AV*, VIII.6. 23)

is what induces the couple to marry. In the scriptures *kāma* is that craving that pushes man to secure women, riches, animals, sons, and heavens.[4] Mythology makes *kāma* the god of love, and it represents him in the Greek Eros manner as a young archer, shooting arrows at the lovers and inflaming them with ardour.[5] The love theme is strictly connected with the symbolism of fire; in India love is fire in the same manner in which fire symbolizes the ascetic heat. Indeed, retaining semen produces the heat (*tapas*) of spiritual ascent; so, inversely the fire of love produces the seed.[6] It is interesting to note how the *gandharva*s, those luminous beings living in the atmosphere and floating like inebriating perfume in the air, represent erotic ardour.

---

4. ". . . . the desire of [having] sons is the desire for wealth, and the desire for wealth is the desire for [conquering the] skies: it's all just one desire . . . .;" *BṛU*, III.5.1.
5. Again the complex symbolism of the bow: we found it already with reference to the definition of *guṇa*. The arrow which is shot by this bow corresponds to *rajas*, that is, to activity and heat. There is no doubt that the arrow of Love's bow is related to this *rājasika* frenzy. At the same time, one must not forget the drill. Even in this case, we find two perpendicular sticks of wood and a cord which transmits the movement. This time the cord imparts a rotating movement to the arrow, allowing its point to pierce. The same movement generates heat through friction, so that this instrument can be used to light a fire. The two woods of the fire drill, with which Agni is given birth, are called *araṇī*s. Their movement has been taken as an erotic symbol even in *śrauta* rites; *see* F. Staal, *Agni* (2 vols.; Berkeley: Asian Umanitas Press, 1983), vol. 1, p. 78.
6. Concerning the production of human seed by Agni, *see* W.D. O'Flaherty, *Asceticism and Eroticism in the Mythology of Śiva* (London, New York, Toronto, 1973), pp. 94-95. For the author's analysis of the separation of the single heat (*tejas*) in *kāma*, erotic ardour, and *tapas*, the heat produced through asceticism; *see* W.D. O'Flaherty, "The Submarine Mare in the Mythology of Siva," In *JRAS* 1 (1971): 9.

Euphemistically speaking, a passionate girl is said to be possessed by a *gandharva.*[7] This is the reason why, in the marriage rites, the king of the *gandharvas*, Viśvāvasu, is invited to leave, ceding his place to the human husband.[8] The erotic ardour of adolescent fantasies gives way after the new carnal experiences but that doesn't occur without reluctance. During the first three nights the newly married couple sleeps together but without consummation, separated by a stick on the bed representing Viśvāvasu.[9]

---

7. Eminent indologists have considered the *gandharvagṛhīta* described in some texts (*AV*, VI.111; *gandharvagraha* = hysteria in *SS*, VI.60. 8) as the case of a demonic possession of a woman by a *gandharva*. However, after a deeper reading, it appears evident that there is the more complex situation of a young woman kindled with love, or — to use a more adequate expression — of a woman 'in heat!' *See Aitareya Brāhmaṇa* (*AB*), V.29.2 and *Kauṣitakī Brāhmaṇa*, II.9. In similar conditions of 'rapture' or amorous ecstasy, she is even able to furnish oracles and teach metaphysical doctrines (*BṛU*, III.3.1; III.7.1).

8. "Now then, Viśvāvasu, we pray to you in all reverence to leave; look for another ardent young girl and leave the bride with her husband." (*ṚV*, X.85.22)

9. Only after three nights Viśvāvasu is able to abandon his lover. The stick symbolizes the *gandharva*'s legitimate property over the woman. Until that moment, Viśvāvasu is the true husband of the woman, symbolized by the stick separating the couple on their nuptial bed. In the *Tristan and Isolde* saga, we find an amazingly analogous detail. The two lovers sleep in their adulterous bed separated by a sword, obvious warning that the bride still remains King Mark's property. In the course of her life as a virgin, the young girl is married to three different entities: Soma, Agni and lastly Viśvāvasu. The *śruti* narrates how the *gandharvas* stole the *soma*, the drink of immortality, from the gods, and how they kept it with them for three days. (*AB*, I.27; *TS*,6.1.6; *MS*, 3.7) It's symptomatic that the number of *gandharvas* is twenty-seven, as many as the lunar asterisms. (*YV*, *Taittirīya Saṁhitā*, I.7.7; *see ibid.*,

→

The *gandharvas* and their female counterparts, the *apsaras*, regulate the fertility of human beings. It is even written that the entire human manifestation sprang from Prajāpati under the form of *gandharvas* and of *apsaras*.[10] In oral traditions these

---

→ III. 4.7) In this case, the three nights of new moon correspond to the abduction of Soma, the moon, by the sun; *see* A. Hillebrandt, *Vedic Mythology* (2 vols. Delhi: Motilal Banarsidass, 1980; 1st edn. Breslau, 1891), p. 251. The three days of new moon may also be related to the days of the female cycle; *see* Esther Harding, *Los Misterios de la Mujer* (Barcelona: Obelisco, 1987), chap. 5. One thus understands what the first three chaste days of Hindu marriage correspond to, waiting for the *gandharva*'s withdrawal. "The menstruating woman is regarded as dangerous and baleful, alike to men and crops, and she is often secluded where the light of sun or moon cannot reach her (light is the progenitive power, and she must not beget at this time). What this seclusion implies is a temporary return to her primordial state, which is not, so to speak, human, but uncanny. Menstruation has often been regarded as a kind of infection or possession; the subsequent purification followed by intercourse is the regeneration of her humanity, and repetition of the nuptial rite by which she was first 'made woman' who had been a 'nymph;' A.K. Coomaraswamy, "On the Loathly Bride," *Speculum,* XX (1945).

10. "Every production of Prajāpati occurs through the intercourse of *gandharva* and *apsaras;*" *ŚB,* IX.4.1.2. Very interesting is the analysis by J.R. Joshi (*Some Minor Divinities in Vedic Mythology and Ritual.* Pune: Deccan College Postg. & Res. Inst., 1977) of all the different hypotheses formulated on *gandharvas* up to the present-day. After having examined them in the light of *śruti,* he concludes confirming the interpretation of *gandharvas* and *apsaras* as *janii* presiding over birth. Thus Joshi confirms the identification with the Kandarpa-Kāma, as proposed by Barnett (*BSOS,* IV, pp. 704-13). He also supports the origin of the name from the root *gandh,* connecting it to fragrances. Concerning this interpretation, he says: "On the background of the discussion regarding the original nature of Gandharva, made above, it may be noted that in the →

mythological figures represent the future generations while, analogously in Buddhism, *gandhabba* (*gandharva*) is identical to the concept of *jīva*:[11] as Cupids they induce couples to choose and to love one another, by piercing them with attraction and desire. They are the same *piṇḍa*s which, desirous of obtaining a body, after having invisibly chosen a future father and mother, torture the couple by sending inebriating fragrances (*gandha*) and sensual solicitations. Their dominion is *taijasa*, because they are vital entities and from their fiery nature they send flames of ardour to the lovers' bodies. Fiery beings, they live in the air and through *prāṇa* they insinuate themselves into the bodies of the future parents, furiously agitating their humour circuits and their breath, provoking the emission of semen. In this manner 'water,' through fire, is said to reach the

---

→ *Bhār-G* [*Bhāradvāja Gṛhya-Sūtra*] fragrance is said to be twofold: divine and worldly. The second type of fragrance, therefore, may suitably be connected with Gandharva. The *Kāṭh-G* [*Kāṭhaka Gṛhya-Sūtra*] has an important rite connected with Gandharva. When a girl firstly sees herself in menses, at a *gandharva* place, sacrifice is to be offered;" J.R. Joshi, *op. cit.*, p. 37. "Lovers would embrace each other and take in each other's body odours. Smell pertains to the Earth element, the most gross, physical element. Sniffing inflames the passions of those who want to enjoy coitus;" R.E. Svoboda, *op. cit.*, 287. Those who oppose this interpretation connected with giving birth, attribute it to Vasubandhu, that is, to a late Buddhist milieu. They wish to interpret the Vedic *gandharva*s merely as spirits of nature connected with some improbable agricultural animism, thus ignoring *ṚV*, X.177: "The bird of the sky [the sun] bears in itself the word which the *gandharva* has once pronounced in the womb."

11. ". . . . the presence of the *gandhabba* is one of the three conditions which are necessary for conception. Presumably, then, if there is a fertilized ovum, then the *gandhabba* was already present . . .;" F. J. Hoffmann, *Rationality and Mind in Early Buddhism* (Delhi: Motilal Banarsidass, 1992; 1st edn. 1987), p. 49.

condition of man.[12] From this point of view, it can be said that *piṇḍa* actively participates in the act of conception.

With the birth of his first male child the *gṛhasthin* obtains the perfection of his individual life. The aim of perpetuating the family has been reached, and at the same time, the continuity of rites to ancestors is guaranteed by the son, the father himself being the first to be remembered. We can say that the *gṛhasthin* in this moment is freed from secular duties, and having paid his debt to his ancestors begins the descending parabola towards the conclusion of his life.

The first doctrine, called *pañcakośavāda,* or the doctrine of the five sheaths, is expounded in the *Taittirīya Upaniṣad.*[13] The *ātman,* the real self, or what we defined previously as the being (*sat*), and what Hindu thought considers identical to *Brahman,* the supreme principle, enters into manifestation giving it reality. A brief description of this doctrine follows, but in a reverse order from that of the *Upaniṣad.* In fact, it is important to describe the involutive process from the absolute to the relative, as if the *ātman* is wrapped in progressively contingent sheaths. The first sheath is called *ānandamaya,* the sheath made of bliss, corresponding to what we have defined in Sāṁkhya terms, *buddhi,* or the first spiritual manifestation.[14] *Buddhi* is considered to be composed of pure light for its quality of dissolving the darkness of ignorance. Precisely for this reason, *buddhi* in the macrocosm constitutes the manifestation of the gods. It's not by chance that the root *div* of Indo-European

12. ". . . Do you know after how many ablutions in fire the consecrated water may be called 'man'? . . . ;" *BṛU,* VI.2.2.

13. *TU,* II.1.1.-5.1.

14. ". . . the non-dual *Brahman,* the extreme limit which denies the dualities interposed by ignorance, is the basis of *ānandamaya-kośa* corresponding to unity;" *TUŚBh,* II.5.1.

languages means both light and divinity.[15] In the human being, instead, *buddhi* is the superior intellect, instrument for true knowledge and for contemplation. The *ātman* can wrap itself in a further sheath known as *vijñānamaya-kośa*; that is, the *kośa* made of distinctive knowledge. Through it, the *ātman* is able to have experiences of the relative in an analytical manner. Without losing sight of the universal cause of this *kośa* it is said that "intention (*śraddhā*) is the head, rectitude (*ṛta*) is the right hand, truth (*satya*) is the left hand, *yoga* is the body, and the tail is *mahat* (*buddhi*)."[16] This sort of analytical lens corresponds to what Sāṁkhya defines *ahaṁkāra*, which permits scientific knowledge (*vijñāna, vidyā*) and ritual action. *Ahaṁkāra* is therefore the principle of individuation, cognition, and activation in the manifest world.

The *ātman* can assume an even more peripheral sheath, the *manomaya-kośa*, made up of the mind. This level manifests the psychic activities of speculative and logical reasoning, of imagination and of memory. The *ātman* can go still lower in the order of manifestation, covering itself in the sheath of *prāṇamaya*, made of air. This psychic sheath is in some measure intermediate between the subtle and corporeal manifestation, since its function is to animate the gross body, or rather to convey vital psychic energy to the gross sheath.[17] This fifth and last *kośa* of the *ātman* is the limit of its manifestation in material life. Its Upaniṣadic definition is extremely important for the theme we are developing. Indeed, it is called *annamaya-kośa*, the body made of food (*anna*) since the elements (*bhūta*) in it — taken from their respective *tanmātras* — deposit and coagulate like

15. It's interesting to note that in the Vedas both *vyoman* and *rocana* — which mean "luminous space" — are used as synonyms of *div*, the sky; *see* A.A. Macdonell & A.B. Keith, *op. cit.*, p. 361.

16. *TU*, II. 4.1.

17. For this reason, its 'tail' is the earth (*pṛthivī*).

those elements taken from the external environment by way of breathing (*prāṇāyāma*) and alimentation (*pītu*). At the same time, *annamaya-kośa* gives back to the environment the alimentary residues through *pāyu*.[18] Now all the alimentary allusions on the part of the *piṇḍa* in the making of the gross body become more understandable.

One can also understand how perfumes (*gandhas*) are perceived above all from the sense of taste (*rasana*) and how the *gandharvas*, *jīvas* waiting for a body, are associated with the vital juices (*rasas*) of the father and the mother. The divinity presiding over conception is naturally *annapūrṇa*, 'full of food'; even the eating of sweets of a spherical shape called *piṇḍa*, during the wedding banquet, is symbolically connected with the idea of *annamaya-kośa* as described in the *Taittirīya Upaniṣad*.[19]

The second doctrine that we will describe, known as the four *pādas* of *ātman*, is developed in the *Māṇḍūkya Upaniṣad*.[20] In this doctrine, the *pāda* of Vaiśvānara corresponds most closely to *annamaya-kośa*. However, this is not considered as a single sheath composed of five *bhūtas* but as the container of all the *kośas* and of the *ātman* itself. In this sense Vaiśvānara is truly the universal man, being *viśva* and *virāṭ*, both universal and particular at the same time.[21] Thanks to the precise analogy of the microcosm (*adhyātma*) and the macrocosm (*adhydaiva*), it is

18. "The *prāṇa* blows on the gastric fire so that in the stomach's crucible the food's nutritive elements may separate from the waste;" *GP*, II.32.48-49.

19. ". . . man, as he is, is truly made of food. . . .;" *TU*, II.1.1. ***See*** G.G. Filippi, "On Some Aspects of the *Bhūtas* . . . . ." *op. cit.*

20. This doctrine has already been expounded in *BṛU*, IV.3.7 38, though in an incomplete form; I shall come back on this *śruti* later on, since it contains important references on the issue of *post mortem*.

21. ". . . Since the universal self in the microcosm is identical to the →

established that the living body of man and the cosmos in its gross form are comparable even among their single components. The cranial box that covers and defines body height represents the starry sky in the cosmos, the firmament covering the *manuṣya loka.* The eyes correspond to the two major luminous bodies: the sun of the right eye and the moon of the left one. Breath and the lungs represent the atmosphere in which the winds blow. The stomach is similar to the intermediate environment between heaven and earth (*antarikṣa*) in which forms are elaborated; where the choice is made of what is to be utilized and what is to be rejected. The kidneys are the clouds that condense steam and make the fertilizing rains fall, while the feet correspond to the earth in its stability. Finally, the mouth of man is the sphere of fire that is all-consuming and transforming. These are the seven parts (*saptāṅga*) in which the regions of this world are classified as well as the parts of the human body.[22]

Vaiśvānara is provided with nineteen orifices with which he makes contact with the external world, bodily organs corresponding to individual faculties: *ahaṁkāra* as the consciousness of individuality, *citta,* or the capacity to associate and to disassociate mental conceptions, *manas,* meant here as

---

→ individual self in the macrocosm, it is reasonably tenable that the first should have seven limbs formed by gross parts, such as the sky, etc. . . . ;" *TUŚBh,* I.3. The most well-known description of the identity *viśva-virāṭ* is Kṛṣṇa's cosmic manifestation in the *Bhagavad-Gītā* (XI).

22. "Precisely of this Vaiśvānara — which is the self — the sky is truly the head, the sun the eye, the air the *prāṇa,* the firmament the diaphragm, the water is truly the bladder, the earth truly the feet, the chest is the altar, the *kuśa* grass is the chest's hairs, the *gārhapatya* fire is the heart, the *anvāhāryapacana* fire is the mind, the *āhavanīya* fire is the mouth;" *ChU,* V.18.2.

the faculty administrating memory data, and finally, *buddhi*, considered not in itself, but in its mental projections, the capacity of intuition and ideation. Besides these four orifices which comprise the internal organ (*antaḥkaraṇa*), there are ten *indriyas* and five *vāyus* or *prāṇas*.[23] We can define these as vital actions operated through breath (*prāṇa*): aspiration (*prāṇa*), inspiration (*apāna*), the air that pushes and moves bodily liquids (*vyāna*), expiration (*udāna*), and assimilation or digestion (*samāna*).[24] Without going into specifics we can describe the vital breath as the principle of both bodily and psychic metabolism.

The dominion in which the activity of Vaiśvānara takes place can be defined in psychological terms as the waking state (*jāgarta sthāna*), in which the human being is conscious of the external world and acts in consequence. This waking state may thus be defined as the situation in which the individual knows the world and takes part in it through his open orifices. During the dream state (*svapna sthāna*), the individual is in a state of withdrawal into himself, his seven parts and his nineteen orifices are closed, forcing him to turn inward. This is the state of subjective consciousness, since external factors do not count and since it is independent from the gross manifestation. Being exclusively psychic, this state is called *taijasa*, the warm, because of the fact that heat (*tejas*) is the vital and prāṇic element.[25]

---

23. In the Purāṇic tradition, to these are usually added the following five: *nāga*, *kūrma*, *kṛkara*, *devadatta* and *dhanañjaya* (*GP*, II.32.45).

24. *See TU*, V.7. The equilibrium and control of these *vāyus* are the object of the science of *prāṇāyāma*, largely resorted to in *yoga* practice.

25. ". . . O heat (*gharma*) give us life (*āyur*), you, O bestower of glory . . . ;" *TA*, IV.7.4. On all the implications of heat in the *śruti* literature, see the exhaustive treatment of Uma Marina Vesci, *Heat and Sacrifice in the Vedas* (Delhi: Motilal Banarsidass, 1985[1]).

The dream state is the reign of a series of incorporeal beings, among whom we can enumerate: *yakṣa, rākṣasa, kinnara, marut, gaṇa, guhya, gandharva,* and *apsaras*, whose lives unfolds as a dream. For them, the length of their lives represents the least compulsory condition, space is more plastic, forms are less rigid, permitting supernatural feats and similar fabulous characteristics.[26] Imagination is the instrument determining the formation of these secondary beings; they are in reality only psychic projections of the one who activates them, whether he be an individual or an analogous macrocosmic principle. In simpler terms, the magic beings that we have just enumerated above don't have a constant form, and may appear under different guises according to the circumstances. They have an indefinite length of life because time doesn't influence their bodily aggregates. They are not even imprisoned in a fixed size, sometimes appearing as giants or as dwarves or with other deformities. If one considers this variety of forms from a psychological point of view he can easily understand that in reality all this change attributed to them is the product of the imagination of whom they come in contact.[27] It can be affirmed that these psychic beings live in forms projected outside of

26. The domain of these beings is the world of fable, in which the adventures of man intertwine with that of fairies and elfs, rather than with the world of myth, which has more expanded cosmic dimensions. However, it would be too schematic to rigidly separate the two domains: one must not forget that the fable of Urvaśī and Purūravas is part and parcel of the *Ṛgveda* (X.95), as the myths of gods and *asura*s intertwine in the *Kathā-Sarit-Sāgar* narrative.

27. The most well-known case is that of "Fata Morgana," which is produced by the imagination of whoever is present to the phenomenon. In India, it is called *gandharva nagara* or city of the elfs: "Just like dreams, magic and *gandharva nagara* appear unreal, so the sage views the entire universe as unreal, in accordance with the *Vedāntin* perspective;" *Māṇḍūkya Upaniṣad* (*MāU*), II.31.

human imagination. This concept is often used to explain the innumerable diversities of iconic forms with which the divinities are represented. An individual belonging to another culture projects onto the subtle being the images he draws upon from his own cultural experience. In other words, if the same subtle being appears simultaneously to a Hindu, a Muslim, and a Christian it would be seen by the Hindu as a *yakṣa*, by the Muslim as a *jinn*, and by the Christian as a demon.[28]

We have already seen that in the macrocosm, Vaiśvānara corresponds to *virāj*; the individual state of *taijasa* in the macrocosm corresponds to the Hiraṇyagarbha, the golden embryo representing the subtle centre of the egg of the world. This centre contains in potency all the forces that it must manifest in the gross domain over the course of its cyclical development. In it, however, other forms are present that are not compatible or possible in the bodily manifestation. The example of the unicorn has been cited, an animal being defined as imaginary. This is the result, elaborated by the imagination; that is, not compatible with the conditions of the domain of the five elements (*pañcakṛta*).

Now we must consider a very important point. There is a close complementary relationship between the macrocosm and the microcosm on the subtle level, in comparing *taijasa* with Hiraṇyagarbha. The latter, we must remember, is the embryo closed within the egg of the world. Thus we return to the aphorism *yathā piṇḍa tathā brahmāṇḍa*. If the *brahmāṇḍa* that contains Hiraṇyagarbha in its interior as mind is analogous to *piṇḍa*, the *piṇḍa* necessarily must contain in germinal form (*bījaka*) *taijasa* in its mind. The result of this important relation-

28. This is often repeated in countries where different religious communities live together. Tibetans have codified this assertion in an actual doctrine, comprised in the *Bardo Tödol*'s traditional commentaries.

ship is that the *piṇḍa* contains both the subtle components (*indriya, vāyu*) and the *tanmātras* in itself.[29] Later myths, in fact, specify that the egg of the world was in an unmanifested state. As soon as the egg shell broke into two parts forming the sky and the earth, the manifestation of the world came about. The world, before this separation, was therefore in a state of subtle latency. Despite being in this condition, within the cosmic egg — not yet open — the yolk can be distinguished from the albumen. The albumen represents the principle from which the gross elements of the manifesting world will be taken. On the other hand, the golden embryo represents the psychic potential of the world. When the egg opens, Hiraṇyagarbha remains substantially subtle as *anima mundi* or lord of the beings ruled over by him.[30] In the same manner, a being not yet manifested with a gross body must be considered subtle, and is composed of two parts: the first possesses the principles needed to develop a gross body, while the other is aimed at animating this same body.

Man, in his bodily life, often transfers his consciousness to the subtle level while in the dream state. His normal life is passed in the waking state in which he spends most of the hours of the day. However, there are some beings that live exclusively in the *svapna sthāna*, as we have already described. These are intermediary beings between men and gods, and we must add a myriad of human individuals not yet born or those

29. "... *taijasa* and *Hiraṇyagarbha* are the same thing because they exist in the mind, as the *śruti* affirms . . . ;" *MāUŚBh, GauḍK*, I.2.

30. This Purāṇic theme is already found in the *Ṛgveda* (X.121.1-2): "In the beginning appeared *Hiraṇyagarbha*, sole Lord of beings who are subject to him; he fixed and established this earth and sky. Who is the god whom we shall honour with our oblation? Giver of vital breath, energy and vigour, at whose command all gods obey, lord of death, whose shadow is immortal, who is the god whom we shall honour with our oblation?"

who have already lived and died. These are *jīva*s who have not yet descended on earth, and *pitṛ*s, the ancestors, who have already lost their bodies on the earth of the living. Their unmoving and vegetative existence remains in the subtle continuation of human life, after the loss of the body. Both are contained in the inexhaustible deposit of Hiraṇyagarbha, the limbo of the *piṇḍa*s and the beyond of the *pitṛ*. We will return to this subject later. We have mentioned this aspect here because the motive is clear for which ordinary men are not able to discriminate between diverse dream representations, magic projections, the appearance of intermediary beings, and visions of disincarnate human beings.[31] This means that an ordinary human being, if he has been witness to a psychic phenomenon, will not be able to determine if his experience has been generated by a dream rather than by the appearance of a ghost or of a genius. It will always be his imagination to give the phenomenon a determinate nature, coherent with his own inclinations or beliefs. The consequences of this conception would be innumerable if it were applied to the experiences of mystics.

Taijasa or *svapna sthāna*, as described in the *Māṇḍūkya Upaniṣad*, is therefore a degree of a composite and complex manifestation, corresponding to three sheaths of the *pañca-kośavāda* of the *Taittirīya Upaniṣad*, and precisely to *vijñānamaya, manomaya,* and *prāṇamaya-kośa*. The highest grade of manifestation of the *ātman, ānandamaya-kośa* corresponds to the

---

31. This confusion has given rise to an extremely popular literary *topos*. An unexpected apparition brings one to ask: "Who are you; a living being or the spirit of a deceased?" At the sight of a woman of astonishing beauty, the hero asks himself: "Are you a woman, a goddess or an *apsaras*?" Witnessing a miracle, the doubt rises: "Are you a magician or a *yakṣa*?" *See* A.K. Coomaraswamy, *Yakṣas*, part I, p. 17.

state of *prajñā* described in the *Māṇḍūkya*.[32] *Prajñā*, represented by the state of consciousness characterized by deep dreamless sleep (*suṣupta sthāna*) is, in reality, the super individual (*arūpaka*) level of the universal manifestation. But, as we have already stated, consciousness (*ahaṁkāra*) is really the principle of individuality, and thus it is not able to transfer itself to the super individual domain. For this reason, upon awakening from a deep sleep an individual does not remember where he has been.[33] If *ahaṁkāra* is not able to take refuge in *suṣupti* during deep sleep, it is due to the fact that the individual has been transferred into that state through *buddhi*, or the super individual component of man. *Prajñā*, from a macrocosmic point of view, is the seat of the gods, of Īśvara himself, the producer God of the entire Universe. These *arūpaka* beings do not possess either a gross body, characterized by the waking state as in man, or a subtle body, characterized by a dream state, as in magic beings.[34]

---

32. The reported analogy of the two doctrines is proposed by Gauḍapāda in the third *kārikā*: "*Viśva* has truly experience of the gross, *taijasa* of the subtle, *prajñā* of the bliss (*ānanda*); know that the experience is threefold;" *MāU*, II.1.3.

33. "Having had various experiences, travelled there, and seen [the effects of] good and bad actions in the deep sleep state, he returns to his original place in the dream state following the contrary way [to his coming]. He is not followed by any of the things seen there, since the *puruṣa* is without attachment. . . . Having had various experiences, travelled there, and seen the effects of good and bad actions in the dream state, he returns to his original place in the waking state following the contrary way [to his coming]. He is not followed by any of the things seen there, since the *puruṣa* is without attachment"; *BṛU*, IV.3.15-16.

34. In this perspective one must consider the gods as real beings, not merely as functions of one's individuality, as in the case of the gods — *indriya*s or of the ritual function invoked in the Vedic hymns.

When a man transfers his intimate essence in *prajñā*, all his individual faculties are concentrated in *ahaṁkāra;* and the same individual consciousness lies abandoned in a *tāmasika* state of oblivion. However, an organic connection is maintained, permitting his reawakening to the world of man. Otherwise, if the tie were cut, the being (*sat, asu*) of that individual would remain prisoner in a world that is characteristic of the divine manifestation (*deva loka*). Now since man must exhaust his particular *karman,* we infer that analogously a *deva* develops a *karman* characteristic of *deva loka*. It follows that a man, 'as such' cannot have experiences of a world different from his own.[35] The cutting of the tie between the person in deep sleep and his organic consciousness which maintained him in life, would purely and simply mean his death.[36]

Similar, but at the same time different, is the situation when one reposes in the dream state. In this case the individual consciousness, *ahaṁkāra,* transfers itself to *svapna sthāna,* demonstrating that dreams are part of the individual human existence. All the mythology of diverse peoples have registered cases of human beings who entered casually into the world of gods, and of the anguish they felt due to this abnormal situation.[37] Equally numerous are examples of persons abducted

35. ". . . because the word *loka* — which can be used even with reference to those beings who simply dwell in them without performing a single action — indicates those worlds offering possibilities of action to their inhabitants;" *BSŚBh,* IV.3.5.

36. However, *manas* can temporarily abandon the body (at least in appearance. . .). This happens especially in dream or swoon states. Anyhow, it finally re-enters the body, bringing back consciousness and knowledge to it. The abandoning of the *asu,* on the other hand, provokes death. *See* C. Della Casa, *op. cit.,* p. 35.

37. It is said that he who has experience of an elfish state in our world, does not wake up after having slept the normal number of hours,

→

by elves or fairies; all these, if they had the good fortune of returning to the land of humans, had the bitter surprise of finding themselves in an epoch much posterior to the moment of their abduction. Their contemporaries and their children were already dead, given that everyday passed in a non-human world, corresponds to a century of earthly time.[38]

It is possible to break the tie between the waking state and the dream state artificially, since these two states are both part of the same individual world, *manuṣya loka*. In this light one can understand the superstitious caution with which, in India, a man is awakened while dreaming. A too brusque awakening

→ but continues to sleep until he is given permission to awake. If this permission doesn't occur, he passes his remaining life sleeping, until death overcomes him. A story of unnatural sleep provoked by a *yakṣa* is told of *mahārājā* Jasvant Singh, who apparently suffered from such condition for few days in 1697; Beni Gupta, *Magical Beliefs and Superstitions* (Delhi: Sundeep Prakashan, 1979), p. 62. The phenomenon of abnormal periods of dream sleep is also said to occur with a certain frequency. Since it is legitimate to consider these interferences amid the dream and waking states as true raptures, one may, in accordance with this doctrine, better understand the significance of amorous ecstasy or mystical rapture.

38. "O Lakṣmaṇa, it is said that the famous *muni* Viśvāmitra, though having his mind fixed in virtue, was so taken by passion for the *apsaras* Ghṛtācī that passed ten years as if they were a single day;" *Rāmāyaṇa* (*Rām.*), IV.35.7. "For the mortal one who enjoys the other world's happiness, time has stopped. When, with the fairy's permission, he is taken by nostalgia and comes back to the world of men, he thinks of having been away just for a few days or weeks whereas entire centuries have elapsed;" L. Harf-Lancner, *Morgana e Melusina* (Torino: Einaudi, 1989; 1st edn. Paris: Champion, 1984), p. 245. To the many cases richly presented in this book, we may add the story of the seven sleeping ones of Ephesus (*Koran*, XVIII), the saga of Cian Ḅolpin (Carlo Felice Wolff, *I monti pallidi*. Bologna: Cappelli, 1982[14], pp. 188-89) and the fable of *Sleeping Beauty* (J. and W. Grimm, *Kinder und Hausmärchen*, I.50).

can, in fact, determine a disorganized return of the *indriyas*, from the state of involution in *taijasa* to their normal bodily abode and may provoke insanity, blindness, stuttering, and so on.[39]

The supreme state of *ātman*, according to the *Māṇḍūkya Upaniṣad*, is the fourth, *turīya*, in which the principle itself is unconditioned not only by *nāmarūpa*, but also by the much more dilated conditioning of the cosmic manifestation in its totality (*sthiti*).[40]

---

39. "They say not to wake him up abruptly. It is difficult to heal he whose self is not able to re-enter . . . ;" *BṛU*, IV.3.14. Śaṁkara comments on this passage as follows: "There is also a popular belief which proves that in dream state the *ātman* is different from the body and the *indriyas*. It's the following: doctors and other people say not to wake up abruptly and violently one who is sleeping. They say so because they believe that the *ātman* leaves the body through the doors of the senses, and then remains blocked outside of it. They say so because they see a danger in this, namely, that if the being is violently awakened, his *ātman* may not find the doors of the senses [so as to re-enter the body]. They express themselves thus: 'If it doesn't find the right organ, the body becomes incomprehensible for the doctor.' The self may not re-enter through the doors from which he had left; thus the body looses its sense faculties or undergoes an alteration of the faculties. In these cases, defects such as blindness or deafness may be produced, from which it is difficult to heal the body;" *BṛUŚBh*, IV.3.14. Certainly the limit of this popular belief is that the *jīva*, before death, cannot actually leave the body: "Sometimes a man tells a dream in which there is no coming back, such as: 'Having gone to bed in the country of the *Kurus*, I fell asleep. In my dream, I went to the country of the *Pañcāla*s and there I awoke.' Had he gone outside his body, he would have really awoken in the country of the *Pañcāla*s, which he thought to have reached, but, in reality, he woke up in the country of the *Kurus*;" *BSŚBh*, III.2.3.
40. "The immutable non-duality is the Lord who uproots all sorrow, the luminous *turīya* who is considered the source of all things;" *MāU*, VII.1.10.

From the above, it can be derived that man, during the course of his bodily life, finds himself in that grade of manifestation that the *Māṇḍūkya Upaniṣad* describes as Vaiśvānara. A restriction is imposed here, however, because if it is true that man as such reassumes the entire manifestation and his same metacosmic principle (*ātman*) in himself, the contingent human individual is much different from this reality. Universal man therefore represents the genius of the species, that principle which manifested on the earth in a single individual, a *pūrṇāvatāra*. In the *Bhagavad-Gītā*, Kṛṣṇa manifested himself in his universal 'form' (*viśvavirāṭa svarūpa*) to the astonished Arjuna, filling sky, earth, and atmosphere with an unlimited growth of his totality. Consciously or not, every man is potentially Vaiśvānara; but only the *avatāra* effectively unfolds all the components of the macrocosm and the microcosm.

7

The End of Bodily Life

OFTEN we read that life is an uninterrupted journey towards death, almost as if it were on a slope in continual descent. According to this idea, death begins to approach us from the very moment of birth, or even before, and precisely from the moment of our conception.[1]

In the Indian perspective this belief is taken into account, but others flank it, reducing this conception to one of the possibilities from which we can approach our discussion about death.

The pre-eminent point of view in this regard starts with the Indian conception of time; not by chance, mythology has established an identity between the god of death and the god of time. Time (*kāla*) is not considered rectilinear but cyclical. The duration of a world is defined *kalpa* from the cosmic cycle that corresponds to it. *Kalpa* is then subdivided into lesser 'geological' cycles called *manvantaras*.[2] Even minor cycles shape

1. Such affirmation is found, for example, in *GP*, II.24.29. This, however, does not exclude the other possiblity already described, namely that human life is an ascending process leading to one's maturity, after which the 'descent' begins, leading to death.
2. Our *kalpa* which, as all others, has the length of one day of Brahmā, is made up of fourteen *manvantaras* or eras of Manu. Each *manvantara* is the field of development of one humanity, that is to say of one special branch of mankind. Having reached the exhaustion of its possibilities, the *manvantara* ends with a deluge →

the historical period of a single humanity, the *yugas*, and so on, until we find the yearly cycle, the monthly cycle, the daily cycle.[3] Bodily life itself is a cycle of major or minor duration, according to the species it belongs to. *Yakṣas*, trees, and other beings live for hundreds of years, even thousands. Turtles, elephants, and man are the longest living animals while the May fly and moth are born and die within a day. From *kalpa* to day, every cycle follows a parabolic development, rising from the darkness of its origin, developing to a peak of splendour and expansion, to then decay, falling into the same darkness which produced it.[4]

Every cycle, once concluded, will necessarily be followed by the manifestation of an analogous cycle, repeating the same kind of development, yet manifesting the powers peculiar to it.[5]

→ (*pralaya*), after which a new *manvantara* follows in which a new humanity develops. The present humanity populates the seventh *manvantara* of the series. I employ the term 'geological' cycle (in quotes, in order to underline its analogous usage), since I have often been confronted with the conviction that whatever comes out from the earth belongs to a past *manvantara*. The fossils of animals and men would thus represent the antediluvian remains of 'possibilities' already exhausted in our world, which have thus been 'buried' by the passage of *pralaya*'s waters.

3. *See* J. Muir, *Original Sanskrit Text*, Oriental Publs. (Delhi, 1972), vol. IV, pp. 90-107.
4. In this way, the *kalpa* is traditionally divided in the day and night of Brahmā. For a selection of texts and a discussion on the length of these cyclical periods, *see* S.P. Basu, *The Concept of Brahmā* (Delhi: Sundeep Prakashan, 1986), pp. 106-09.
5. Having said this, one can easily see how the conception of an 'eternal return' is a typically Western conception, which finds its followers in G.B. Vico and F. Nietzsche. The extension of such a conception to Indian doctrines concerning time, is the exclusive responsibility of those historians of religions who have based their theories on second hand sources.

Human bodily life is understood in this precise perspective: growth can be considered as the distance from that threshold of death which is in fact the entrance into this world. The early part of life thus appears as an affirmation always qualitatively more elevated in potentiality, as was previously illustrated through the series of *saṁskāras*. The apex of life is the maturity which man attains in his stage of *gṛhasthin*. Man is then in his full force, with all his physical and psychic powers fully active and in expansion.[6]

The birth of his first son is the first sign of the imminent retraction of his energies and of a psychosomatic decline; from this moment the individual begins his downward path, at first almost imperceptibly, progressively augmenting in speed, towards the moment of his death.

As we notice, this conception is integrated, but not extinguished, in the belief that life is a descending race towards the direction of death. Since its most remote historical roots, Hindu thought has never caressed the illusory idea of bodily immortality.[7] With cyclical contraction, the life of

---

6. For the same reason, all significant events are believed to take place "Nel mezzo del cammin di nostra vita. . . ." According to various traditions, a being having a mission, like an *avatāra*, cannot start operating before having reached perfect maturity.

7. "Sage or ignorant, *brahman* or whatever, all men must die" (*GP*, II.24.30), ***see also*** R. Lazzeroni, *op. cit*. "In the future no one will be immortal in the body; when you will have taken the body to be a part of yourself, you, who are to become immortal through knowledge or through ritual, will become immortal after you will have separated yourself from it" (*ŚB*, X.4.3.9). This is not in contrast with the various traditions which tell how in the past *yuga*s the human life had a much longer length than in the present age. "The human body is equally subject to this law of time. In the *Satya Yuga* — the Golden Age of original time — a man's vital breath (*prāṇa*) resided in his bones; he subsisted on air alone, enjoyed a lifespan of 100,000 years and reproduced sexually. In *Tretā* the vital →

ordinary men has shortened, but men of immense powers — accumulated through asceticism — have reached longevity (*āyuṣya-cirajīvan*) in recent epochs.[8] This phenomenon is not exempt from physical decline, so we should not confound the longevity obtained by spiritual means with what is improperly termed 'eternal youth.' Artificial prolonging of an eternally youthful aspect undergoes a brusque interruption as soon as the ascetic or magician is distracted from his concentration, turning his attention towards worldly things. When his condition of magical youth has exceeded the amount of time ordinarily conceded to him, he undergoes a sudden ageing bringing him to decrepitude or death.[9]

→ breath was situated in his bone marrow, and he lived for 10,000 years; in *Dvāpara* it was in the blood, and life expectancy was reduced to a thousand years. But now in *Kali Yuga* the vital breath resides in the grains we eat, we live to a maximum age of 125, and few are virtuous enough to attain even this modest target," J. Parry, "The End . . .," *op. cit.*, II, pp. 496-97.

8. According to the Siddha school, the yogic and alchemic practice known as *kāya sādhanā* (a term which J. Parry translates with "physical culture" in the work quoted above), leads to an artificial extension of one's lifespan, with the aim of augmenting the possibilities for the attainment of living liberation (*jīvanmukti*).

9. The search for 'eternal youth' is a characteristic feature of some Tāntric schools like the ones of the Siddhas and Nāthas, and of other sects derived from them like the Kāpālikas and Aughars. All these resort to *rasāyana*, that is, alchemy. "When she came to me she looked like a fifteen-year-old girl, but she is much, much older than that. Death cannot come to take her until she herself desires it. She remains naked, but covers hereself with her long matted locks, and she carries a trident, Shiva's symbol. Once I playfully asked her, 'Why don't you let me see your real form?' She showed me — and my God! I was horrible! I was nauseated by the sight: all her skin was wrinkled; her eyelids dropped down onto her cheeks, and she had to pick them up with her fingers in order to see me. She has become immortal [sic] through the use of mercury," R. Svoboda, *op. cit.*, p. 291.

Sometimes the ascetic, having reached his aim, after qualifying the great austerity tests and having obtained the postponement of bodily death, recognizes the uselessness of remaining in this sheath made up of food, and lets himself die. Other times, the dying ascetic or wounded hero prolongs the moment of his death through his powers, so as to leave this world in the most favourable astrological conjunction.[10] However, the majority of these extraordinary episodes occurred in the remote past when gods walked the earth in the midst of ordinary mortals, times in which conditions regulating our world were not yet so rigid. In the present period of man's history, the *kali yuga*, the dark age, restrictions are more inflexible and man is severely bound by precise limits. Humanity in its present space-time condition has a lifetime that does not exceed one hundred years.[11] Only those who pursue a life of

---

10. This is the well-known case of Bhīṣma, the pure hero of the *Mahābhārata*, who, although having been wounded by innumerable arrows, prolonged his agony till the summer solstice, so as to die in *uttarāyaṇa* (*MBh*, VI.120.5662-5672). Parry has noticed the contemporary survival of this ancient custom, though in the opposite sense, of voluntarily shortening one's lifespan: "Death must therefore be a *voluntary* renunciation of life, a *controlled* evacuation of the body. It should happen at the right place (ideally in Benaras on the banks of the Ganges with the lower limbs in the water), and at the right time (ideally in "the fortnight of the ancestor [*pitṛ pakṣa*]. In the paradigmatic case, the dying man forgoes all food for some days before death, and consumes only Ganges water and the mixture in which in image of a deity has been bathed (*charanamrit*), in order to weaken his body so that the vital breath may leave it more easily, and in order to make himself a worthy sacrificial object free of foul faecal matter," J. Parry, "The End . . . .," *op. cit.*, p. 503.
11. The *śruti* gives a hundred years as the maximum limit for human life within this cyclical period (*ṚV*, VII.10.161, VII.66.16). This limit is also said to be very difficult to reach (*GP*, II.24.1-2) due to the effects of negative *karman* (*GP*, II.24.10). This *karman* may be →

spiritual realization based on yogic or alchemical techniques which alter and slow down their metabolism can partially elude this age limit. Even for these the extent limit is one hundred and twenty years. Given the present conditions of existence, over and beyond that age, life is impossible.[12]

At this point, we must consider the problem of immature death due to illness or violence. Certainly these types of death are considered inauspicious, or 'bad' deaths.[13] The 'good' death, according to the norm, should arrive in a 'normal' way, with old age as the cause.[14] Why then, these deaths occur during youth? The difficulty represented by this eventuality is overcome upon consideration that bodily life, whatever its length, has the aim of furnishing a support to the real self for the actualization of an eschatological design. Premature death, in some rare cases, may even be interpreted as a positive sign of a complete realization.[15] From this point of view, prolonging bodily life would be senseless because nothing else could occur

→ dissolved by cautiously performing the correct ritual acts: rites thus help reach the limit of a hundred years.

12. The wisest among Western scientists agree on this point; *see* G.G. Filippi, *Salute Malattia e Morte* (Milano : IPL, 1991, pp. 299-300.

13. Even the death caused by a cobra's bite (*nāga, naja-naja*), belongs to this category. However, those who have performed *nāga* worship in the course of their lives, annul the negative effects of death caused by snake's poision; *see GP*, II.44.24.

14. Peculiar is the case of Kṛṣṇa, who was accidentally killed by a savage hunter named Jara (*VP*, V.37). Now, the term *jarā* actually means old age: Viṣṇu's *avatāra* was thus killed by the 'good death' (*MBh*, XVI.5.19-25). Arora (*op. cit.*, p. 87) notes the assimilation of *jarā* to the Greek. γερας For a comparison of the savage hunter's theme with Prajāpati and Yama, *see* my "On Some Sacrificial . . . ," *op. cit.*

15. Positive premature deaths are rare and exceptional as the causes of Śaṁkarācārya, Caitanya, Mīrābāī, etc. Extraordinary instances, due to the special sanctity of these figures.

when "all has been consumed" : living in the body beyond this limit would be an impossibility.

Premature death, even though in apparent contradiction to the average length of life, can never be considered causal: that is why it inspires fear.[16] The length of one's life is determined as we have seen, at a seminal level, even before conception, being the result of actions performed in a preceding existence. In the same way, deformities and amputations should also be considered as real potentialities of the individual undergoing them; if they are not consciously confronted and dissolved, they will develop and be fulfilled in the precise moment in which all the required kārmic circumstances are co-present. All this will be discussed presently, when we deal with *karman*.

But let's return to the man who has reached his prime, his full individual maturity. From this moment on he begins the declining phase, at first slowly and imperceptibly, and then at progressively greater velocity. During childhood, the individual's powers are manifested quickly and frequently, slowing down during of youth and again gets reabsorbed during middle age, at a faster and faster rate. The first signs of decadence are the greying or falling of his hair. The unpleasant discovery of the first grey hair at his temples puts him, for the first time, before the spectre of death.[17] From this moment on

---

16. An exception is death in battle, which leads to the *guhyu loka*. "Presented by mere luck, an open door of heaven — happy the *kṣatriyas*, son of Pṛtha, that get such a fight," *BhG*, II.32. *Gaṇas* and *kinnaras* say that he who survives in battle must be considered dead (*GP*, II.48.37). This is different, however, from that most unfortunate case when one comes back after his funeral rites have been performed. Battle survivors are considered with the same esteem of the initiated, of these who have performed a descent to the underworld, or who have experienced ritual death.
17. *See* Sinclair Stevenson, *The Rites of the Twice Born* (New Delhi: Munshiram Manoharlal, 1971[2], 136; 1st edn. London, 1920).

he begins to prepare himself to affront his remaining life in a different manner. The ideal of Hindu life requires passing into the state of *vānaprasthin*. As already noted, nowadays there are few who abandon their homes to retire into the forest alone or with their wives, in order to interiorize the *gṛhasthya* rites. The current usage is to enter into some *sampradāya*, going around dressed as *sādhus* or *sants* to holy cities (*pīṭha, tīrtha*), living off alms near temples and *āśramas*.[18] Others directly assume the condition of *saṁnyāsa*, without passing through the stage of forest-dweller.

With the passing of time, the weakness of individual faculties becomes ever more evident.[19] The loss of the woman's fertility, with analogous masculine decline, leads to sterility and a lowering of passions, in an inverse sense to those before puberty. A character involution begins, transforming the elderly man into a capricious and naïve being, suspicious and defenceless, almost a backward puberty crisis.[20] In this manner a subtle alliance is formed between the elderly and the child, the grandfather and grandson. The child lives through his imagination, the old man through his memory. The child sleeps many hours a day, while the aged sleeps less and less. The senses begin to weaken; his ear becomes deaf, his sight grows dim.[21] Sometimes his mind vacillates due to a deteriorating

18. The term *āśrama* is intended here as the seat of a school of spiritual discipline, since these *sādhus* are already *saṁnyāsins* and thus beyond distinctions of caste and stage of life (*ativarṇāśramī*).

19. For this reason, *GP* insists that one should enter *saṁnyāsa* fairly early, not in old age.

20. This happens especially after *bhīmarathī*, the night of fear, which falls on the seventh day of the seventh month of the seventy-seventh year of life. After this night, the old man is freed from all social obligations, being viewed as one who has lost his mental faculties.

21. This is still the phase of the organs' weakening, not yet the phase →

brain. As a child manifests *manas* activities by his incessant and tormenting questions, so the old man ceaselessly repeats his exasperating explanations.

When he sleeps the old man no longer takes the foetal position, but stretches out like a corpse; he dreams of old deceased friends and relatives, of the events of the past. He dreams of walking south in the direction of the abode of Yama, and dreams of garlands, flowers, incense, and songs.[22] Premonitions (*kāladūta*) become insistent, as his gait becomes uncertain and his hand trembles.[23]

Popular tradition has also created magic spells to verify if his end is near. One of these consists in the old man going out on a full moon night. He turns his back to the moon, while staring fixedly at his throat in the shadow he projects on the gound, all the while reciting *mantras*. After this recitation he looks up, and by an optical illusion he sees his own gigantic, pale form against the background of the dark sky. If the vision appears to be headless, his death is imminent and inevitable. Another simple test consists in staring cross-eyed at the point of his nose. If he does not see the point of his nose, it means that death is already upon him, turning his nose downward.[24]

→ of retraction of the corresponding faculties. Nevertheless, presbyopia is often related to the loss of brightness of one's eyes.

22. *See* Sinclair Stevenson, *The Rites of the Twice Born*, *op. cit.*, pp. 135-36.

23. A death omen is the apparition of certain species of doves (*kapota*) and of owls (*ulūka*); *see* *R̥V*, X.165.1-5. The seventh night of the seventh month of the seventy-seventh year of life is called *bhīmarathī*, "the night of fear or panic," since from that moment on all unexpected events are to be viewed as *kāladūtas*. Thus, death can arrive immediately.

24. *See* Sinclair Stevenson, *The Rites of the Twice Born*, *op. cit.*, pp. 137-38. Even the *Āyurveda* employs analogous techniques for achieving the same purpose. Not being able to see the polar star, the Milky →

All these stratagems, in reality, are superfluous, given that in India a man realizes by himself when his hour is near.[25] Just as in old European fables, the dying Indian calls his sons, relatives, and intimates around him in order to give last instructions, his will, and recommendations for what will take place after his departure.[26] Then he abandons himself to death,

→ Way or the *arundhatī* star, is an omen of imminent death (*SS*, I.287). To see the polar star or the *arundhatī* intermittently, indicates that death will occur in the course of a year (*MBh*, XII.318.9).

25. *See* R.B. Pandey, *op. cit.*, p. 246.

26. "As things go, it seems like we have forgotten how people used to die just about thirty years ago. In the countries of our Western civilization, this happened with great simplicity. First of all, the feeling (more than the presentiment), that one's time had come: 'A rich farmer, feeling his death near. . . .' Or an old man: 'Finally, feeling himself near to the end of his days. . . .' A feeling that never deceived: everyone was the first to be informed of his own imminent death. This recognition was the first act of a family ritual. The second was the public ceremony of bidding farewell, which the dying presided: 'He had his sons come to him, he spoke to them without any witnesses . . .' or on the contrary, in front of witness. The essential thing was that he say something, make his will, repay his debts, ask for forgiveness, express his last wishes and finally take leave: 'He grasps the hands of all, he dies.' This is all. This is how things would normally go. It was important that the dying died without any haste but also not slowly, so that the moment of bidding farewell would be neither avoided nor prolonged. Physiology and medicine would almost always recognize the medium length of allotted lifetime for the dying. This standard length was disrupted only in exceptional cases: the unexpected and sudden death (*a subitanea et improvisa morte, libera nos, Domine*), the trick of the dying person who refused to recognize always clear signs of approaching death (a practice denounced and ridiculed by moralists and satirical writers), an irregularity of nature, when time passed and the dying never died. Today one realizes that these cases, once rare and viewed as an aberration, have become exemplary. One must die like once one was not supposed to. But who determine the custom? First of all, the lords →

not leaving his house, or getting up again.[27] It is not rare in these circumstances that the man decides to assume *saṁnyāsa*: he shaves his head, puts on saffron robes, and undergoes initiation rites. He must be conscious and respond coherently to the anticipated questions.[28] The assumption of the state of renunciation on the death-bed is called *ātura saṁnyāsa*.

With death at hand, the old man sends for a brāhmaṇa whom he gives a series of goods which are strongly allusive to the trip he is about to undertake:[29] several empty cotton balls[30]

→ of the new kingdom of death with its mobile frontiers, the staff of hospitals, doctors and nurses, to whom is always guaranteed the complicity of family and society," B.G. Glaser & A.L. Strauss, *Time for Dying* (Chicago, Aldine, 1968); quoted in Ph. Aries, *Storia della morte in Occidente* (Milano: BUR, 1978[1]), I regret the impossibility of having direct access to this interesting work. In India it is said that if an old man refuses to die or to recognize the coming of death, death will strike a child of his family as substitute, one who is unable to defend himself from the attacks of the *yamadūtas*; *see* J. Parry, "The End . . .," *op. cit.*, p. 503.

27. "Having previously predicted the time of his going, the dying man gathers his sons about him and — by an effort of concentrated will — abandons life. He is not said to die, but to relinquish his body," *ibid.*, pp. 503-04. In Varanasi, some prefer to ask for hospitality at the two existing shelters that facilitate one's passing away: these are the *Kāśī Mukti Bhavan* and the *Kāśī Lābha Bhavan*. Here one is not given medical assistance, but exclusively ritual assistance; *see* L.P. Vidyarthi, B.N. Saraswati & Makhan Jha, *The Sacred Complex of Kashi* (Delhi: Concept Publishing Company, 1979), p. 59.

28. A ritual's efficacy increases when the person performing it is aware of what takes place in the process. If the person finds himself in a state of unawareness, the ritual has no little effect; if he's aready dead, the ritual has no efficacy whatsoever (*GP*, II.16.2-3).

29. Even in this case, the gifts have greater efficacy when the *indriyas* are operating (*GP*, II.30.3-4). The gift is the most direct means for obtaining merits during the *kali yuga*. In older epochs the means were different, in accordance with the characteristics of humanity: *tapas*, the ascetic discipline, was the means to directly obtain merits →

that probably constitute a 'viaticum,' given that in remote times these were exchanged as money. Another gift consists in iron pots: this metal is considered full of subtle impure influences, for which it is well accepted by the envoys of Yama (*yamadūta*).[31] The third gift is of salt, an element of complex significance; it is not only the residue of āsuric oceans and symbol of death and sterility. Salt has the power of conserving corruptible foods. When sprinkled on food, it gives flavour. Therefore, salt is a substitute for the dying man who is becoming mineralized, and who will remain in a state of preservation until the moment in which he will return to a new existence.[32] The custom of buying salt to celebrate the Indian new year has the analogous significance of the renewal of the solar cycle. A gift of land may also be given to the brāhmaṇa.[33] A poor man may be limited to giving the priest a handful of earth, along with a few coins, signifying that the old man is registered to leaving the earth. He also gives the priest a

→ in the *kṛta yuga*, knowledge was the means in the *tretā yuga* and sacrifice was the means in the *dvāpara*; *see GP*, II.34.2.

30. The gift of cotton balls, according to *GP*, II.30.15, has the function of keeping away the *piśācas*. I have been told that nowadays this custom is no more in use, having been substituted by the offering of a few coins, according to the usage of *niśkraya bhūtam dravyam*, "things of scarce value," which gives even poor people the opportunity to participate in the rituals.

31. The dying one, by offering iron, touches the earth with his hand. Yama is armed with an iron rod, with which he beats the sinners. Thus, one may even offer him iron weapons (*GP*, II.30.24-25). Sesame and iron are the gifts that Yama welcomes most (*GP*, II.30.14). In northern India there used to be the custom of offering small iron statues of Yama. This custom has come to an end only recently: today formless pieces of iron are offered instead.

32. The negative and āsuric aspects are represented by salt, the use of which is discouraged. On the contrary, positive aspects are attributed to rock salt; *see Kāṭhaka Gṛhya-Sūtra*, I.8.

33. "He who donates a property will be reborn as a King", *GP*, II.30.16.

handful of cereal and legume seeds (*bājarā*). These seeds represent his last vital powers which he disperses in order to take his last trip. Together with the seeds he also gives some clarified butter. We can note an analogy between the gift of *bājarās* and the *śrāddha*[34] which we mentioned earlier. The seventh gift is of *laḍḍū*, the golden sweet of spherical shape, which the Lord Gaṇapati loves: the elephant headed god is the lord of passages and the destroyer of obstacles, so through this gift, the man guarantees his exit from earthly life without difficulties or hindrances. On the *laḍḍū* even the most indigent try to apply a fragment of golden membrane,[35] in order to pay their passage to the world beyond. The final gift is that of a cow, called Vaitaraṇī,[36] or "she who crosses over" or "she who makes one cross over."

The animal is accurately prepared to take part in the rite: her horns are painted gold, her hooves are painted silver, and her behind, copper. Her back is adorned with a *sārī*, her neck with bells, and her tail is braided with pearls. This cow must not have any physical defects, and she must be accompanied by her calf.

---

34. *Śrāddha* means that which rests on *śraddhā*, faith. This is indeed an apt term since, in the rituals for the dead, the *pitṛ*s delegate brāhmaṇas to represent them in the meetings with their living relatives. Faith is certainly needed in order to believe that, by offering gifts and food to the brāhmaṇas, the positive effects of the rituals will reach one's *pitṛ*s. The gods, for instance, never use any mortal to represent them in the world of humans; *see* Charles Malamoud, "Les morts sans visage," In G. Gnoli & J.P. Vernant (ed.) *La mort, les morts dans les societiés anciennes* (Cambridge: Cambridge University Press, 1982), pp. 441, 451.
35. "The gift of gold produces happiness in heaven;" *GP*, II.30.16.
36. *See* R.B. Pandey, *op. cit.*, p. 246. This custom is still alive in the old neighbourhoods of big cities. Sometimes, this cow is mentioned in texts with the epithet of *utkrānti*, "she who makes free."

Vaitaraṇī is brought into the old man's room, and her tail is held mightly in his right hand. He then consigns the gift to the brāhmaṇa. The dying man held the cow's tail with all his strength, in order to be pulled along for a few meters. The animal's function is to conduct the deceased along the road that leads to the kingdom of the dead. Sometimes, when the dying man is too ill to be disturbed, a cord is put into his hand, tied to the cow that remains outside in the street. If the dying man does not have sufficient means to buy a cow, he can donate five coins of diverse value, symbolizing the price of a cow. Certainly the gift of a cow (*godāna*) is the most important one of all, since the animal serves the function of a psychopompus. Vaitaraṇī is also the name of the river of blood and excrements that, at the southern extremity of the human world, marks the boundary line with the kingdom of god Yama.[37]

In the past, those of *śrauta* cults did not give these gifts directly to the brāhmaṇas; the offerings were thrown into the sacrificial fire which transformed them into smoke and vapour, going upwards together with the soul of the deceased.[38]

37. The funeral gift is needed in order to easily cross the Vaitaraṇī river. For this purpose, it is better to offer the gift during an eclipse, an equinox, at dusk, or at the sun's passage from one zodiacal sign to the next; *see GP*, II.47.22-23. Sometimes elderly people, even if still strong and in good shape, anticipate the gift of the Vaitaraṇī so as to have it coincide with some important astrological event. In this case, the gift of the cow will not be repeated when death is impending.

38. The Kalpa-Sūtras are ritual texts which, unlike the *Brāhmaṇas*, are not included in the Śruti. They are viewed as one of the six Vedāṅgas, the sciences necessary for the correct understanding of the Vedas. The Kalpa-Sūtras comprise three collections: the Śrauta-Sūtras, which describe the solemn collective rites, the Gṛhya-Sūtras, pertaining to the obligatory daily rites, and the Dharma-Sūtras, listing caste rules and the laws of social behaviour. The Śrauta-Sūtras are often improperly defined as "texts of Vedic

→

Regarding *godāna*, certainly in its origin, the psychopompus animal was sacrificed. It is extremely difficult to establish the epoch of the adaptation of the *ahitāgni*'s tradition to the prescriptions of the Gṛhya-Sūtras. However, during the first Islamic sultanate in India, this was already common. During the funeral of an *ahitāgni* an Anustaraṇī cow was chosen, "she who is laid down,"[39] an euphemism meaning that she would be killed.[40] Anustaraṇī was sacrificed and its organs sectioned; each organ was placed on the corresponding organ of the deceased, lying on the stock of wood.[41] The cremation (*upoṣaṇa*)

→ ritual," though for instance even the Gṛhya rites are of Vedic origin. The Śrauta-Sūtras describe solemn rites and other ritual activities which were seldom performed even in the oldest times. Given the rarity of these ritual performances, only a few Brāmaṇical families have succeeded in transmitting — from time immemorial — the sacred fire for the excecution of these rites. These brāhmaṇas called *ahitāgni*, are still present in some areas of Uttar Pradesh, Maharashtra, Kerala and Tamil Nadu. They can perform all Vedic rituals, though they have substituted animal sacrifice with natural or symbolical elements; ***see*** J.A.B. van Buitenen, *The Pravargya: An Ancient Indian Iconic Ritual: Described & Annotated* (Pune: Deccan College, 1968). ***See also*** U.M. Vesci, *op. cit.*

39. The Anustaraṇī, unlike the Vaitaraṇī, must have been an old cow, in bad physical shape and with only one horn, ***see*** A. Hillebrandt, "Death . . .," In *op.cit.*, 476b.

40. The funeral ceremony with the Anustaraṇī is more complex. The way of the funreal procession is marked by three halting moments. At each of these stopovers a goat is sacrificed and the participants circumambulate counter clockwise (*prasavya*) the dead body, ventilating it with the border of their *dhotī*s and *sārī*s. Finally, three *pradakṣinā*s are performed without ventilating the corpse; ***see*** A. Hillebrandt, "Death . . .," in *op. cit.*, 476b-477a.

41. Kidneys were placed in the hands of the dead, as an offering to Yama's two dogs; ***see*** *ibid.*, 475b. Instead of the cow, a billy goat (*chāga*) could also be sacrificed. The animal's bodily parts had to be placed on the corpse exactly in the same way as in the Anustaraṇī →

took place. In this manner, Anustaraṇī served as a guide to the deceased; the smoke arising from his burnt flesh would be food for the soul of the deceased during his long journey.[42] After the medieval period, a custom arose in which the cow was made to flee from the sacrifice site, in conformity with the progressive reduction of bloody rites. It's probable that the skin of the Anustaraṇī was used to wrap around the corpse to be cremated. Even today the straw mat enfolding the dead body is called antelope skin or the placenta for a new birth. It is interesting to note that in archaic Hinduism, still alive in Bali, the remains of brāhmaṇas are enclosed in wooden coffins sculptured in the form of a cow. In this coffin they are delivered to the flames of cremation.[43]

Going back to the main tradition of the Gṛhya-Sūtras, the gift of a Vaitaraṇī cow substitutes a sacrifice to the gods with a donation in favour of the brāhmaṇas, the real divinities in human form.

After the series of gifts,[44] the successive passage immediately precedes death: an illusory improvement after which the dying man loses consciousness. The relatives then delicately

→ rite (*ṚV*, X.16.4; *ŚSB*, VI.2.1.5). The billy goat represents Agni, of whom it is the vehicle. *Pitṛs* are believed to be particularly fond of the meat of billy goats; *see Matsya Purāṇa*, CXLVIII.83.

42. *See* R.B. Pandey, *op. cit.*, p. 246.

43. *See* Miguel Covarrubias, *Island of Bali* (London-New York-Sydney-Henley: KPI, 1986[3], London 1937[1]), pp. 371-77.

44. To end our discussion on gifts, it should be noted that offerings must be given with great generosity. They are thought to guarantee a rebirth in a prosper condition. He who has no money, tries to procure it in fraudulent ways, with the risk of ending up in hell (*GP*, II.24.46). In the past, numerous families were ruined by celebrating expensive funeral rites. The Muslim kings of India emanated various laws in order to minimize these wastes. Recently, even the Government of Indonesia has intervened against the custom of performing expensive funeral rites.

lift his body and place it on the purified naked earth, with his head facing north and his feet south, so that he can depart towards the southern reign of Yama. The closest angle to the domestic fire is chosen,[45] above all for the majority who do not practice the cult of the three fires.[46] The old man should not expire suspended between heaven and earth as he would on his bed; between heaven and earth there is the atmospheric environment (*antarikṣa*), populated by subtle beings, demons (*piśācas*), vampires (*vetālas*), and nightmares (*uragrahas*),[47] ready

---

45. *See* R.B. Pandey, *op. cit.*, p. 246. It is interesting to remember that in India the archaeological excavations have revealed the popular custom of burying the dead under the domestic floor, near one's fireplace. This custom, rarely resorted to in the Indus valley civilization — in which the corpses or their ashes used to be buried in cemeteries located to the south of inhabited centres — used to be all over India, from Kashmir to the whole of Deccan, from the sixteenth to the seventh century BCE. *See* P. Singh, *Burial Practices in Ancient India* (Varanasi: Prthivi Prakashan, 1970), p. 171. The majority of skeletons which have been found are of children. They were buried in embryonic position, in order to facilitate their rebirth. "Thus on several sites, children have been found buried in pottery urns in embryonic position and sometimes under the house floors. The burial in embryonic posture was accorded possibly in the belief that as a man came out of his mother's womb, so shall he return whence he came," *ibid.*, p. 174. Curious is the analogy with archaic Chinese customs: the ceremonies of both marriage and of ancestores,' burial took place inside the house; *see* Marcel Granet, *La religion des Chinois* (Paris: P.U.F., 1951), pp. 2, 4.
46. *See* R.B. Pandey, *op. cit.*, p. 246. *See also* *Āśvalāyana Gṛhya-Sūtra* (*AGS*), IV.1. The *ahitāgnis*, on the contrary, are placed on the ground in the open space where he used to perform sacrifices.
47. "Pressing the chest," a term which, as already pointed out in note 146, appears identical to the French *cochemare* and to the Spanish *pesadilla*. It should be remembered that these are spirits who sit heavily on the chest of sleeping people, causing suffocation and erotic fantasies; *see* G.G. Filippi, "Alcune note . . .," *op. cit.* *Bālagraha* appears to indicate a series of nine different kinds of infantile →

to invade the body of whoever is still inexperienced in his new aerial condition.[48] The soul itself, if suspended between heaven and earth would find itself in a dream state (*svapna sthāna*), where it has no contact with an objective environment, and is prey to its unbridled imagination. There consciousness is not vigil, does not distinguish between real and unreal, can confound the dream visions created by itself with psychic interferences of other beings who are probably evil, badly intentioned. The dying man, lying on the ground, can better grip onto an objective reality, remain in the waking state, and die lucidly while concentrated on the phenomenon he is experiencing.

Around the dying man sacred water from the Ganges is sprinkled, seeds and *kuśa* grass (*dūrvā*)[49] are scattered, symbolizing promises of a new existence. Cow excrements are sprinkled, representing the land in its rawness.[50] Relatives are gathered around him; if he is a *brahman brahmavid*, the priest officiating recites some passages from the *Āraṇyaka*s, or some hymns from the Vedas of his family tradition.[51] For other castes, the priest

---

→ nightmares. *Grāhī*, on the other hand, defines the female spirit seizing men, and is the female equivalent of *grāha*.

48. *See GP*, II.29.10, "These were the common sources of help, but they were greatly outnumbered by a variety of supernatural entities which could cause harm. Chief among these were *bhut-parhet* (ghost), *churel* (the ghosts of young women who died in childbirth), *dayen* (female witches), and *jadu-phoonk* (malign sorcery)," G.M. Castrairs, *Death of a Witch* (London-Melbourne-Sydney-Auckland-Johannesburg: Hutchinson, 1983), p. 54.

49. *Desmostachya bipennata* or *Saccarum cylindricum*. According to O. Viennot (*op. cit.*, pp. 275-76), *dūrvā* would be the *Cynodon dactylon*, whereas *kuśa* would be the *Eragrostis cynosuroides*.

50. Because of the often noted anlogy between birth and death, pregnant women should lay on the ground thus purified at the time giving birth; *see GP*, II.2.6-8.

51. *See* A. Hillerbrandt, "Death . . .," *op. cit.*, p. 476b.

chooses sacred and efficacious verses from the *Bhagavad-Gītā* and the *Rāmāyaṇa*.[52] So it is in this atmosphere, consecrated by vibrations of sacred texts, by the perfumed air of flowers and incense, near the sacred *gārhapatya* fire, sprinkled with Ganges water, and lying on the naked and fertile earth, or rather lulled by the five *bhūtas*, that man concludes his earthly existence.

---

52. *See* R.B. Pandey, *op. cit.*, p. 246.

8

Agony and its Rites

WHILE all these events are taking place with the ritual implications just described, the dying man undergoes a complex modification of his faculties, which permitted his contact with the human world up until then.

The first signs of physical decline leading up to old age have already been described. The weakening of the senses is followed by the partial retraction of the faculties of sensation and action. This is considered the beginning of the transferral of the gods, who had taken abode in his sense-organs, towards the central seat from which they emerged after conception. The sense-organs, the doors of communication with the outer environment, become obtuse and progressively occluded. The mind begins to withdraw from its functional organ, the brain (*mastiṣka*), progressively closing the flow of solicitations from the outside world, actively intervening less and less. The mind is engaged in reorganizing data stored in memory, beginning with the most recent, then reconsidering the most remote. The person takes refuge in his past memories, and as he grows still older, he recalls his youth, his adolescence, and his childhood. While recalling he consumes and exhausts a great part of the registered data, cancelling the most recent memories so as to appear forgetful, a prisoner of punctilious memories from the remote past.

When the old man feels death at hand, he calls his family members around him, thus beginning the rites just described.

However, he does not enter into a state of agony until the retraction of the *indriyas* of his bodily organs pass into their conclusive phase.[1] As we have seen, the process of reabsorption of the individual faculties goes in reverse order to those which were manifested at the moment of birth. The first faculty to withdraw is odour, followed by speech. The retraction of *vāc* is the first impediment to communication which the agonizing person experiences.[2] In this phase he is panic stricken because he realizes that he is about to leave the certain for the uncertain. The loss of the taste faculty follows, and the body loses its last capacity to move from its resting place. He feels fear mixed with frustration over his lack of potency, while his desire to continue living remains keen.

His vision is weakened right from the first phase; if he is able to speak he often declares to see only darkness. This passage is crucial in the agony process. In fact, the loss of vision is the most acute and bewildering moment, severing the principal tie between the person and his surrounding environment. In respect to the other four senses, vision is the most developed in human beings. It is probably that superior animals experiences an analogous sense of panic with the retraction of their sense of smell, if this is their most highly specialized sense faculty.

---

1. The agony is preceded by a phase of mental oblivion, made worse by the progressive retraction of individual faculties. This syndrome is known as *ariṣṭa*, from the name of the bull demon of Kṛṣṇaite mythology, furious because of its mental isolation from the ambience; ***see*** *VP*, V.14. Analogously, the *Viṣṇudharmottara Purāṇa* explains the use of the buffalo as a symbol of Yama and death, due to its characteristic confused mental state; ***see*** G.G. Fillippi, *On Some Sacrificial, op. cit.*

2. During the agony phase, fever (*jvara*) is unfailingly present, gradually wearing out the dying, *Jvara* is identified as a female deity, daughter of Śiva's wrath, ***see*** *SS*, III.

The faculty to generate retracts along with vision. Fertility already ended by the conclusion of middle age. But here by the term 'generate' we mean the pleasure principle (*kāma*) that oversees all emotional life. With the retraction of this faculty, the dying person feels a sense of indifference to the human environment he is about to leave. This is the beginning of a psychological detachment that takes over from his sense of panic, heretofore predominant.

In the succeeding phase, the dying person loses his sense of touch and grasping ability. With the retraction of touch, any relationship with physical pain is annulled, while the sense of detachment begins to change into an attitude of serenity. The dying person lets his hands rest, and lies in abandon upon his death-bed. At this moment, the people present are in doubt whether he is dead or alive, so someone tries with a mirror to see if he is still breathing. In reality, he is still present and partially conscious; in fact, he is listening to the voices of those present, even if his participation is exclusively passive.[3] Along with the retraction of hearing, his digestive and excretive faculties are arrested, with the consequent relaxation of the muscles of control.[4]

3. "When an ill person is about to die, the ones surrounding him ask: 'Do you recognize me? Do you recognize me?' But he continues to recognize them until the moment he leaves the body," *ChU*, VIII.6.4.

4. ". . . 'I will speak,' said the word; 'I will see,' said the eye; 'I will listen,' said the ear. The same said all the others, affirming their function. Death, beginning its action, won over them all, it pressed them and it neutralized them. For this reason the word weakens, and the same happens to the eye and to the ear. Death, however, did not succeed in subduing the *prāṇa*, which lies in the centre [of the *indriyas*]. The others thought: 'The best of us all is he, who does not suffer any danger or harm, either if he moves or remains still. Thus, may each of us become one of his secondary components . . . ," *BṛU*, 1.4.21.

In this way, all the faculties of sensation and action are enveloped in *manas*. As we have repeated, the process of retraction of the *indriya*s towards *manas* occurs in an inverse order to that of their inception during infancy. The mind, which supervises this phenomenon, controls the experiences that the *indriya*s have subordinated to its revision during the course of life. Thus the dying person has brief sequences of visual memory of the events of his life,[5] but inversely to their chronological order. It is as if he sees a flashback of his life.[6]

Once this enveloping of the senses has taken place, and the doors of communication with the outer world have been closed, the mind no longer experiences the external environment. *Manas* now finds itself in a situation analogous to the dream state. A return to the waking state is almost impossible due to the inefficiency of the bodily organs and of the body in general. This condition of the dying man's individual consciousness corresponds to that of the foetus during its life in the uterus, especially in the period that would permit its survival in case of a premature birth. His mind is busy revising memory data in a turmoil of incongruous impressions. These dream representations are forced by the mind to a *reductio ad*

---

5. This phenomenon has been well described by C. Della Casa, although — within the context of his study — it is attributed only to Buddhists: "According to the Buddhists, at the time of death life in its entirety presents itself to the consideration of the dying person: thus, there is no difference in saying that destiny is determined by the conduct of one's life or affirming that what is essential is what one thinks at the time of death, since these two are identical;" C. Della Casa, *op. cit.*, p. 51.

6. "When the body decays due to old age or illness, as the mango, *udumbara* and fig fruits detach from their branch, exactly in the same way the Puruṣa — detaching himself from the body — goes in the opposite direction towards his cause, that is, to the *prāṇa*," *BṛU*, IV.3.36.

unum, ending his mental activity. *Manas* withdraws into the *prāṇas*, here intended not only in their aerial composition to guarantee the continuation of breathing, but as the principle of vegetative life. When *manas* merges in the *prāṇas*, individual consciousness leaves the dream state, without however passing into the state of deep sleep (*suṣupta sthāna*).

To remain on the threshold, putting two diverse states in communication, is a grave risk.[7] In the Indian viewpoint of passage rites, the place of communication between two stages may also be unexpectedly a tangential exit. For example, the temporal hiatus between two cycles not only puts two domains into communication but it may also be the exit door from the cosmos. Thus, the lunar door may be the exit from earthly life and the entrance to another dimension of the earth, as well as the door to go up to the heavens. In the myth of the descent of Viṣṇu as man-lion, the Supreme God hides himself on the threshold of the door in order to devour "whoever is neither at home nor outside." And Indra kills Namuci at the door of sunset, because the demon could not die either by day or by night.

An analogous suspended condition occurs during fainting spells. In this case, consciousness is arrested between two domains, the waking state and the dream state, or the dream state and deep sleep state. If the individual is not induced to stay in one of the three states of consciousness, rapidly and gently leaving the pass over limit, his death will be extremely unfavourable.

The death process passes into a further stage when the mind is deactivated and immersed in the vital prāṇic forces.

7. Sleep, in Indian mythology, is presonified by Nidrā Devī, the younger sister of Mṛtyu. In order to lengthen life, the *yogin* tends to reduce the hours of sleep; *see* J. Parry, *The End*, *op. cit.*, p. 500.

Individual consciousness then transfers itself into the state of deep sleep, with always minor possibilities of returning to the waking or dream states. To use modern terms, the dying man enters into an irreversible coma, with no psychic activity except for his reflexes. From this moment *prāṇa* also retracts into *tejas*, or that vital heat composed of the five *tanmātras*. This phase culminates with the arrest of respiration, the first external sign of bodily abandon. For the same reason, one pays attention to all the interruptions in the process of breathing: yawns, coughs, etc., which are exorcized through the quick invocation of divine names.

In popular fantasy, death principally consists in breathing one's last breath. This is due to the fact that, at birth, the vital force, the air of Viṣṇu, penetrates into the baby by means of the first energetic inspiration, activating the animal energies of the infant. Death, as described in myths, is one who steals breath away from the living, suffocating and strangling the dying. Difficulties in breathing, pulmonary diseases, or the oppression of regular breathing caused by a nightmare,[8] are all considered premonitions of one's own death.

The end of respiration causes the consequent arrest of the circulation of bodily fluids, first of all the blood. In absense of respiration, the heart misses beats and then stops; the blood no longer irrigates the bodily organs and neither there is the exchange of external elements nor the consequent expulsion of wastes which are necessary for life. This favours and determines

8. It will be remembered that nightmares (*uragraha*) are thought of as beings oppressing the chest of sleeping ones. They cause difficulty in breathing, to the point of determining death by suffocation, with the same erotic implications which are noticed in death by strangling; ***see*** chapter 5 footnote 34. ***See also*** *MU* I.4 and VII.8. For further details, ***see*** G.G. Filippi, *Alcune considerazioni sui bhūta, op. cit.*

the beginning of putrefaction, starting with the most delicate organs.

According to the Indian 'science of death,' at this point even *tejas* retracts into the divinity governing the individual aggregate, which is the same *ahaṁkāra* withdrawn within itself.[9] The envelopment of *tejas,* or the heat constituting the essence of the *tanmātras,* also shows a progressive cooling of the body.

Generally, this cooling begins with the hands and feet and moves towards the heart. After the end of respiration and cardiac arrest, *rigor mortis* is the ultimate evidence of death. As long as there is the slightest of warmth, the *tanmātras* remain in the body to conserve life, because *ahaṁkāra* continues to dwell therein as the principle of individuality. At this time, even though highly improbable, a return to life is still possible through an inversion in the tendency to retraction of the individual faculties. But when the *rigor mortis* sets in, it is assumed that *ahaṁkāra,* after having gathered its production around itself, as a sovereign does with his vassals, has abandoned the body. This is the actual death of the body. This does not imply that every tie with the *jīvātman* has been cut off, but simply that a return to life is by now impossible.[10]

9. This condition of mental disorder, which was mentioned in relation to the buffalo, is called *mada,* etymologically cognate to the English 'mad.'

10. ". . . The cut down tree grows again from the old root. The man who has been cut down by death from which root may be reborn? Don't say from sperm, because this comes only from another living being; this would be like saying that a tree already cut down could rise again from a seed. But when it is uprooted, even a tree can have no rebirth. The man who has been stricken by death from which root may he be reborn? He who has been born is not reborn anymore; who could ever bring him back to life . . .," *BṛU,* III.9.28.6-7. "Nobody who has died can come back [to life], be he a King, a →

Thus, after having described the death throes,[11] as experienced by he who undergoes the phenomenon, let's see what happens to the family members and friends gathered around the deathbed. Everybody follows the phases of his agony with apprehension. With the help of a mirror held near his nose and mouth, they try to determine if he is still breathing. In this phase, the man's head is carefully shaved, except for the sacred pigtail, *śikhā*, almost repeating the *cūḍākaraṇa* rite, which had purified his body in his infancy. When even his heart stops beating, they call him by name.[12] If he still recognizes himself by that name, it means that he will come back to life, abandoning the state of apparent death.

→ beggar or a *brahman;* who dies in battle is dead, and even he who survives, is dead;" *GP,* II.48.36. This assertion fits with the following: "When alive one may reap the results of possive *karman*: one may obtain a village, a property, a house, a horse or wealth; but one can never gain back a human body;" *GP,* II.49.19. In this way, the prospect of reincarnation — at least as it is popularly understood in the West — is excluded.

11. The torment of impending death and the grief caused are vividly described in *GP,* II.2.54-55: the envoys of Yama, the *yamadūtas,* violently pull away the soul from the body.

12. "When your soul reaches the abode of Yama, o son of Vivasvān, we recall it here, at your home, to life;

    "your soul reaches the Sky and the Earth; we recall it here, at your home, to life;

    "your soul reaches the quadripartite earth, we recall it here, at your home, to life;

    "your soul reaches the four directions of the atmosphere; we recall it here, at your home, to life;

    "your soul reaches the ocean of clouds; we recall it here, at your home, to life;

    "your soul reaches the luminous rivers; we recall it here, at your home, to life;

→

After this last attempt (in case it fails); all witnesses promise, with vows and mortifications, to help the deceased reach the highest goal in his posthumous condition. A bit of clarified butter is placed on his forehead, and is replaced a few times as it melts. When the butter no longer melts, it is the proof of the cooling of the body. This moment onwards, the house as well as family members of the deceased are struck by impurity, whereas the corpse is declared sacred.[13]

This impurity, *aśauca*, that hits brāhmaṇas for nine days, kṣatriyas for twelve days, vaiśyas for fifteen days, and śūdras for a month, is due to the psychic unbalancing caused by the death of a family member. In this period, the *sapiṇḍa*s go through a crisis, because the discarnated no longer possesses a covering as was the body, and a new psychic covering has not yet substituted the body.[14] This is a period of weakness in the

---

→ "your soul reaches the Sun and the Dawn; we recall it here, at your home, to life;

"your soul reaches the great mountains; we recall it here, at your home, to life;

"your soul reaches this world; we recall it here, at your home, to life;

"your soul reaches the furthermost horizon, we recall it here, at your home, to life;

"your soul reaches the past and the future; we recall it here, at your home, to life."*ṚV*, X.58.

13. The image of the family God is immediately brought out of the house and given to a neighbour, with great precaution, so as to save it from the impurity which is about to fall on the family; *see* S. Stevenson, *Rites of the Twice-Born* (London, 1920), p. 163.

14. At this stage, known as *ativaha* (beyond the covering), the deceased finds himself in a transitory condition, which is extremely vulnerable; *see GP*, II.30.30. In case be does not succeed in obtaining a new 'body' and thus become a *preta*, the deceased will be condemned to remain in this condition as a *piśāca*, that is, as a soul →

family's defences, in which subtle attacks of evil spirits such as *vetālas*, *piśācas*, *bhūtas*, or living wizards (*yātudhāna*) may insinuate themselves. Their aim of infesting the home, or of utilizing the mortal remains or psychic residue of the deceased, would cause grave repercussions to his *post mortem* condition, plus fear and damage to the family.[15]

From a biological point of view, the beginning of *rigor mortis* manifests with the contraction of the pupils which become oblong in shape. The eyelids of the deceased are lowered, to avoid the horror of his glassy gaze. His elongated pupils are similar to the eyes of cats, cobras, *yakṣas*, and of all those beings living in darkness who must sharpen their sight in order to catch even the dimmest flash of light. The eye of the dead, however, does not see the surrounding darkness. In reality, it is the living one who, through the eyes of the dead, can see the darkness of the hereafter through the corpse itself.[16]

→ in pain or a ghost. "The body which the deceased is to wear in his other existence, cannot be the same which the flames have consumed, or the earth covered up: it may not even be one like it, for he is to dwell henceforth in the company of divine spirits, and must be clothed like these to be able to claim a right among them;" R. Roth, "On the Morality of the Veda," In *JAOS*, III, p. 343.

15. In order to avoid these dangers, a *maṇḍala*, a magic circle of protection, is drawn all around the corpse; *see GP*, II.2.12. It is believed that if the deceased is not protected this way, he will be reborn in the air, and thus will become a *piśāca*; *see GP*, II.2.14.

16. A different interpretation, based on the mythology of the *Itihāsas*, says that the gaze of the dead is comparable to that of the gods. Indeed, these latter ones may be recognized because they don't bat their eyelids or, to be more accurate, because they bat them much more rarely than human. The batting of eyelids (*kṣaṇa*) is, according to Indian cosmology, the tiniest speck of time perceptible to man, that, the moment, the instant. Now, since for the gods the six months from the spring equinox to the autumn equinox →

The long and composite rite that follows is the last *saṁskāra*, *antyeṣṭi*, or 'the last sacrifice,' the funeral.[17]

→ amount to just one day, even their *kṣaṇa* will have a duration three hundred and sixty times greater than that of humans.

17. "By means of the *saṁskāras* which follow birth, the Earth is gained; by means of the *saṁskāras* which follow death, the worlds [are gained];" *Baudhāyana Pitṛmedha-Sūtra* (*BPS*), III.1.4. The Brāhmaṇical ritual divides itself in sacrifices (*yajña*) and *saṁskāras*. Malamoud notes that the *antyeṣṭi* is the only rite which involves both types of rituals; *see* Ch. Malamoud, *op. cit.*, p. 452.

9

The Last Sacrifice
The Offering of the Body

THE first act in the long process of funeral rites is the shaving and washing of the body.[1] Families following the Śrauta tradition, that is, ritual Vedic prescriptions, then make their offerings to the domestic fire called *gārhapatya*.[2] The sacrificer, generally the eldest son, takes the right hand of the deceased in his own, and pours a spoonful of *ghṛta* into the fire. Those Hindus, who limit themselves to the prescriptions of the Gṛhya-Sūtra, continue with the preparation of the body: a few *tulasī* (basil) leaves, are placed in the mouth of the deceased, along with some drops of water from the Ganges or Yamunā rivers. His forehead is smeared with clay and ash, or, if the deceased is an unmarried young man or a married woman, not a widow, the forehead is painted red. The persons present begin to repeat the sacred syllable *oṁ*, first in a whisper, then louder and louder, almost a cry, decreeing the official death of the person. From the loud repetition of the *mantram*, the neighbours learn the news and come to participante in the mourning.

After this invocation if the deceased awakens from his catatonic state, then such return would be regarded as

1. Hair and nails should be buried in an unknown spot; *see Gautama Gṛhya-Sūtra*, II.24.
2. If the deceased was the depository of the cult of the three fires, the *homa* offering in the *āhavanīya* fire is obligatory only later on; *see* R.B. Pandey, *op. cit.*, p. 246.

inauspicious, as a ghostly return from the kingdom of the dead. When his earthly departure has been ascertained, the corpse becomes the object of a sort of deification. As images of the gods are prepared for *pūjā*, in the same way the dead body is washed, dressed, and bedecked with flowers. The family, on the contrary, falls into *aśauca*, the time of impurity connected with the mourning period, due to the psychic imbalance provoked by the death of a relative. There is an emotional continuity with the psychic ties of the deceased. Relatives and friends make a sacred circumambulation, *pradakṣiṇā*, around the body, almost as around the tomb of a god, while incense and camphor are burnt. This tribute takes place in respectful silence. It is only after this ritual that everyone leaves the room of the deceased, weeping and giving way to sorrow.

An elderly relative or a friend remains in the room, someone who has had an analogous experience, to vigil over the deceased. This person is therefore able to defend the mortal remains in this delicate moment in which the individual soul is transferring itself from its bodily sheath. As already stated, the deceased leaves his body by degrees, before undertaking his posthumous journey.[3] During this stage, he can be compared with an unmoving embryo; thus, the apotropaic cures act as a backward *puṁsavana*. At this point the individual can no longer return to life, but is in danger due to a feeble relationship which he still maintains with his body.

As previously commented, it would be frightening if some subtle being or an act of witchcraft should interfere in this movement towards a conception in a reverse sense. Black magicians and vampires could profit from this last travail to take over the psychic residue of the deceased and use it for their evil aims. Thus, the delicate balance of a non-vigil

---

3. *Preta* means "he who goes on," "he who travels."

conscience could be altered, perhaps negatively conditioning his posthumous evolution. The vigil serves to protect the deceased from psychic assaults of harmful beings, which try to accost the corpse under shamanic forms as cats, snakes, owls, or other impure animals living in darkness.[4]

The waiting period, from ascertained death to the elimination of the corpse by cremation, can extend up to three and a half days. However, the climate furnishes the definite unpleasant proof of the *jīva*'s detachment from his gross body (*sthūla śarīra*). Often, when putrefaction is evident, the funeral takes place a few hours after death. Because of the horror provoked by bodily corruption, it is now the custom to carry the corpse to the cremation site as soon as death has been ascertained.

The corpse is laid on a straw mat[5] on top of a stretcher in the form of steps, made of *udumbara* wood. This mat substitutes the black antelope skin[6] or perhaps the skin of the sacrificial

---

4. *See* *R̥V*, VII.104.22. It should be remembered that precisely for this reason a *maṇḍala* or magic circle is drawn, so as to protect the corpse; *see* *GP*, II.2.12-14.
5. Even in the Indus Valley civilization, it has been possible to exhume corpses that were enveloped in straw mats similar to these. It is worthwhile noticing that, in this latter case, the burial practice was that of inhumation; *see* Stewart Piggott, *Prehistoric India to 1000* BC. (Harmondsworth: Penguin Books, 1964), ch. 5. Nowadays the straw mat is used as a substitute for the antelope skin in Hindu funeral rites in Bali; *see* M. Covarrubias, *op. cit.*, pp. 363-68. The straw mat is believed to possess the power of protecting the corpse from the attacks of *piśācas*; *see* *GP*, II.35.42.
6. *See* R.B. Pandey, *op. cit.*, p. 247. The black antelope or *nīlagau* (*Antilope picta*) is a bold animal, very similar to a bovine. Its dark skin (*kr̥ṣṇājina*), decorated by a half moon and by two white circular spots, is used as a placenta to envelop the body of he who is about to return to the uterus, from which he will be reborn in →

anustaraṇī cow, which represented the placenta in which the being was enfolded while awaiting a new birth, during ancient times. The dead man is invited to take off his old clothes and wear new and purer robes.[7] Clothing always alludes to the body in this instance. Then his big toes and also his thumbs are tied together, his arms are tied tightly along his sides, and his legs in their winding sheet are tied together.[8] The shroud must be of unused new silk, and the body is tied to form a bundle resembling an Egyptian mummy. For this reason, tying the toes and fingers together is not so common nowadays. The silk chosen for men is white, sometimes yellow, while it is always red for women, symbolizing the whiteness of semen and the redness of blood, in view of a new conception.[9]

→ a superior state of existence. The *kṛṣṇājina*, besides being present in all the *saṁskāra*s I have described, has been used as a substitute of leopard and tiger skin by *yogī*s for their carpet, and as a substitute of *tārpya* in rituals of royal consecration as well as in funerals; *see AV*, XVIII.4.31. Since the *kṛṣṇājina* is also decorated with drawings of stars, it is evident that the black spotted skin is thought to represent the sky garment. On these issues, *see* Asko Parpola, *The Sky-Garment* (Helsinki: Finnish Oriental Society, 1985), p. 203.

7. *See* R.B. Pandey, *op. cit.*, p. 247. Nowadays this change of dress, indicating the wish to be reborn in a more favourable condition, is symbolically highlighted by the rich golden cloths covering the corpse when it is laid on the stretcher.

8. This is a precautionary measure, to avoid the possibility that the deceased transform himself in a *révenant* and try to go back to his house. This same fear drove the inhabitants of the cities of the Indus Valley to bury the skeletons of their deads — their flesh having been pulled out — with their femurs in inverted position. Analogous precautions were taken by most other civilizations to prevent the return of the ghost; *see* P. Singh, *op. cit.*, p. 173.

9. According to Indian beliefs, death — which in the large majority of cases conditions one's rebirth in another species — does not →

The officiating brāhmaṇa supplies five sweets of a spherical shape (*piṇḍa* or *pūraka*) made of flour and water, to celebrate the traveller's rite (*pathika*). The first sweet is offered to the 'genius' living in the floor of the room in which death took place, the second to the spirit of the threshold of the house, the third to the divinity of the cross-roads via which the funeral procession will pass by. The fourth *piṇḍa* is donated to the earth spirit where the coffin will be placed in the cremation field (*śmaśāna*), and the fifth to the fire of the funeral pyre.[10] In Vedic times the body was carried out of the house through an opening in the wall, which was then closed again. Therefore, originally the second *piṇḍa* was offered to the spirit of the wall of the house. The wall was closed up again to impede the ghost of the deceased from finding his way back and disturbing his family members. This custom is still in use in Dravidian countries and in the island of Bali.[11]

The funeral procession is led by the eldest son,[12] who often carries a clay lantern with burning coals from the domestic

→ facilitate sex changes. Usually a soul is reborn maintaining the same gender. If there is a change in gender, this does not typically concern the dominant aspects of one's personality. On these issues, *see* Sri Aurobindo, *Renacimiento y Karma* (Barcelona: P&J, 1989; Pondicherry, 1952[1]), Ap. IV.

10. The *Garuḍa Purāṇa* mentions a sixth sweet which is offered to the earth when the bones are gathered; *GP,* II.4.48-49.

11. *See* M. Covarrubias, *op. cit.*, ch. 11. In olden times, two bundles of branches (*kūḍī*) were fastened to the corpse's feet. The deceased, when journeying would thus erase his footsteps and be unable to retrace his steps; *see AV,* V.19.12.

12. The eldest son performs all funeral rites from this moment onwards. ". . . Thus is defined a learned son 'the one who procures the worlds,' and it is for this reason that he is given education. When the one possessing this knowledge dies, he leaves all his competence to his son. If there remain some negative actions →

fireplace with which he will light the funeral pyre. The corpse — as the sacrificial victim destined to the holy fire — follows on a coffin carried by six or more servants.[13] Close relatives

→ performed by him, the son frees him: for this reason the son is called *putra*. He has an aid in this world in the son and the immortal celestial winds support him," *BṛU*, I.5.17. "He who saves his father from the hell is called *put*, who is known as *putra* here and hereafter," *GP*, II.21.32. This verse is obviously concerned with 'posterity.' The posthumous destiny of the deceased will be the subject of a future study.

If there is no son, he can be substituted by the closest relative of male sex. In exceptional cases, if parental ties are too loose, a Yajurvedic priest (*adhvaryu*) is nominated to preside over the funeral; ***see*** R.B. Pandey, *op. cit.*, p. 249. ***See also*** J. Gonda, *Le Religioni*, *op. cit.*, vol. 1, p. 184.

GP, II.8.2-4 gives the following list of substitutes, authorized to celebrate the funeral in the absence of a son: the nephew, the great-nephew, the brother, the brother's male descendants, any descendant of a *sapiṇḍa*. In the case of the extinction of all the males in the family, a female relative may officiate. If the family is totally extinct, the King may take upon himself the duty of performing the funeral rites of his subjects. Even nowadays, many *mahārājā*s perform the *sapiṇḍīkaraṇa* ritual for their ex-subjects. Myth attributes the origin of the *ekoddiṣṭa* — a term designating the ritual offerings of the *piṇḍa*s up to the *sapiṇḍīkaraṇa* at the end of a year — to Agastya. One day the *ṛṣi* saw some men, all skin and bones, hanging to a thread by their heels, in the imminent danger of falling into a chasm. He was told that those men were his ancestors, who lacked descendance due to his asceticism. Thus, Agastya broke his vow of celibacy and had a son who could perform the *śrāddha* rite for his ancestors. Another myth in the *Mahābhārata* attributes the founding of the *ekoddiṣṭa* ritual to a different *ṛṣi*, Jaratkāru, "he who brings to old age."

13. The corpse (*śava*) is usually carried with its feet forward. Sometimes, however, the opposite posture is adopted, with the head facing south to indicate that the deceased has his head downwards, like a foetus waiting to be given birth in the *pitṛ loka*. Anyway, when →

follow in the order of their age: first the eldest, then the younger, the members of the same clan and friends.[14] Women remain at home,[15] except for the widow; however today her participation at the funeral is very rare. Often the procession is preceded by several priests, who sprinkle water on the ground to purify it from the footprints of untouchables. In the Śrauta tradition, the corpse is placed on a cart driven by one or two oxen, and servants may not approach the mortal remains. In this case, relatives are in charge of loading and unloading the coffin from the funeral cart.[16]

Repeating the name of Rāma — *rāma, rāma bolo, bhāī* or *śrī rāma nāma satya hai* — the procession reaches the cremation field. This land, especially consecrated for funeral rites, is always situated outside the city gates.[17] Usually it is situated to

---

→ the corpse is on its bed, at the halting places along the way, and on the pyre, it must always be laid with its head facing the northern direction.

14. *See* R.B. Pandey, *op. cit.*, p. 249.

15. Women remain at home and mourn, loosening their hair and beating their chests and thighs; *see* H. Oldenberg, *Die Religion des Veda* (Berlin, 1923), p. 582.

16. On this occasion, the eldest son repeats the following verse: "Pūṣan, who knows the way well, has well trained the animals to transport you; he who is the protector of the place, may he take you with him. May he thus take you to the region of the ancestors. May Agni, who knows what's your due, take you away with him. . . ." *ṚV*, I.42.1-10. Pūṣan is a deity in charge of nutrition, I shall later discuss the topics of the hunger and thirst of the deceased.

17. The place chosen as cremation ground has opposite characteristics to that where people sacrifice to the gods. It must face the south-western direction, it must be limited by water on the western side but not on the eastern, and it must also have a pleasant view towards the east; *see* J. Gonda, *Le Religioni, op. cit.*, vol. 1, p. 185. *Śmaśāna* literally means burial-place, cemetery. According to Yāska's tradition (*Nirukta* III.5), it would be compound made up →

the south, towards the kingdom of Yama. If the *śmaśāna* is situated in another direction, the funeral procession leaving the city must pass through the southern gate.[18] The procession, from the home of the deceased to the *śmaśāna,* halts at three spots. At every stop the *Yama Sūkta* is repeated. However, the invocations to the god Yama are so feared by the population, that nowadays these recitations are done away with, to avoid the possibility of the invoked god appearing on the scene.

The first ritual that the members of the procession perform is digging a hole, in the middle of which is put the wood to build the funeral pyre. This wood is stacked on the surface as per tradition: sandalwood being considered the best, although being costly today it is used only by the rich. The dimensions and the direction of the pyre are rigorously regulated by laws derived from sacred texts.[19] Up until not too long ago — though nowadays completely removed from memory — the internal organs of the deceased were sometimes taken out, to avoid rapid decomposition or free the body from the faeces. The abdominal cavity was purified with clarified butter.[20] Today this custom would be considered repugnant, and the only custom is to shave the corpse and cut his nails. In Bali such archaic customs persist; the body is buried for a long time, until the flesh has totally disappeared from the bones. Then the skeleton is exhumed, put into a coffin and cremated.

→ of *śman,* body, and *śayan,* bed. With the prevalance of the cremation rite, it has come to mean cremation ground.

18. In Vedic times, the corpse of a brāhmaṇa was taken out from the eastern gate of the village, that of kṣatriya from the northern gate, and that of a vaiśya from the western gate. In those days, as now, it was forbidden to turn one's head back during funerals; *see* J. Gonda, *ibid.*

19. These rules are contained in the various *Gṛhya Sūtras*; *see* R.B. Pandey, *op. cit.,* p. 251.

20. *See* A. Hillebrandt, *Death, op. cit.,* p. 476b.

When the fire is ready, the carriers plunge the corpse into the holy waters of the river up to its knees.[21] After this last purification, the body is taken off the stretcher of *udumbara* and is laid upon the pyre, with his head to the north and his feet facing south.[22] Then the circumambulation around the corpse is made counterclockwise, with the funeral pyre to one's left. This processional direction, *prasavya,* is used in all funeral rites, to honour the *pitṛ*s, to heal snake bites, and in general, during all inauspicious rituals. Even the Vaitaraṇī cow, with its calf, circumambulates the pyre counterclockwise.[23] Similarly, the *dvija*s assist the *antyeṣṭi* holding the sacred thread on the right,[24] instead of on the left.

The shroud is loosened and the ropes tying the fingers and toes together are cut. If the deceased was a brāhmaṇa, a piece of gold is placed in his hand. If he was kṣatriya, a bow is placed

---

21. *See AGS,* IV.4.10. The texts do not specify if the body must be plunged up to its knees, as used until some decades ago, or almost entirely as nowadays.

22. In Varanasi one walks counterclockwise, taking on mourning, and the deceased is considered unquestionably dead only after the performance of the *kapāla kriyā, see* J. Parry, *The End, op. cit.,* p. 506. Another noteworthy custom is that sometimes the bodies of men are placed face downwards on the pyre, while the bodies of women are placed supine. This symbolizes sexual union, since the funeral fire is understood as a union from which a rebirth will ensue; *see ibid.,* p. 507.

23. *See* R.B. Pandey, *op. cit.,* p. 250. In Varanasi I've noticed that the counterclockwise movement during funeral rites is not so strictly followed anymore. Even the *karmakāṇḍin*s do not seem to attribute much importance to the issue. On the contrary, the *prasavya* is still rigorously performed in the rites of *piṇḍa* offering.

24. Della Casa observes that this practice hints at the opposite rules governing the kingdom of the dead; *see* C. Della Casa-P.A. Carozzi, *op. cit.,* ch.5.

in his hand,[25] if he was a vaiśya, a jewel. The body is covered with sweets representing the dismembered parts of the *anustaraṇī* cow of the Śrauta tradition. Originally in this ritual the intestines of the sacrificed animal were placed on the corpse's face and each organ was placed upon the corresponding organ of the deceased; then the whole body was wrapped in the skin which acted as a 'placenta.'[26] Nowadays, even for funerals of the *agnihotṛs*, sweets are offered in place of the obsolete practice of animal sacrifice. In this case, however, with the corpse are placed the objects of cult which he used when alive, to be burned along with him: wooden spoons, clay pots, household goods.[27] This custom has very ancient origin. We know that in pre-Vedic times, food, weapons, and domestic animals were burned to help the deceased during his long journey leading to the land of the dead: this was called funeral

---

25. Gonda notes that if the deceased was a kṣatriya, the bow placed in his hand was subsequently taken away from him. The officiating priest would then break the bow and through it in the fire with its cord; *see* J. Gonda, *Le Religioni*, *op. cit.*, vol. 1, p. 186. Nowadays, politicized priests avoid caste symbolism so as to avoid their 'democratic faith' from being questioned.

26. "Then the cow (or a goat) is slain, the face of the deceased is covered with its intestines and the verse of *ṚV*, 10.16.7 is recited:

    "Use this as an armour,
    against the Fire cover yourself with fat,
    so that the bold, aggressive god of fire
    may not seize you, bringing distruction."

    — C. Della Casa-P.A. Carozzi, *op. cit.*, pp. 45-46.

27. On the head of the deceased the ritual cup called *iḍāpātra* or *kapāla* is placed. This is why the *tāntrikaṣ* known as *kāpālikas* justify the ritual use of the human skull as bowl: indeed, *kapāla* means both bowl and skull. On this issue, *see* what is said below about the *aghorīs*.

'according to the ancient custom.'[28] We know from the passages of the *Ṛgveda* that in preceding epochs, even the widow was burned along with her husband. To avoid this cruelty, in Vedic times a substitute rite, still practised today, was created. The performer of the rite, generally the eldest son, addresses the deceased thus:

> O deceased, your wife desires to be united with you in the future world and is lying with your corpse. She always observed the duties of a faithful wife; concede permission for her to remain in this world and to leave your riches to your descendants.[29]
>
> — *ṚV*, X.18.7-9

At this point a man from the procession, taking the widow's left hand, invites her to come down, saying:

> Stand up, o woman, you who lie next to the deceased, come to the world of the living, far from your husband, and become the wife of he who will take your hands and will want to marry you.[30]
>
> — *ṚV*, X.18.8

In even older epochs, a brother of the deceased would help the widow descend from the pyre and then marry her. Thus he could procure a male descendent for the deceased, who would assure him ancestral rites. We derive from this that widow sacrifice was abrogated since archaic Vedic times. However

---

28. ***See*** *AV*, XVIII.3.1. Paṇḍey reports the hypothesis that in Vedic times, on the pyre of the deceased, even slaves were sacrificed with food, weapons, cloths and domestic animals; ***see*** R.B. Pandey, *op. cit.*, p. 252. Due to the practice of cremation, no archaeological evidence can support the hypothesis. Moreover, there are no written documents to endorse such a theory.
29. ***See also*** *BPS*, I.8.3-5 and *AGS*, IV.2.16-19.
30. ***See also*** *AGS*, IV.2.16-19. Since several centuries, marriage of widows is not in practice. Nowadays, it is tolerated only within Westernized circles.

satī, the voluntary sacrifice of widows, remained in use among certain warrior families until 1835.[31] When the widow left the pyre, she took a piece of gold or a jewel from her dead husband, pronouncing hopes of prosperity to living relatives. This ritual hinting at *satī* is very rare today; it was restricted to funerals of members of princely families who reigned in kingdoms before the birth of the present Republic.

The first son, holding a handful of *kuśa* grass in which the embers burn, performs five circumambulations counter-clockwise (*prasavya*) with his closest relatives. Then he lights the fire, offering his father's body as a sacrificial victim to the god Agni,[32] invoking the following *mantram*:

> Agni, devour this body into ashes; do not harm it, don't disperse its skin and parts. O Jātavedas [Agni], when this body will be correctly burned, lead its soul to the ancestors.[33]
>
> — *ṚV* X.16.1

---

31. For the recent history of *satī*, very useful is the collection of articles in Arvind Sharma (ed.), *Satī: Historical and Phenomenological Essays* (Delhi: Motilal Banarsidass, 1988).

32. "From him you [o Agni] were born; may he now be born from you in the sky," *AGS*, IV.3.27. ***See also*** *ṚV*, X.16.5. Fire can be of two kinds: *kravyāda*, 'eater of raw meat,' or *jātavedas*, 'familiar to humans.' The first kind has only a destructive power, whereas the second kind can transform the raw into cooked, that is, in food for the gods. For this reason, if the fire bursts out too violently it must be put out. The son of the deceased will rekindle it, being careful to keep the flames in check; ***see*** W. Caland, *Die altindische Todten-und Bestat-tungsgebrauche* (Amsterdam, 1896), p. 178. "Agni, send away the fire devourer of raw meat, drive out the fire devouring corpses, have the fire which cooks for the gods come here;" *TS*, I.1.1.7. The *bhūtas*, spirits of the decomposition of the body — to be also identified with the *ignis fatuus* — are also called *kravyāda*, and are iconographically represented as corpse eaters.

33. From the *mantram* one understands that the funeral pyre must slowly consume the body, without leaving any residue. "Pour →

And then, turning towards the deceased:

> May your vision go towards the sun, may your *prāṇa* mix with the atmosphere, may you proceed, according to the virtuous actions that you made, towards heaven, earth, watery regions, towards any place pleasing to you. That you may, provided with food, lead a bodily existence.
>
> — *AV*, XVIII.2

Then the participants await the destruction of the corpse, which normally takes from three to five hours. Due to the heat, after a brief period the cranial box explodes. If it doesn't, the son must break the skull with a golden axe — according to the texts — or, more realistically, with a bamboo stick, permitting the exit of the last *prāṇa* from the body, the *dhanañjaya vāyu*.[34] This *kapāla kriyā* rite, which probably makes most Westerners

→ détourner l'aggression du feu dévorant et l'empêcher de détruire ce qui, de la personne du mort, doit être preservé, on lui offre un bou que l'on immole au moment des funérailles, et surtout on le repaît da la graisse ou de la moelle de la vache dite *anustaraṇī* qui enduit comme d'une cuirasse le cadavre. Sauvé par le feu sacrificiel, cuit et maintenu intact, le corps devenu oblation subit une transformation complexé au term de laquelle il est a la foi ouvert aux Manes, dispersé dans l'Univers, convoyé jusqu'au séjour 'des êtres aux actes bons,' enfin recomposé et prolongé dans sa progeniture (*Ṛk-Saṁhitā*, X.16.5);" *see* Ch. Malamoud, *op. cit.*, pp. 444-45.

34. This appellation belongs to Tāntric terminology. It means 'permitting the conquest of the treasure.' Adepts of various Tāntric schools — Hindu, Jaina and Buddhist — try in all possible ways to secure the intact skull of a dead person. From it they derive a cup from which they eat and drink, at the same time benefiting from the potency released by the *dhanañjaya vāyu* still present in the skull. The treasure, conquered thanks to the fruition of the psychic power of the dead, may consist in material wealth or spiritual rewards. None the less, the deceased runs the risk of becoming a *piśāca*. For this reason, it is thought to be wise to perform the *kapāla kriyā*. To this same cultural climate, one must →

shiver, is done with great serenity and with the awareness that the human remains are no longer the beloved relative or friend.[35]

If the fire dies down before finishing its job, spoonfuls of clarified butter are thrown on the pyre to augment the flames. When it is evident that the corpse has been consumed, the remains of the fire are put out by pouring water on it. To give the sensation of coolness to remaining calcified bones, aquatic plants are scattered around and, in antiquity, a frog (*maṇḍūka*)[36] was liberated on it. Often the ashes hide bone fragments resistant to the fire's heat. On cremation day, or on the third or tenth day of mourning depending on local traditions, these fragments (*asthi sañcayana*) are collected, taken delicately between the thumb and ring finger, and put into a clay jar which is then immersed in the Ganges or any other sacred

→ refer the practice of skull drilling. "Thus, in one case each at Burzahom and Kalibabgan, the skull of the deceased has been drilled. What the precise significance is of such a ritual can only be guessed. This may have been done to free the soul which is supposed to reside therein," P. Singh, *op. cit.*, p. 173.

35. ". . . But when life has left these persons, then one can turn them over on the pyre with a poker, so that they may consume themselves completely, thus preventing anybody from saying: 'you are hurting your father, your mother, your brother, your sister, your teacher, a *brahman*,' because all these exist as long as they are alive. . . ." *ChU*, VII.15.2.

36. "[Earth], return to be fresh and pleasant in this place; may the frog be comfortable here. Satisfy this *agni*," *ṚV*, 16.14. ***See also*** C. Della Casa-P.A. Carozzi, *op. cit.*, p. 47. Frogs, in the Indian tradition, are believed to resist the fire's heat, like salamanders in the Hermetic Western tradition. Those who follow the Śrauta tradition, dig a trench about one foot deep, which is then filled with water, and a marshy flower is planted therein. "The tradition explains this custom in this way. The dead man rises from the trench and ascends along with the smoke to heaven," R.B. Pandey, *op. cit.*, p. 254.

rivers.[37] In some parts of India there is still the old custom of burying the jar of bones among the roots of a sacred tree, or to scatter bones and ashes in a desert place (*haviryajñīyanivāpa*).

Richer families have a cow milked for ten days in a row at the cremation site. Most of these rites are not possible on the crowded *ghāṭ*s of Varanasi, where coffins are awaiting their turn for cremation. The extraordinary sacredness of the site allows the simplication of the rites. Up to the end of the Gupta period, jars containing the remains of bones had coarse representation of sexual feature, so that the ashes of a woman were collected in jars with breasts carved upon them. The jars were then buried, and thus diverse specimens were preserved and have come down to us. Today jugs with spouts are dedicated to women, while a round form of vase is used for men.[38]

---

37. Some have seen in the *asthi sañcayana* the proof of the historical passage from inhumation to cremation. To support this theory the example of the *Mahābhārata* is adduced, which ignores such custom. J.N. Tiwari, however, proves through two citations that in the Epic period, bones, once collected, were laid in rivers; *see* J.N. Tiwari, *Disposal of the Dead in the Mahābhārata* (Varanasi: Kishor Vidhya Niketan, 1979), pp. 23-24. Tiwari also notes that the description of the ritual of cremation in the Epic is identical to how it is performed nowadays.

    It's curious to note that P. Singh views the inhumation of reassembled corpses as more archaic than the burying of ashes and bony remains in earthenwares; *see* P. Singh, *op. cit.*, p. 171. From recent excavations, however, it has been discovered that in the Harappan epoch inhumation and funeral urns coexisted, as, for instance, in Kalibangan. In the excavations of Mehrgarh — which predate the origin of the Indus Valley civilization by some millennia — the most ancient human remains had been inhumed without reassembling the corpse; *see* M.A. Halim, "Les practiques funeraires a Harappa," In *Les Cités Oubliées de l'Indus* (Paris: Muśee Guimet, 1988).

38. *See* Jeannine Auboyer, *La vie quotidienne dans l'Inde ancienne* (Paris: Hachette, 1961), II.3, n. 89.

Human ashes, mixed with the firewood of the pyre, are collected and dispersed in the water of the nearest river. At this point, anyone who has attended the funeral ceremony, feels the need to purify himself by taking a bath in the river. Sometimes special trenches are dug for this purpose.[39] Afterwards, a beam is put up, under which the funeral participants must pass, the last one being the eldest son. He concludes the rite by giving praise to the Sun god, who dies and is reborn daily. Everyone returns home, accompanying the closest relatives to their door. This return is sad and accompanied by the recitation of the sacred syllable *oṁ*. When the procession reaches the entrance of the home of the deceased, the women who did not participate at the funeral cry and lament, invoking the name of Rāma. On the discretion of the priest who conducted the funeral ceremony, the procession breaks up. Everyone washes his feet before entering his own home, and touches purified and blessed objects.[40] Then they take a complete bath to free themselves of acquired impurities, and will put on clean clothes while reciting the *Yama Gāthā*.[41]

---

39. "According to the practices of other Vedic schools, the mourners leave the funeral pyre to burn itself away, and the chief mourner excavates three trenches to the North of the pyre, lines them with pebbles and sand and fills them with water brought in an odd number of jars. The people who joined the procession are now requested to purify themselves by bathing in the trenches," R.B. Pandey, *op. cit*, p. 254. On the dry gravel banks of some rivers, as for example in Gayā, it is not necessary to fill up any trenches, since water crops up from the subsoil.

40. These objects and materials are stones, fire, cow dung, various kinds of seeds, oil and water. It's also common practice to purify one's mouth by chewing *nimba* leaves (*nīm*) and burn incense sticks. Some also rub themselves with a plant called *apāmārga*, 'she who dries up,' thus hoping to prevent the return of the psychic force of the deceased under the guise of a ghost; *see ŚB*, XIII.8.4.4.

41. *See ṚV*, X.14. *Also*, *GP*, II.34.26.

Only after returning to his family may the eldest son give vent to his sorrow, in private, with reserve.[42] For nine, twelve, or thirteen days, according to one's caste, the family will fast, refusing the noblest and purest foodstuffs.[43] Almost as if a curse had fallen upon the home, social life is avoided, as well as all signs of daily routine; hair is left uncombed, one does not wash, nor put sacred signs on the forehead. Above all, rites cannot be performed. During these days of *aśauca*, neighbours, friends, and relatives come and make brief and comforting visits.[44] They come so as to distract the family of the deceased from their sorrows, although they remain for not more than ten minutes. Only those who have been present can understand what this human solidarity means. The day after the funeral and for all the days dedicated to the rite of *śrāddha*, a brāhmaṇa comes to the home to read the *Preta Mañjarī*, the section of the *Garuḍa Purāṇa* dedicated to the journery of the soul in the afterlife, so often mentioned herein. Listening to the fabulous adventures that the deceased is undertaking comforts the members of the family, and distracts and interests them deeply.

---

42. One must restrain from crying. It is believed that tears have the power of augmenting, the sultriness of the deceased (*Raghuvaṁśa*, VII.86), probably because of their salty taste.

43. The most appropriate food for the mourning relatives is thought to be barley, due to its supposed apotropaic properties. The Sanskrit word for barley, *yava*, comes from the root *yu*, 'to drive out'; *see* C. Della Casa-P. A. Carozzi, *op. cit.*, p. 47nl.

44. '*Aśauca* is obligatory for all *sapiṇḍas*, that is, for all those who are blood relations of the deceased, up to the seventh generation. Instead, "the observance of *aśauca* is left to one's own judgement in case of the death of the family priest, the father-in-law, a friend, acquaintances, a maternal uncle, or the sister's sons"; *Pārāśara Gṛhya-Sūtra*, III.10.46.

10

Transformation of the Deceased into Ancestor

THE day after cremation, or after three, ten, or thirteen days, depending upon family traditions and the regions,[1] the *sapiṇḍas*, that is, all those who have one or more ancestor in common going back to the seventh generations,[2] go to the river banks or to a pond, to make purification rites and an offering of the *udakakarman* water. Covered with ashes and with the *yajñopavīta* cord on their right shoulder, they immerse themselves in the

1. The days of *aśauca* differ in number depending on one's caste, age, and sex. The length of thirteen days is purely indicative. In reality, caste and regional customs vary enormously in the Indian complex social environment. According to the Gṛhya-Sūtras, *aśauca* lasts ten days for brāhmaṇas and kṣatriyas, fifteen days for vaiśyas and a month for śūdras. An *ahitāgni* brāhmaṇa that is, a brāhmaṇa keeping the sacred fire, leaves behind him an impurity which lasts one sole day. The younger the age of the deceased, the shorter the period of impurity for the family. The same rule applies for females; *see* R.B. Pandey, *op. cit.*, pp. 257-59.
2. "Taken in its original sense, the word *sapiṇḍa* appears to designate those obliged to perform together certain funeral practices in honour of a father, grandfather or great-grandfather, and their wives with them," J.H. Hutton, *Les castes de l'Inde* (Paris: Payot, 1949), 71 nl. "According to one authority, all the relatives of the dead down to the seventh or tenth generation bathe in the nearest stream and purify themselves offering a prayer to Prajāpati;" R.B. Pandey, *op. cit.*, p. 255.

water, while praying to Prajāpati.[3] Facing south, in the direction of the kingdom of the dead, they take some water in the cup of their hands and, with a gesture of offering, raise their hands towards the sky, calling aloud the name of their beloved deceased.[4] Traditionally they consider the dead one to be atrociously thirsty, almost as if he finds himself in the other world in a feverish state. He cannot yet satisfy his thirst, but can be at least pacified by this attention accorded to him.

Emerging from the water, the *sapiṇḍa*s change into dry and pure clothing, squeezing out their wet robes and laying them on the west bank to dry in the sun. Then they throw boiled rice and peas to the crows, calling them aloud. This ancient rite is based upon the Vedic conviction that the souls of the departed still appear to their family members under the guise of birds.[5] While performing this ritual the following *mantram* is pronounced: "as birds the *marut*s hasten to the offering."[6]

---

3. The hair must be uncombed and no kind of ornament used; ***see*** *ibid*.
4. This is the last time that the deceased is publicly called with his name. From this moment onwards, he will develop a new individuality. *GP*, II.10.12 states that the efficacy of the rite reaches the deceased because of the utterance of his name and *gotra*. This utterance acts as a *mantram*.
5. "This recalls the primitive notion that the dead appear as birds, and the comparison of the *marut*s with birds, for the *marut*s are an offshoot from the cult of the dead;" A. Hillebrandt, *Death, op. cit.*, p. 477b. ***See also*** W. Caland, *op. cit.*, p. 78. D.N. Shastri highlights the identification of the dead with birds on the basis of the authority of *BGS*; ***see*** D.N. Shastri, "Cult and Images of the *Pitṛ*s," In *JISOA* (VII): pp. 301-11.
6. *ṚV*, I.85.7. The *martu*s perform the function of psychopomps during the cremation rite: "In the sun may your eye go, in the air your soul; may you proceed, in harmony with your virtuous actions, towards the sky, or the earth, or the watery regions; may all places be beneficent to you. May you exist there with a body, →

It is interesting to note that even today Indians conceive of the souls of their ancestors in the form of crows, which takes us back to the theme of the *maruts*. From this point of view, we come to the conclusion that disembodied souls, before birth in

---

→ supplied with food; may the *maruts* lead you on High;" *AV*, XVIII.2.7. Gonda notes that the pyre's fires were lit with this invocation; *see* J. Gonda, *Le Religioni, op. cit.*, vol. 1, p. 186. It should be recalled that the *maruts*, on a macrocosmic level, represent the celestial forces causing the rain to fall, causing the storm clouds to lighten themselves of reddish colour, causing the gathering of clouds as the wind. All functions which are strictly related with the 'downpour' descent of the souls on earth. We leave aside, in this context, a detailed characterization of these primordial deities and their activities. By the term *marut*, are to be understood the winds, the celestial waters, and the bright light of the sun filtering through the clouds. What most matters here is the microcosmic significance of the *maruts*. They are the *prāṇas* accompanying the soul of the deceased outside the body: in this way one understands why they are associated with steam and light (*tejas*). The *maruts* are not the actual 'being' of the deceased, but rather the psychic vehicles leading him in his *post mortem* journey. It is precisely in this sense that the identification of the *maruts* with the *vāyus* must be understood. Dumézil is thus right in rejecting the identification of the *maruts* with the souls of the deceased. His denial of all connections of the *maruts* with the *post mortem*, is however excessive. It is also prompting enough to hold that the *maruts* were exclusively a brotherhood of warriors of the Indo-Āryan *Mannerbund; see* G. Dumézil, "Viṣṇu et les Maruts a travers la reforme zoroastrienne," in *Journal Asiatique*, 1953, pp. 1-25. Dumézil's study has led G. Gnoli to distinguish the *maruts* from the Iranic *fravašis* much too neatly; *see* G. Gnoli, "Le "fravaši" e l'immortalità. In G. Gnoli-J.P. Vernant (ed.), *La mort, les morts dans les societiées anciennes* (Cambridge: Cambridge University Press, 1982), p. 343.

It is in this perspective that crows, that is, *maruts*, are even nowadays believed to represent the *pitṛs*. The food which the crows eat is thought to be miraculously devoured by the ancestors themselves.

a body, are comparable and sometimes identifiable with those mysterious mythological figures called *gandharvas*. Analogously, disembodied souls which have left the body are compared and sometimes identified with the *maruts*.[7]

The crows, that is, the *prāṇas* or *vāyus* of the ancestors, are the beneficiaries of the offerings of water and food; as stated, he who has just died cannot enjoy those offerings.[8] Because when a soul leaves the body, composed of gross elements, it finds itself in the condition of mere psychic existence, or of *tejas*.[9] In this situation, the individual still has the faculties of sensation and action, of *prāṇa*, of reason and of consciousness. But because these components are deprived of their corresponding organs, they are in a state of envelopment.[10] It is therefore necessary for the deceased to create another sheath around himself, to substitute the gross body he lost with death, in order to enjoy or suffer the experiences of the after world in a way comparable with that which he experienced while living.

The ten days following the funeral ceremony are dedicated to the formation and development of this subtle body, by means of ritual feeding. Each of these days corresponds to a lunar month, ending with birth in the world of ancestors.

---

7. *See MU*, VI.30, where the *marut* begins the posthumous journey towards North (*uttarāyaṇa*).
8. *See* R.B. Pandey, *op. cit.*, p. 256.
9. "The dead is regarded as still living in a sense;" R.B. Pandey, *op. cit.*, p. 265. The fact that he is made up of *tejas* explains why he feels thirsty.
10. Indeed *piśācas*, constantly in this situation of lack of balance, are thus described in *Garuḍa Purāṇa*, II.22.34-36: ". . . They are hungry and thirsty, can't speak, are without mental balance, don't recognize their position in space; distressed, they wander without knowing where they are going. They have neither father nor mother [they lack a body] . . .."

If we consider this process from a different viewpoint, we can affirm that the formation of a new body is not the main concern here. The rites made during the ten-day period create the instruments to adapt the *liṅga śarīra* of the deceased to a new condition of existence. When in the course of life the *liṅga śarīra* was situated in the *sthūla śarīra,* it was organized in such a way as to occupy and animate the body as a whole and in its single organs. Lacking this sheath,[11] the individual consciousness retreats into the unmanifest (*prajñā*) until the psychic sheath becomes an instrument of consciousness in the subtle domain.[12] To better understand this concept, we can use the classic example of the snake shedding its skin. The new skin was previously live skin within his body. Having shed this sheath, a new skin appears on the surface which is adaptable to new aims. Or we can refer to the already cited example of the caterpillar and the butterfly. When the carterpillar 'dies,' closing itself in a chrysalis, a retraction of its consciousness in a state of deep sleep occurs. Meanwhile, a metamorphosis takes place and when consciousness returns it takes over its new vehicle.

11. "The usual theory of the process of death was the separation of the soul from the body. The soul may separate from the body before death as in dreams. . . . Thus, the deceased, though disembodied, was supposed to be still living;" R.B. Pandey, *op. cit.*, p. 235. This last consideration is important, since the defunct has not yet ceased to be in some way involved in life. One might define this *post mortem* condition as an 'extension' of human life, beyond the bodily form. The disembodied person continues to carry on a sort of existence in the same world of humans, albeit limited to a psychic sphere. Thus, he is not yet subject to transmigration in another world. Some of these people will not need to incarnate again having reached *krama mukti*, 'the liberation which is postponed to the *post mortem*.'

12. ". . . When one dies, discriminative knowledge (*saṁjñā*) does not exist anymore . . .;" *BṛU*, IV.5.13.

These analogies to explain the phenomena of the creation of a body adapted to the new conditions of posthumous life, must not be taken literally. In fact, the snake and the butterfly wake up to a state of vigil consciousness, that is, in the same conditions of life in the gross body to which they have previously 'died.' The deceased, instead, transfers his consciousness to another domain altogether, characterized by the dream state.[13] It is as if the deceased goes to a dream state to enjoy deserved serene dreams, or to suffer horrible nightmares.

After these necessary clarifications, we now analyze what happens during the ten days following the funreal, to better understand in what way the deceased succeeds in gaining a body suitable to obtain subtle experiences, called *yātanā śarīra*.[14]

---

13. "Above this state is the *Swapna* (dream) state. In this state the *Jīva* or the vital principle retires into the subtle bodies. Normally this state is attained in sleep. Subtle bodies freely experience the conditions of subtle planes. The beings inhabiting these planes really live. The so-called dead man dwells in this subtle plane waiting to resume a physical form. After death just as the material body reverts to nature and serves again to build the physical supports of life (e.g., vegetable, animal and human bodies) so the subtle bodies dissolve into the planes of matter corresponding to those to which they impart a very strong impregnation proceeding from the beings whose envelopes they were;" D.N. Bose & Hiralal Haldar, *Tantras: Their Philosophy and Occult Secrets* (Calcutta: Oriental Publishing Co., 1956[3]), p. 172.

14. This term literally means 'body of suffering,' even in case of not unfavourable conditions. It is the result of the aggregation of two different components: the first is known as *vāyuja śarīra*, that is, covering produced by *vāyu*. This conception is of Yogic and Upaniṣadic origins: it is believed that the *jīva*'s exit from the body is enacted through the impulse of the *udāna*; *see Praśna Upaniṣad* (*PU*), III.9. Already *Atharvaveda*, XI.8.31 stated that, at the time of death, the *prāṇa* reabsorbed itself in *vāyu*. Soon after abandoning →

The rite made by the eldest son after the offering of water to the ancestors is called *śrāddha*.[15] He goes to the Śiva temple to purify himself, and in front of the image of the god, he prays for the posthumous peace of the deceased. The temple priest offers him a lighted lamp, representing the new vital essence.[16] Wearing pure clothing on which is traced a red *svastika*, with a

---

→ his earthly body, the deceased finds himself solely enveloped by this covering originated by the *vāyu udāna*, which is not sufficient for enjoying his new condition. The *vāyuja śarīra* is also called *adhideha*, or intermediate body.

The second component results from the assimilation of the food (*piṇḍa*) ritually offered during the ten days following the funeral. Fed in this way, the subtle covering, becomes *piṇḍaja śarīra* and, by the end of the tenth day, is 'born' as *yātanā śarīra*. As one may notice, this process is analogous to the making of an embryo: indeed, the fecundated ovum, lacking nourishment, would soon be aborted; **see** *GP*, II.10.83. I may here anticipate that the *piśāca* is endowed with the *vāyuja śarīra* only, that is, of a subtle covering still associated with the body process. This is why the *piśāca* is sometimes referred to as a 'psychic corpse.' Lacking the *piṇḍaja śarīra*, the *piśāca* is condemned to perpetual hunger and thirst, making him malevolent and aggressive; **see** *GP*, II.9.53. Often, the *yātanā śarīra* alludes to the subtle body of the *pitṛ*. In this case, the subtle body of *preta*s is defined as *piṇḍaja śarīra*, while that of *piśāca* is defined as *vāyuja śarīra*.

15. In the Śrauta tradition these rites are called *piṇḍa pitṛ yajña*s: offerings of rice *piṇḍa*s to the ancestors, identical to those offered in the *gṛhya* ritual. In this solemn rite the making of the subtle embryo is constantly followed for the duration of ten lunar months. The offering of *piṇḍa*s is made during the day of the new moon; **see** J. Gonda, *Le Religioni*, *op. cit.*, vol. 1, p. 189. This day is especially consecrated to the birth of a *preta*, since the intense lunar attraction on fluids and steams is particularly favourable to giving birth.

16. The lit earthen lamp illuminates the dark path which the deceased must follow in order to reach the city of Dharmarāja; **see** *GP*, II.18.5.

vertical line adorning his forehead, he walks with the family's brāhmaṇa towards the river banks to a secluded spot. This site must be pleasing to the eye, far from any cremation field (*śmaśāna*). The earth is purified by sprinkling water and a few handfuls of sesame and barley seeds on it. The priest and the eldest son of the deceased sit on two straw mats, with a third mat placed to the side. The presence of Viṣṇu is invoked upon this mat, and, representing this god, some long and thin *dūrvā* leaves are placed. The brāhmaṇa announces the reason for the rite: to provide the deceased with a 'body of suffering.' Then a subtle trail is drawn — along the north-west south-east direction — on which ten round sweet balls made up of barley flour, sesame seeds, sugar, milk, yoghurt, butter and *ghī* are placed.[17] An invocation is repeated to each sweet on the trail. Laying the first *piṇḍa* (or *pūraka*): "May this form the head." Laying the second: "May this form the neck and the shoulders." And so on with the third, fourth, fifth, etc., repeating: "May this form the heart and chest; may this form the back; may this form the abdomen and the stomach; may this form the groin; may form the intestines; may this form the legs up to the knees; may this form the legs, the ankles and the feet." And lastly, laying the tenth sweet ball on the trail, the priest followed by the *sapiṇḍa* of the deceased for whom the ritual is performed, says: "May this give birth to the faculty of nutrition, and satisfy hunger and thirst."[18]

The *pūraka* sweets are made up of four parts: the first is dedicated to Yama, two parts are offered to the five elements, and only the fourth part is nourishment for the deceased.

17. "The ball was called '*piṇḍa*,' because it was supposed to constitute the body of the *preta*;" R.B. Pandy, *op. cit.*, p. 265.

18. This spell constitutes the umbilical cord through which the deceased can feed himself of the ritual offerings. The rite described is an abbreviated variant, the effect of which must be considered virtual.

Water is poured on the *piṇḍa*s and a long cotton thread is placed upon it, to weave together the different parts just created into a sole *yātanā śarīra*. Now this subtle 'body' will receive water for the first time, to extinguish its thirst. Water is dripped from a shell (*śaṁkha*), ritually and symbolically connected with the uterus. This ritual gesture alludes to the embryonic formation of the subtle body. From this moment on, the disembodied one becomes a *preta*,[19] that is, a subtle embryo, living in hereafter, waiting to be born as an ancestor. After an invocation to Viṣṇu asking for the god's intercession so that the deceased will not remain a prisoner of Yama — thus avoiding the eventuality that the *preta* will be held in hell — sweets are collected and thrown into the river. The rite is concluded with a generous offering of *laḍḍū*s to the brāhmaṇas, of hay to the cows, and of bread (*roṭī*) to the dogs who represent the infernal gods.

This rite commonly performed in ten days,[20] is considered

19. "The dead, in ten days of *piṇḍa* offerings, acquires the body of a *preta*, as the child in ten [lunar] months in the mother's womb acquires his human body;" *see GP*, II.34.44. Worthy of interest is a different description of the ten days, found in a few lines preceding the above cited text. Herein, the soul of the deceased is said to remain in water for the first three days, in fire for the next three days, and in ether for the last three days: on the tenth day it ascends to the sky of Indra; *see GP*, II.34.39-40. Thus the sky of Indra corresponds to the situation of the *preta*. This intermediate state between the *manuṣya loka* and the *pitṛ loka* is, according to our text, a necessary stopover during the *kali yuga*, due to the unfavourable conditions of the cycle. In any case, the *Garuḍa Purāṇa* states that the souls of the dead pass through the stage of *preta*s only at the beginning of a *kali yuga*; *see GP*, II.20.13.
20. On certain occasions, through an abbreviated ritual, the offering of these *piṇḍa*s is performed in one sole day. In the uncertainty of the rite's efficacy and to perfect its outcome, some funeral sweets (*piṇḍa dāna*) are offered in a particularly sacred place.

inferior, or as an impure *śrāddha*; its only scope being to provide the formation of some kind of subtle body.[21] However, if this rite were not performed, the psyche of the deceased would be transformed into a *piśāca*,[22] a ghost desiring only to satisfy his hunger and thirst, due to his fiery condition of *tejas* in which he is kept prisoner after the loss of his physical body.[23] Without the *śrāddha*, that at least furnishes him with a body of suffering, the *piśāca* tries desperately to procure the necessary organs with which to satisfy his thirst by penetrating into living bodies and possessing them.[24] This is easier to do with non-

21. As we shall see shortly, the *jīva* of the deceased, considered to be the dimensions of a thumb, is waiting to obtain the embryonic body of a *preta*. He is able to assist at his funeral rites by 'associating' himself with an insect like a butterfly or a scarabaeus (***see*** H. Jacobi, "Death and Disposal of the Dead. In *ERE*, IV, p. 480) or by 'associating' himself to a crow, a spider or a monkey" (***see*** J. Parry, *The End, op. cit.*, p. 512). This is a belief widely attested to even among Indian tribals. There is the custom of finding shelter for the *jīva* in a small earthen pot (*ghaṭa, kumbha*) hung to the branches of a *pīpala* tree. The earthen pot will be broken by the *Brahman* officiating the funeral rites on the eleventh day after death, when the *jīva* takes up the embryonic body of a *preta*; ***see*** J. Parry, *ibid.*, p. 508.

22. ***See*** *GP*, II.9.47-49 and *GP*, II.21.24. The *piśāca* of a kṣatriya is called *kaṭapūtana*, a ghost causing illnesses of the abdomen.

23. Thirst (Tṛṣṇā) is the daughter of Kāma, passion, and Rati, pleasure.

24. A case causing sensation in the fifties was that of a girl living a few miles outside Delhi, said to be possessed by the *piśācī* of a woman who had died of a violent death. This case was studied by Western anthropologists; ***see*** S.A. Freed-R.S. Freed, "Spirit Possession as Illness in a North Indian Village," In *Ethnology* (III), 1964. Indian popular religion views some illnesses as being due to the possession of the dead who have suffered a violent death: "For example, Moti Surat fell ill while working at a cotton-mill in Ahmedabad; this happened in the summer of 1948, eighteen months before we first met. For three days he suffered severe headache and fever which →

vigilant beings, who have their defences relaxed, in other words with the mentally ill, with weak characters, or those prostrated by fatigue or illness. Often the *piśāca* takes over the bodies of sleeping persons, of foetuses in the womb of unworthy mothers, of infants who are not sufficiently watched over.[25] The result of this intrusion in the body of the living is comparable to the situation of the obsessed, of the one possessed by demons, or of the victim of vampires. Of course this occurrence, which to Western eyes appears 'diabolical,' is enacted by the *prāṇa*s of the *piśāca* and not by his real being, which is imprisoned in a condition of deep sleep. These instances, in the West, have been well defined as cases of 'souls in torment.'[26]

→ was not relieved by two injections given to him by a doctor, and after this he suddenly became quite psychotic, talking incoherently and striking his room-mates for no reason. He became so violent that he has to be admitted to the city madhouse for ten days, after which Devi Singh brought him back to Sularupa by train and on foot, with his arms tied with ropes. He remained severely disturbed for three months, during which time he was led, still with his arms bound, to Danaji's shrine, whose Bopa told him that the illness was due to his having passed water at the spot where a man had been killed in a road accident, and it was the ghost of this man who must be propitiated. This was done, and the madness gradually left him;" G.M. Carstairs, *op. cit.*, p. 55.

25. Analogous to these cases of possession (*āveśya*) are those of ghosts inhabiting a corpse recently abandoned by its soul. In this case the artificially animated body is thought to be possessed by a *vetāla*, which is a generic term. Indeed, it is difficult to establish when the corpse is possessed by a *piśāca*, a deity, or the magic power of a sorcerer. The most famous story about *vetāla*s is that of the *Vetālapañcaviṁśati* in the *Kathā Sarita Sāgara* collection, a text which has been translated in various European languages under different titles.

26. The *jīva* of one who is in such a tragic situation is motionless and incapable of proceeding in his posthumous evolution. The →

The imperfect rite of *śrāddha*, as described, is also called *malina ṣoḍaśī*, the sixteen impure, as it adds the offerings of the ten *piṇḍa*s to the six already made to the earth spirits during the funeral procession, from the home of the deceased to the cremation ground. The dead one has become a *preta*, a sort of subtle embryo, and from this moment on, in the next nine solar months (ten lunar months), he undergoes a process of transmutation in which he will become an ancestor.

→ impossibility of becoming a *preta* and a *pitṛ*, condemns him to remain tied to his psychic corpse. If this situation is not ritually cured, the *piśāca* will remain in this condition until the *pralaya* (*see GP*, II.22.4-5) and will then be reborn as a worm, an insect or a locust (*GP*, II.13.23-24). Since this mortal remain is subject to infestation or, worse, is utilized by magicians for sinister purposes, even the *jīva* risks becoming involved in all this, accumulating bad *karman* and worsening his rebirth prospects. The living realize the *piśāca* condition of their relative by anomalous happenings in the site where the deceased died or in its immediate vicinity (*see GP*, II.9.58-62). It is thus necessary to obtain the dissolution of the psychic corpse (*piśāca mocana*) through a *piṇḍa dāna*. This rite, which is performed collectively on the banks of a sacred river, imitates the offering of sweets already described. The chosen locales for this 'recovery' rite are Varanasi, Allahabad, Gaya, and Badrinath (Brahmakapāla). The learned Maharaja of Ramnagar told us that similar sites are even performed on sea banks, as near Madras and Rameshvaram. Moreover, H.H. Dr. Vibhuti Narain Singh knows of a site in Gujarat called Matrigaya (which we have not been able to identify), where the *piṇḍa dāna* is offered to the female line of ancestors. The *piṇḍa dāna* obtains a sure effect if performed on the day of the new moon, during the *pitṛ pakṣa* of the month of Āśvina (September-October), an equinoctial festival analogous to the Western festivities of All Saints' Day and Halloween. On this occasion the ones believed to be possessed by *piśāca*s are exorcized, thus dissolving the psychic corpse and giving form to a *preta*. In the Vedas the night of the new moon, propitious to the dead, is called *anumati*; *see ṚV*, X.59.6.

The eleventh day, the day following the celebration of the *malina ṣoḍaśī*, the *śrāddha* called *ekādaśa*, the eleventh, is celebrated. The name *ekādaśa* refers to the number of *pūrakas* offered on this occasion. These sweets are made of water, sugar, milk, yoghurt, honey, *ghṛta* (*ghī*) and sesame. This last cereal is present in all funeral rites, for its power in opening the doors to the kingdom of the dead. This is the significance of the expression 'open sesame!' of the Arabian fable.[27] This rite is analogous to the one already described. However, if the *malina ṣoḍaśī* is comparable to a *garbhādhāna*, the rites that follow appear analogous to other *saṁskāras* that take place during embryonic life, propitiating the regular development of the embryo and then of the foetus.

Returning to the river with the brāhmaṇa, the eldest son purifies the ground with barley, sesame, and sprinkles of water. Digging a furrow, in which some *dūrvā* grass is laid, the son deposits eleven spherical sweets made of rice. He covers the *piṇḍas* with a thread, which always represents a unifying principle, and again he waters them by pouring milk and water from a sea shell. He invokes the names of eleven gods, and finally, reciting passages from the *Yajurveda*, the priest asks for the power of alleviating the thirst of the *preta*. This offering is done very rapidly, as if to lighten the thirst of the *preta*. Then the *piṇḍas* are thrown into the river or given to a cow to eat.

After a bath in the water, the son gives an ulterior offering of five *piṇḍas*, the so-called *pañca śrāddha*, following the outline of the preceding rites. Also this time, in the furrow in which *dūrvā* is laid, five rice balls are added, with cotton thread on top, sprinkled with water. After the ritual invocation,

27. J. Gonda relates the use of sesame in funeral rites to the black colour of its seed; *see* J. Gonda, *Le Religioni*, *op. cit.*, vol. 1, p. 189. The *Garuḍa Purāṇa* states that sesame has the power of consuming the faults of the deceased; *see GP*, II.2.17. Sesame is also said to have originated from Viṣṇu's perspiration; *see GP*, II.2.16.

everybody prays that the deceased may not linger in the embryonic state of *preta*. These *piṇḍa*s are also thrown into the river, and the celebrant purifies himself with another bath.

Then a series of rituals are performed to avail the protection of gods and goddesses upon the deceased. Two clay altars are erected: on one of these, offerings are made in favour of *śakti*; on the other, in favour of Rudra, Pūṣan,[28] and Agni. A bull and a young mare are brought to the site, and their marriage is celebrated, after which they are let free. They are an added help to the *preta* for his passage across the Vaitaraṇī river. This ancient rite is called *vṛṣotsarga*,[29] the abandonment of two

---

28. In Purāṇic accounts Pūṣan, god of food and roads (*see TS*, I.2.4), and guide of the deceased towards the domain of *pitṛ*s, is substituted by the Goddess Annapūrṇā. This deity, whose name means 'giver of food,' is identified with Pārvatī and Gaṅgā: In the course of the *preta*s' journey towards the *pitṛ loka*, Annapūrṇā provides them with the *piṇḍa*s offered during the *śrāddha* rite. Annapūrṇā, as Gaṅgā, had originally come down from the northern hemisphere to the southern one in order to 'nourish' with water the austral sea, which had been drunk up by Agastya; *see Mbh*, II.109.20.

29. The ritual is quite complex and includes various aspects of Tāntric origin, as for instance the constellation of stars and the worship of *mātṛkā*s; *see GP*, II.14.19-24. Many passages insist on the efficacy of the *vṛṣotsarga*, believed to have the power of freeing the soul from Yama's power; *see GP*, II.6.121-122, *GP*, II.6.133-140, and *GP*, II.13.13-14. This ritual is believed to represent a powerful start in overcoming the condition of *preta*; *see GP*, II.13.3-4. The ritual is often accompanied by the gift of a bed (*vilakṣaṇā*) to a brāhmaṇa, or, more frequently, to a newly-wedded couple, reproposing the inverse analogy between death and conception. Originally, the *vṛṣotsarga* ended with the killing of the cattle, which were tied to the sacrificial pole (*yūpa*). To remember the *yūpa*s of those ancient epochs, in some parts of India — especially in the eastern regions — a wooden sculptured column (*vṛṣa kāṣṭha*) is erected. Usually the pole has a *mūrti* of Śiva on its top, indicating the bliss to be reached;

→

calves, since these were made to enter into the jungle, the inhospitable domain of Yama. Today the bull and the cow are often substituted with two lumps of *dūrvā* grass.[30] This eleventh day, so full of ritual offerings, is concluded with the oblation of a sole and important *piṇḍa*. In the Śrauta tradition, the rite is performed at the end of a year from the day of death, and signs the moment in which the *preta* will be born into the *pitṛ loka*. In the abbreviated rite, the *preta* is already virtually considered as a *pitṛ*, who is represented by a bunch of *dūrvā* to the south, in front of the celebrant. He makes the gesture of handing the *piṇḍa* to the *preta*, puts it into the furrow, and sprinkles it with water. After having thrown in this *piṇḍa*, and having purified himself, the eldest son invites fifty-two brāhmaṇas to feast. They represent the weeks of the year required by tradition for the fulfilment of the rite. This banquet is possible because, on the same day, the period of mourning and thus of impurity (*aśauca*) is over for the entire family.[31] The brāhmaṇas can therefore sit at the table and accept food from them. From this moment on, they can begin celebrating the *saṁdhyā* rite in its complete form at dawn and dusk.

→ on its base the figure of an ancestor with folded hands (*añjali-mudrā*), and in its middle the figure of a bull acting as psychopompus; *see* D.N. Shastri, *op. cit.*

30. Originally this ritual was probably a bull sacrifice, to provide the *preta* with the necessary nourishment for reaching the *pitṛ loka*. The offering of buffalo or rhinoceros meat was held to be even more efficacious, to guarantee the full success of the ritual; *see ibid.*, p. 162.

31. This celebration marks the return of the family to its normal state (*ṛtviya*). In fact, from the moment of their relative's death to this banquet of reconciliation, the relationship between the living and the line of ancestors had been interrupted. The deceased, in the condition of *preta*, finds himself in a hiatus between the *manuṣya loka* and the *pitṛ loka*, which prevents the living from normal access to the rites of the ancestors, or to the rites *tout court*. When, →

The last day, the twelfth, is dedicated to the offering of *piṇḍas*.[32] At dawn, the eldest son with the priests return to the river bank to celebrate the passage of the *preta* into the world of ancestors. Fifteen *piṇḍas* are offered in favour of the twelve months that the deceased must pass through.[33] We must remember, in fact, that everyday after death represents a month of subtle gestation of the *preta*.

The funeral rite immediately following is called *saṁyojana śrāddha*. In its origin this rite was much simpler and was called *sapiṇḍīkaraṇa*,[34] as it placed the deceased among his ancestors, represented by the souls of his father, grandfather, and great-grandfather, if deceased.[35] Water was poured in equal parts into three jars to indicate the new *pitṛ*'s access to the community

---

→ however, the condition of the deceased changes from that of *preta* to that of *pitṛ*, the family is readmitted to its normal ritual life. When a brāhmaṇa eats the *piṇḍas*, the *pitṛs* enter him and participate in the meal. The father goes in the stomach, the grandfather places himself to the left of the stomach and the great-grandfather to the right of the stomach; *see GP*, II.10.26-28.

32. This is the array of rites known as *sapiṇḍīkaraṇa*, which, depending on if the sacred fire is kept or not, is performed on the twelfth month or on the twelfth day after cremation; *see GP*, II.26.9-15. The end of this period is marked by the gift of the bed; *see GP*, II.34.39-40.

33. What is symbolically celebrated here is a transformation which has not yet taken place, since it will become effective only at the end of the twelve month period after death.

34. "After the great path, which lasts one year, he sojourns in the *pitṛ loka* together with the [other] *pitṛs*;" *GP*, II.26.6-7.

35. He thus loses his identity, becoming a member of the community of *pitṛs*; *see GP*, II.26.10-12. Among *pitṛs*, three categories can be distinguished: the *agnisvātta*, the *barhisada*, and the *somapa*; *see GP*, II.5.38. After having ended their existence in the *pitṛ loka*, they transmigrate in order to become humans, gods, and birds; *see GP*, II.10.1.

of ancestors, represented by his three past generations.[36] The *sapiṇḍīkaraṇa* is still performed by those who maintain the sacrificial rite of the three fires.

Nowadays the *saṁyojana śrāddha* has brought modifications and additions to the ancient *śrauta* ritual. Five brāhmaṇas participate in it, three impersonating the father, grandfather, and great-grandfather of the new *pitṛ*. The other two represent witnesses of the event, the gods Kāla and Kāma, Thanatos and Eros. The deceased is represented by a bunch of *dūrvā*, tied together. From a jar of water, one-third is poured on the ground in front of each brāhmaṇa who represent the ancestors. Boiled rice is distributed to the five priests, along with numerous other vegetables. Then the celebrant mixes the rice with the usual ingredients; when it has formed a homogeneous dough, it is divided into two equal parts. With one part he makes one big *piṇḍa*, and with the other half, three *piṇḍa*s of usual dimensions. The first and biggest *piṇḍa* is consecrated to the deceased and the other three to his ancestors whom he wishes to unite with. Thus a total of fifty-two *piṇḍa*s offered in different moments during the twelve days following death — a symbolical and ritual allusion to the weeks of gestation of the *preta* — is reached. After the usual offering in the furrow of ground, the largest *piṇḍa* is removed and divided into three equal parts, which are added to each of the three *piṇḍa*s offered to the *pitṛ*. The deceased is assimilated to his ancestors through these rites. The three rice sweets, again kneaded, are placed in the furrow, covered by thread, and sprinkled with water. At the end of the ceremony the *piṇḍa*s are thrown into the river, closed in a copper amphora or offered as food to a cow. The usual bath follows, plus offerings of food and money to the priests. Again food is offered to the crows, upon returning

36. This rite may be related, albeit in an inverse sense, to the myth of the ṛbhus and their cup; *see* *ṚV*, IV.33-34.

home. The lady of the house throws different vegetable seeds on the roof, loudly calling birds, who represent the *maruts*, as we have seen. It is a bad omen if the crows do not appear, and the women sometimes spend hours attempting to attract the souls of their deceased under the black appearance of these birds. And this time, in the company of crows, the deceased himself participates in the meal.

It is interesting to note that the new ancestor is called by a new name from the moment in which he is born into the *pitṛ loka*. In most cases he is called Śarmā if he was of the Brāhmaṇical caste, Varmā, if he was a kṣatriya, Gupta if he was a vaiśya, and Dāsa, if he was of a servile caste. In this way the ancestor assumes the function of family spirit, having lost the individual characteristics which identified him during earthly life or immediately after death.[37] Up to this moment, the transformation of the soul into ancestor has been compared to the

---

37. In India, funeral rites tend to make the deceased's individuality disappear, rather than exalting it in the memory of posterity, as happens in the West. The loss of individual characteristics, instead of relegating the ancestor in an anonymous group, includes it within the circle of the chosen ones, who have overcome or are in the process of overcoming the domain conditioned by name and form (*nāmarūpam*); *see* chapter 9 n. 36. This process of loss of personality develops in stages: we have seen that, among *pitṛ*s, only three are still identifiable as individuals: the father, the grandfather, and the great-grandfather. When the son dies and from *preta* becomes *pitṛ*, he takes his father's place, and the father takes his grandfather's place. In this way, the great-grandfather disappears from the troop of oldest ancestors, uniting himself to the family totem; *see* Ch. Malamoud, *op. cit.*, pp. 446-47. The stelae of heroes fallen in battle (*vīra kāla*) and of widows who freely chose to burn themselves on the pyre of their husband (*satī kāla*), are exceptions. These kṣatriya customs maintain a certain consideration for the individuality of the deceased, who distinguished themselves for their martial virtueṣ.

gestation period. Summarizing, right after the death of the body, the soul appears as a subtle seed. With the first offering of *śrāddha*, an embryonic psychic 'body' begins to develop, becoming a *preta*. In a year's time, thanks to the nutrition which the living send him through the umbilical cord of rites, the dead one completes his subtle body and is born as a *pitṛ*. This symbolism is very ancient and faithfully adheres to the Śrauta conceptions.

This transformation undergone by the deceased in his first year is described in Purāṇic myths as the journey of the soul from the land of the living to the kingdom of Yama. The *piṇḍa*s offered by the son with different *śrāddha* rites are considered to be stopovers in the journey. This description of the posthumous transformation of the deceased, of Purāṇic origin, was superimposed on the preceding one, not without generating some confusion in popular beliefs, as we shall shortly see.

Before continuing, we must ask what would happen in the absence, interruption, or negligent performance of the *śrāddha* rites. In these cases, the soul of the deceased, the *jīva*, remains indefinitely prinsoner in the dream state, incapable of enjoying the conditions of his new subtle existence.[38] The condition of

38. "He who does not obtain funeral rites, is condemned to perpetually remain a *piśāca*," *GP*, II.9.47-49. As we have already explained, the term 'perpetual' refers to a temporal length which extends itself until the *mahāpralaya*: *see GP*, II.22.4-5. Naturally, the persons who are more exposed to the eventuality of becoming *piśāca*s are those who die while travelling, away from home and at a young age. Relatives may interpret their absence as a delay, and continue hoping in their return. Thus, his corpse is not searched for. Other cases are those of people who commit suicide, who died of an infectious disease, who were burned alive; *see GP*, II.22.8-13. In general, all those who suffer a 'bad' death, risk remaining prisoners of their psychic corpse. An exception is those killed in battle and pilgrims who died at sacred places, who are believed to reach the heavens; *see GP*, II.38.19 and *GP*, II.48.12.

piśāca is generally described as that of a being unable to breathe, eat, or drink, blind and deaf, dull, deformed, and ugly,[39] in a state of great sufferance. At the mercy of the subtle elements in which he is enveloped, he sometimes comes into casual and unknowing contact with the world of the living. In fact, humans and animals can feel his presence through smells, noises, cold touches caused by unnatural draughts.[40] Rarely it is even possible to see the grotesque form created by the fire element as a mirage. In other words, the *piśāca* indirectly provokes all those phenomena of infestation[41] which one can get rid of by beginning the funeral rites all over again, including the *piṇḍa dāna*. When one becomes *preta* and then *pitṛ*,

39. ***See*** *GP*, II.22.34-36. Due to the derangement which has brought them to such terrible condition, *piśācas* have serious 'physical' anomalies, sometimes bearing animal traits; ***see*** *GP*, II.22.46-47. Although the unhappiness of *piśāca*s is caused by the inability to feed themselves, a great voracity is popularly attributed to them. They are believed to eat mucus, faeces, urine, pus, waste and all sorts of revolting rubbish; *GP*, II.22.55-56.

40. These phenomena are always unpleasant and manifest the bad mood of the *piśāca*; ***see*** *GP*, II.21.5-7. As already noticed, the malevolence of the soul in pain is due to the hunger and thirst to which he is condemned; ***see*** *GP*, II.9.53. Some *piśāca*s may become dangerous for the life of men. The *cuṛel*, that is the *piśācī* of a woman who died at delivery, is particularly fearful: "Encounters with a churel (who could be recognized at once because her feet were turned backwards) were a much more serious matter, because their resentment at being cut-off when they were enjoying sex and looking forward to rearing children was so great that they were set upon killing their victims, whether male or female;" G.M. Carstairs, *op. cit.*, p. 55. Interesting is the detail of the feet turned backwards which, together with palmate feet, is found in European tales as a distinctive sign of certain fairies and witches.

41. "The *piśāca*s infest the houses where the sacred *mantram*s are not recited, where rituals are not performed, where knowledge is not cultivated;" *GP*, II.22.58.

suffering ends and he stops disturbing the living, and in particular the members of his family and those who now live in his house.

These phenomena of infestation are often produced involuntarily, by individuals in imbalanced psychic conditions, who act as a support to the suffering *piśāca*. They may be permanent mental disorders or temporarily altered psychic states, as those occurring during adolescence. It is the same living being who unknowingly puts his psyche at the *piśāca*'s disposal, with which the *piśāca* is believed to manifest those phenomena that today are commonly defined as *poltergeist*.[42]

---

42. Another psychic phenomenon believed to be caused by *piśācas* is that which is called split [personality. In general, whoever experiences it has a vision of himself as if he were outside his body; *see GP*, II.23.5.

11

Funerals Without Cremation

THERE are three different cremation rites. In the first case, the deceased had performed worship of the three fires. In the second case, he had only kept the domestic fire burning. Thirdly, as in the great majority of Hindus, he had no family tradition regarding the sacred fire.[1] In the first case, the funeral pyre is lit from embers coming from the three hearths, and carried to the cremation site in three clay jars.[2] In the second case, the flames lighting the pyre come from the embers of the domestic fire. In the third case, the pyre is lit by fire taken from a temple near the cremation site. The texts thus affirm: "May the *ahitāgni* be cremated with the three fires,[3] the *anahitāgni*

1. A fourth case is those who fall in battle. For these a mass cremation is provided for, which however must be considered exceptional and destined to the members of the kṣatriya caste; *see* J.N. Tiwari, *op. cit.*, pp. 48-59. This war ritual, going back to the *Mahābhārata*, was also in use during the campaigns in India in the last decades.
2. Before the funeral, relatives perform an *agnihotra* in honour of the deceased, characterized by the offering of milk of a cow nursing a calf which is not her own; *see* J. Gonda, *Le Religioni, op. cit.*, vol. 1, p. 187.
3. The three fires represent earth, atmosphere and sky. Great attention is given to identify which of the three fires reaches the mortal remains first. If it is the earth fire, his destiny will be to return to the earth; if the atmosphere fire, the deceased will follow the path of his ancestors (*pitṛ yāna*). If touched first by the celestial fire, he will follow the way of the gods (*deva yāna*); *see* A. Hillebrandt, *Death, op. cit.*, p. 477b.

with one, and all the rest with *laukikāgni*,"[4] meaning the fire of this world.

Although the three cremation rites differ in rituals but certainly not in effectiveness. In each case, the common element to destroy the body is fire. But Hindu tradition considers other possibilities of disposing the corpse.[5] In Vedic times and also

4. R.B. Pandey, *op. cit.*, p. 269. A perennial fire is kept in the vicinity of various cremation grounds in Varanasi. A bundle of burning *dūrvā* grass is taken to the funeral pyre. This fire is considered impure and is accessible only to the untouchable ḍoms who control all *śmaśāna* activities in this sacred locale. Even more impure is the fire sprouting here and there from a pyre in extinction, because the last residues of physical and psychic elements, known as *bhūta*s, are believed to remain in it. Magicians try to possess these sinister embers, so as to utilize them in their witchcraft, and the *kāpālika*s for the performance of their dangerous ascetic feats (*śmaśāna sādhanā*).

5. Until not long ago, Indo-European populations were thought to be characterized by certain rites performed to destroy the corpse. Although A.B. Keith had already taken a critical position on this issue, it is only recently that such a vision has been corrected, given that no one any longer gives a homogeneous ethnicity to the reconstructed Indo-European language; ***see*** P.J. Ucko, "Ethnography and Archaeological Interpretation of Funerary Remains," In *World Archaeology* I, 2 (1969): pp. 273-76. Recently, Colin Renfrew has returned to the issue; ***see*** *Archaeology and Language* (London: Jonathan Cape Ltd., 1987), ch. 1.

   As to our field of research, it appears that Indo-European populations having a common linguistic origin practised different types of rituals, diffused also among populations of different linguistic stocks; ***see*** J. Gonda, *Le Religioni, op. cit.*, vol. 1, p. 183. As to the funeral customs of early Greece, ***see*** Emily Vermeule, *Aspects of Death in Early Greek Art and Poetry* (Berkeley: University of California Press, 1979), chs. 1, 3. For the funeral rites of the Romans, ***see*** Georges Dumézil, *La religion romaine archaïque* (Paris: Payot, 1974), chs. 1.6, 2.4.2; Javier Arce, *Funus Imperatorum* (Madrid: Alianza, 1988), ch. 1; Carlo Pascal, *L'oltretomba dei pagani. . . .* As to ancient Germanic populations, ***see*** Jan De Vries, *Altgermanische Religionsgeschichte*, 1956, vol. 1, p. 148.

cited in the ancient Saṁhitās, burial[6] ushers as another equally important ritual. We remember the celebrated verses of the *Ṛgveda*:

> Go to your mother earth, the vast and delicious earth, this virgin as soft as wool for its generous worshipper; may she protect you from proximity to Nirtti. Cover him, earth, do not oppress him, be kind and gentle to him. Cover him as a mother covers her child with the hem of her robe. May the earth piled over him cover him lightly. May thousands of grains of sand enfold him. May this resting place distil clarified butter for him. May it be a refuge everyday of this world. I pile earth over you to cover you with this tomb. May I not run this risk. May the ancestors maintain your monument, may Yama condescend to make a refuge here for you.[7]

Besides these two funeral customs, others are mentioned, such as the following: "O Agni, lead all the ancestors here, whether they were buried, thrown, cremated, or exposed, so as to enjoy the offerings."[8]

---

6. On this issue, see the complete monograph of S.P. Gupta, *Disposal of the Dead and Physical Types in Ancient India* (Delhi, 1972). Prof. Gupta gave me precious informations when he was Director of the Government Museum of Allahabad. The tombs of the *ārya*s were quadrangular, while the *anārya*s built circular funeral monuments; *see ŚB*, XIII.8.1.5.
7. *ṚV*, X.18.10. Of interest here is the mention of the grave (*stūpa, thūpa*) kept by the *pitṛ*, corresponding to *ṚV*, X.18.10. Compare this *mantram* with the initials *STTL* (*sit tibi terra levis*) engraved on Roman sarcophagi. It is interesting to note that the Greek sarcophagus, 'eater of meat,' corresponds to the Sanskrit *kravyāda*.
8. *AV*, XVIII.2. To these four different rites must be added the disappearance of the corpse (*brahmalīna*) and mummification; the only scriptural example is that of Nimi, son of Ikṣvāku; *see VP*, IV.5.7.

We deduce that in Vedic times bodies were destroyed through all four elements; earth, water, fire, and air.[9] The destruction of the body by water and by exposure to air appears in the Vedas just one other time.[10] As for exposure to air, the *Śatapatha Brāhmaṇa* offers an ulterior indication. This ritual text highlights that the corpse had to be raised and fixed upon the branches of a tree.[11]

9. Even the bones, when collected after cremation, are entrusted to the four elements. In the case of the *ahitāgni*, the bones are ground up, mixed with *ghṛta*, put on another pyre, and burned to a complete incineration; *see* A. Hillebrandt, *Death, op. cit.*, p. 476a. In other cases, the bones are buried, thrown in rivers, or abandoned in places not frequented by human beings. Gonda notes that even sacrificial gifts, although usually offered to the fire, may be thrown into water, hung on trees, or offered to anthills; *see* J. Gonda, *Le Religioni, op. cit.*, vol. 1, p. 156. The ants are believed to carry the offerings to the subterranean world. In Tamil country, offerings are still made to the anthills in favour of subterranean deities, that is, the *nāgas*; *see* G. Eichinger Ferro-Luzzi, *The Self-milking Cow and the Bleeding Lingam* (Wiesbaden: Otto Harrassowitz, 1987), pp. 93-98.

10. *See* respectively *ṚV*, X.14 and *AV*, XVIII.2.34. Some scholars have explained the scant mention of these two funeral practices in Vedic texts, with the fact that they were rarely performed. In our opinion, Vedic hymns dedicate greater attention to cremation and inhumation simply because they are the canonical texts for those living in society as *gṛhasthins*.

11. *See ŚB*, IV.5.2.13. This description agrees with one of the modes of disposal of the corpse, practised by the Tibetans, the origin of which is unknown. Tiwari notes that the episode of *Mbh*, IV.5 testifies to the existence of this ritual use: the five Pāṇḍavas, before entering the city of Viratanagara, decided to hide their weapons. To be sure that no one could steal them they laid their weapons in the hollow of a *śami* tree, near the site of a *śmaśāna*. From the cemetery, they took the corpse of a woman who had been exposed in that place 'according to the tradition of her family,' and they tied it to the *śami*. Then they left, sure that no one would challenge the macabre guardian of their weapons; *see* J.N. Tiwari, *op. cit.*, pp. 28-29.

In the *Chāndogya Upaniṣad* we find a significant reference to water burial, especially among *vāṇaprasthins*.[12] Today *vāṇaprasthins* and *sādhus* are still thrown into the water as soon as they die. Often, just before abandoning the body to the currents, the deceased's brethren cross his legs in the lotus position (*padma āsana*) and break the summit of his skull with a coconut, to ease the exit of the *prāṇas* from his body.[13] The departure of the deceased in the waters is celebrated with a banquet in which the members of the same school (*sampradāya*) and brāhmaṇas participate.[14] In certain cases, children who die before the age of two are thrown into the waters, as those who die from epidemics. Their images in *dūrvā* are regularly burned on the funeral pyre. Burning bodies of the plague-stricken is avoided for fear of offending the gods who sent the calamity. Water, in fact, does not destroy the bacilli sent by the gods as fire does.

Usually, however, children who die before the age of two are buried. Burial, in this case, has an evident relationship with the concept of *regressus ad uterum*. The aborted foetus, or the stillborn child are considered beings who could not be exposed the possibility of realizing any real action or ritual *karman*.[15]

Saṁnyāsins were also buried in Vedic times, and this usage is protracted up to the present. In this case we must not confuse the burial of innocent babies with that tributed to *saṁnyāsins*: these latter are considered free from every *karman*. Their death

12. *See ChU*, VIII.66.
13. *See* W. Caland, *op. cit.*, p. 95.
14. *Sādhus* do not produce the impurity of the *aśauca*.
15. Death occurring in infancy guarantees a human rebirth; *see GP*, II.24.4. Children less than four years old are believed to be incapable of performing evil actions. This is why no ulterior expiatory rites are necessary, and the mourning period following their death is very brief; *see GP*, II.43.3.

corresponds to a liberation of individuality and identification with the Absolute.[16] Thus the burial of a *saṁnyāsin* is not followed by any ritual.[17] The body of the holy man is laid in a

16. À vrai dire, les textes ne donnent pas de raison positive pour l'inumation des renonçants, mais ils s'expliquent, ou sugg erent des explications, quant a l'impossibilité de les incinérer: le sacrifice de la crémation ne peut s'accomplir que dans des feux prélevés sur les feux domestiques du mort; or, le renonçant, en se dépouillant de tous ses biens, s'est dépouillé aussi, et au premier chef, de ses utensiles cultuels, et le moment crucial de la cérémonie d'entrée en *saṁnyāsa* est celui o u il éteint ses feux sacrificiels. Mais en les éteignant, il ne les abolit pas vraiment: bien plutôt il les absorbe, ou, selon l'expression sanscrite, il les fait monter dans son ême. Et la flamme qu'il porte en lui désormais entretient le *tapas*, la brûlure ascétique qui ne cessera qu'avec sa mort, et qui consumera, de son vivant, les souillures et les conséquences des actes qu'il a accumulés: en sorte que, quand vient la mort, il peut s'évaporer compl etement, parvenir à la "délivrance" (*mokṣa*) c'est à dire gagner l' absolu (le *brahman*), puisque rien ne subsiste de lui qui le retienne dans le cercle des renaissances. Cuit et même consumé par avance par la flamme du *tapas*, il n'a pas a soumettre tout son corps a ce perfectionnement ultime qu'il n'a pas à être transformé en victime sacrificielle. En fait, cela n'est pas seulement inutile, c'est impossible: les victimes sacrificielles sont en principe des animaux domestiques. Or, le renonçant, en rompant solennellement ses liens avec la societé (avec son village, sa famille, ses rites), en se plaçant, comme il est dit *Vaikhānasa-smārtasūtra,* V.8, en-dehors du *dharma* et de *l'adharma*, en-dehors des r egles et des crit eres sociaux, et en se ritirant dans la solitude de la forêt, devient lui-même un être forestier, semblable à un animal sauvage et donc impropre au sacrifice;" Ch. Malamoud, *op. cit.*, pp. 448-49. On the sacrifice of domestic (*paśu*) and wild (*mṛga*) animals, *see* G.G. Filippi, *Some Sacrificial, op. cit.*

17. "The *Taittirīya-Āraṇyaka* speaks of the rite of brahmamedha, performed on the death of a brahman who had realized brahmanhood;" R.B. Pandey, *op. cit.*, p. 268. The *saṁnyāsin* is exempted from funeral rites for the reason explained in the previous note, as well as because the rite of initiation at this fourth stage of life involves the preliminary performance of the *śrāddha* rites.

grave, with his begging bowl on his lap.[18] His wooden drinking vessel, *kamaṇḍalu*, filled with water, is placed in his right hand. The grave is then covered with earth to protect it from animals. Above the tomb, as above the place where the jar containing the bones of a universal sovereign (*cakravartin*) is buried, a monument[19] is later erected called *samādhi, stūpa,* or *loṣṭaciti.* Tradition envisages the *samādhi* as a monument to a saint, and the *stūpa* or *loṣṭaciti* as a monument to a king. The moment for the construction and the number of bricks utilized are established by astrological calculations. The building is made at night, accompanied by sacred music and dance. These rites are called *śmaśāna*[20] for the *saṁnyāsin,* and *pitṛ medha* for the king.[21] In the Ganges valley one can still find some *stūpa*s of protohistoric kings. Over the centuries they have been viewed as the burial sites of companions of Gautama the Buddha, or of the Jaina Tīrthaṁkaras, predecessors of Mahāvīra, or even as

18. "The funeral of the *parivrājaka*s, retired ascetics and mendicants, form another class. They are those who have given up all worldly attachments and have realized the *Brahman* or Universal soul;" R.B. Pandey, *op. cit.*, p. 271.
19. *See* G.G. Filippi, *Cakravartin, op. cit.*, pp. 133-34.
20. The term literally means burial. In the course of time, however, *śmaśāna* has come to mean cremation site.
21. With the construction of this monument, the deceased king is promoted to collective ancestor of the surrounding district of *genius loci.* This is why the rite of construction of the *stūpa* is called 'obtain of the ancestor;' *see* R.B. Pandey, *op. cit.*, pp. 263-65. It is interesting to observe that the monument can be erected only when the memory of the deceased has been purged of every individual information. When memory of individuality has been exhausted, it is exterior proof that the psychic corpse (evil) of the deceased has dissolved: "The tomb should not be built too soon to not reinforce evil. One must wait, thus avoiding evil. The tomb must be built [for example] when the year of death is no longer remembered. Thus evil can be eliminated through oblivion;" *ŚB*, XIII.8.1.2.

the abode of *yakṣas* and *nāgas*.[22] In India, the custom of erecting *stūpas* and *samādhis* has never been abandoned.

The destruction of the body by exposure to air is of difficult interpretation. It seems that young men who died by violent means[23] were left exposed on tree branches. In all other cases, *brahmacārins* were cremated.

In the course of thousands of years, the use of fire became generalized. Except for *saṁnyāsins*, even those who have been buried, or thrown into rivers, or those whose corpses have not been found, are all burned on the pyre under their image of *kuśa* grass (*dūrvā*).[24]

Mention must also be made of strange cases in which a person left home,[25] and died without the family's awareness. After a certain number of years, when they think he is deceased, the family may perform funeral rites for him. The body, always represented by *dūrvā* leaves, is burned on the pyre,[26] according to the usual ritual. Then the eldest son, or

22. *See* John Irwin, "The Stūpa and the Cosmic Axis. The Archaeological Evidence," in M. Taddei (ed.), *South Aisan Archaeology* (Naples, 1979), col. 2, pp. 800-802.
23. *See* R.B. Pandey, *op. cit.*, p. 273. From some passages in the *Atharvaveda* it seems that corpses were laid in the hollow of a tree; *see AV*, XVIII.2.25 and *AV*, XVIII.3.70.
24. *See* R.B. Pandey, *op. cit.*, p. 274.
25. Persons dying far from home, in a traditional Hindu environment, are regularly cremated. Their bones are collected and sent to the family that recomposes the remains and folds them in a shroud (the skin of a black antelope). Then a second cremation takes place; *see ŚB*, XII.5.1.13-14. This is the case of double cremation of Pāṇḍu (*Mbh*, I.116.31 and I.117.1-7), which greatly baffled *Mahābhārata* scholars; *see* J.N. Ṭiwari, *op. cit.*, pp. 60-79.
26. In case the deceased is of a high caste; then a *mahābrāhmaṇa*; else if of a low caste, then a barber makes an effigy in human form using fifty-six different materials, of which *dūrvā* grass is the most significant. A camphor lamp is lit at the level of the navel of the →

closest relative, performs the *śrāddha* rites. It might happen, at the conclusion, that the presumed deceased unexpectedly reappears. Now he is considered ritually dead, and as such, comparable to a *piśāca* in pain, carrying with him every sort of disaster. Therefore all *saṁskāra*s must be performed for him, from that of birth to that of marriage.[27] Only in this case can the unfortunate man be reborn to social life.[28]

Considering what we have examined here with extreme caution, we get the impression that, at least in principle, the body is destroyed by different elements in accordance to the stage of life (*āśrama*) in which his death occurs. The earth, by burial, is due to *saṁnyāsin*s or those who have overcome their *karman*, and also to infants, given their inability to produce actions.[29] Water is the element designated to destroy the bodies of *vānaprasthin*s, and of those who died from infectious diseases. Next comes fire, for the adult who conducts a social life (*gṛhasthin*) and who normally offers oblations to *agni*.[30]

→ dummy, with an invocation to the deceased's *prāṇa* to occupy that body's substitute. When the lamp goes out, the dummy is considered dead. Then the effigy can be cremated according to the canons of the customary funeral; **see** J. Parry, *The End, op. cit.*, p. 507.

27. "In such a case, sometimes, a few of the supposed dead persons came back. They had got to be revived again with the proper *saṁskāra*s, from the conception to the *vivāha*, as they were socially dead and nobody would keep contact with them. At present the same ritual is followed but people do not evince any hurry about the funeral of missing persons, and their *antyeṣṭi* is performed when the possibility of their return is over;" R.B. Pandey, *op. cit.*, p. 272.
28. *See* J. Gonda, *Le Religioni*, vol. 1, pp. 187-88.
29. "A child, whose teeth have not come out, should be buried with the recitation of *praṇava* denied to the abortive child;" **see** R.B. Pandey, *op. cit.*, p. 270.
30. This funeral is canonical both in the Gṛhya-Sūtras and the Śrauta- →

Premature and violent death, corresponding to the youth of *brahmacārins*, one time required exposure to air. However, this custom fell into disuse several centuries ago and has been substituted with cremation.

The attentive reader will realize that the element of ether has been overlooked. In reality this element bears some characteristics distinguishing it from the other four, being more subtle in comparison with other *bhūta*s, and so abstract as to be confused with space and with emptiness or void. Thus, *ākāśa* seems almost unmanifest occult. With reference to the death of some Hindu saints, according to tradition their bodies dissolve directly in the ether. The saint who departed from the world in this way leaves an object for the veneration of his devotees in place of his mortal remains: a bouquet, a *śālagrāma* stone, a sword, or other items.[31]

→ Sūtras, which establish the daily and solemn rites of *gṛhasthins*. This is also why cremation is considered as a characteristic rite in the Vedic Saṁhitās, these latter ones containing the hymns to be pronounced during the rites of the *sūtra*s above-mentioned.

31. The cases of Dattātreya, Kabīr, Karurāma and others are well-known. This extraordinary death, defined *brahmalīna*, disappearance in *Brahman*, or *antardhāna*, invisibility, takes place in the case of saints who have followed a path of realization (*sādhanā*) utilizing the alchemical method (*rasāyana*). My informant from Varanasi told me of a similar recent disappearance of the master Svāmī Rāma. This disappearance of the corpse is also well-known in the Tibetan milieu: ". . . Even more recently, in 1952, my uncle was a witness to one of these events. Near my town lived an old man, who earned his living by engraving *mantra*s on stone. He had been a tailor in his youth, then squire of a famous master, Dodrub chen (rDo.grub chen), whose teachings he probably heard. Before dying, he gave all his belongings to the monastery where his son was a monk, and announced that within a week he would die. Everyone was amazed, as no one considered him a religious adept. But when he gave orders to close himself in a tent for seven days, they understood that he would attain the body of light. On

In one way or another, great care is observed during the ritual, destruction of the corpse,[32] the intention being to prevent the deceased from returning home and disturbing the family. An abandoned corpse decomposes in its gross elements and in prāṇic components that are unable to follow the *jīva* together with the other vital breaths. As the body begins putrefying, so do these lower constituents.[33] This putrefaction provokes the passage from the solid state to the liquid and to the gaseous, with the production of the *ignis fatuus*, that represents the restitution of these bodily instinctive elements (*bhūtas*) to nature.[34] In all world populations, these *bhūtas* are

---

→ the eighth day, many people came to be present at the event, among them some Chinese officials, convinced that once and for all the superstitions of the Tibetan people would be demonstrated. Also in this case, however, they found only nails and hair;" Namkhai Norbu, *Dzog-Chen, lo stato di Autoperfezione* (Roma: Ubaldini, 1986), pp. 51-52. I have discussed analogous cases with the Dean of the Tibetan Institute of Higher Studies at Sarnath, Lama Sandong Rinpoche.

32. ". . . les cérémonies funéraires, quand on les examine pour elle-mûemes, paraissent n'avoir d'autre raison d'être que de donner une réponse, abondante, minutieuse, acharnée, a cette question que la collectivité se pose quand elle est en présence d'un cadavre: comment s'en débarasser?;" Ch. Malamoud, *op. cit.*, p. 441.

    Certainly, as we have seen, this is not the principal aim of funeral rites. The effect sought is the formation of the *yātanā śarīra*. "The *agnidagdha* (burned by Agni) and the *anagnidagdha* (not burned by Agni) like to offer the *svadhā* (the libation presented to the ancestors) in the brazier of the flaring being. With it he takes on your splendours and you furnish him with a body carrying his soul where it wants;" *Ṛ̥V*, X.15.14.

33. "That the sight may return to the sun and the *prāṇa* to Vāyu. Give back to the sky and the earth what you owe them. Give back to the waters and the plants the parts of your body belonging to them. But there is also an immortal part . . . . .;" *Ṛ̥V*, X.16.3-4.

34. *See* G.G. Filippi, *Alcune note, op. cit.*

considered to be the real ghosts of the deceased, automatically attracted to the daily life of the family in which they lived. These cadaveric elements are particularly dangerous because situated between bodily and psychic modalities: their use by wizards is especially sought after. Through them it is possible to pass from the psychic to the gross, and one can harm an enemy's body at a distance. But the lack of consciousness is a serious limit to their utilization, as is the incapacity of the *bhūtas* to move any way but in a direct line.[35] For this reason, once all over the Indian subcontinent — but still today in Tamil Nadu and Bali — the body was made to exit from the house through a hole drilled in the outside wall, which was then quickly closed again. Thus, the *bhūta* was no longer able to find its way back. To this same conception one must attribute the expedient of inverting the femur bones upon burial in the ground, and other similar practices. At the popular level, the *bhūta* is confused today with the *piśāca*. But we shall return to this topic shortly.

35. *See* G.G. Filippi, *Il culto del Meru a Bali, op. cit.*, pp. 173-74.

12

The New Conditions of the Living Soul

THE most diffused belief in India today, and a belief that has influenced the Islamic milieu, is that the deceased is immediately brought before Yama, King of the underworld, to be sure he is the appointed vicitim, as mistakes are always possible in such a delicate matter as death. The *yamadūtas*, helpers of death, are sent into the world to carry away the souls of those who have exhausted their vital breath.[1] It might occur that these diligent envoys carry away the wrong soul, or that they choose the wrong moment to do their unpleasant task.[2] The most frequent cases in contemporary legends are those of errors of homonymy.

For example, it is narrated that a certain woman named Jana, who belonged to the Jain community, was robbed of her

1. The soul is pulled out with pain from the body and, once reduced to the size of a thumb, it is brought into Yama's presence; *see GP*, II.2.44-45.

2. In March 1993, Paṇḍit Vaikunthnath Upadhyaya, a well-known teacher of the Śāstras in Varanasi, told me how 'death' had come to him at the inappropriate time. In 1978, the Paṇḍit was returning to Varanasi on a boat from Ramnagar where he had been witness to the solemn *Rāmalīlā* led by the local *mahārājā*. The small boat, being too crowded, sunk and all its thirteen passengers were drowned. The apparently lifeless body of Paṇḍit Upadhyaya was found fifteen hours later. During the shaving of the body, he woke up and remembered being in Yama's presence. The King of the dead had ordered his helpers to bring him back to life, since he was the only one amongst the passengers whose hour had not yet come.

soul by an error of *yamadūtas*: they should have caused the death of a Muslim woman with the same name. Jana underwent the long and tortuous way towards the kingdom of Yama. When Yama saw her, he realized that she was not the woman predestined to die, so she was sent back into the world. Her body, however, has already been cremated. The god of death found an expedient to overcome the grave error committed by his assistants: he got the soul of the Muslim woman with the same name stolen and, then guided the Jain woman's soul into her body. This was even worse because the poor woman had to live with great repugnance in a family of meat-eaters, and was condemned to not enter the Jain temple because she was a Muslim. The story does not tell us if this case of *āveśya* or possession ended with the woman being condemned to damnation in hell for being obliged to live in an impure manner in the eyes of orthodox Jains.[3] Numberless stories describe cases concerning what is called apparent death in the West.

As soon as the dying one enters into a state of deep sleep, his *jīva* is concentrated in the summit point of his heart. According to a very ancient version, the dimensions of the individual in this stage are comparable to that of a thumb.[4] In

3. My Indian editor, Mr. K. Rai Mittal, told me of an incredible and similar case. In the fifties, his aunt Janaki suddenly died. Before the funeral rites begun, Janaki came back to life, causing general panic. She narrated of having dreamed to be in front of a gigantic and dreadful man. He was terribly angry and scolded the group of assistants surrounding Janaki, saying that they had taken away the wrong person's soul. He then commanded them to take Janaki's soul back to its body and to come back with the soul of the right person bearing the same name. Mr. Mittal was particularly touched when, reading this manuscript, he found the similar story of Jana.

4. The Indian tradition is grounded in ancient and illustrious texts. The thumb dimensions of the souls of the dead are mentioned in

→

a few hours, this 'Thumbalino,' flying rapidly, almost as if it had boots of the seven leagues of the European fable, goes to visit the Ogre-Yama. If he is the right person, he is sent back home in order to enjoy the benefits of funeral rites. If Yama notices an error, he is sent back the same, but to continue living for the rest of the time allotted to him.[5] It is interesting to verify what speculations can be developed around this type of story, a literary disguise of ancient doctrines which are still alive today.

Chāndogya Upaniṣad, VI.8.6 affirms that "when a man is dying, speech (*vāc*) re-enters into his mind (*manas*), reason into the vital breath (*prāṇa*), *prāṇa* into vital heat (*tejas*), and *tejas* into the Supreme Divinity." To better understand what is meant by Supreme Divinity, we must examine another passage of equal traditional authority: "When the *ātman* weakens and seems to disappear, then all the senses crowd around him; the *ātman*, reabsorbing these vital elements in itself, concentrates itself in the interior of the heart. When the essence living in the eye goes back to its source, the eye no longer distinguishes forms. Then we say that the person doesn't see, doesn't smell, doesn't taste, speak, listen, think, touch, know, because all these things have become one in the *ātman*.[6] Then the summit of his heart shines. Through this shining summit, the *ātman* exits, or through the eye, or the head, or any other part of the body.[7]

→ *TA*, X.38.1, *KU*, II.4.12 and II.6.17, *ŚU*, V.8, etc. *Garuḍa Purāṇa*, II.10.74 states that a bodyless soul is like a fireless flame, having the dimensions of a thumb.

5. 'Death' is indeed only apparent and Purāṇic sources are clear on this: it is impossible to obtain another human body after death; *see GP*, II.48.36 and II.49.19.

6. In other words, this state is characterized by the envelopment of the eleven *indriyas*. If this condition should become permanent after the loss of the body, then the *jīva* would turn into a *piśāca*.

7. The principal openings of the body are the nine 'mouths,' that is, →

When it is gone, the *prāṇa* follows it, and when the *prāṇa* leaves, all other vital breaths follow the *prāṇa*."[8]

Clearly, the Supreme Divinity is the same *ātman* of the dying man. Withdrawal takes place in the entity which supports the individual as a whole from within, to paraphrase the axiom of the *Brahma-Sūtras*.[9] As *Chāndogya Upaniṣad*, III.14.3 states: "This *ātman* which is in the heart is smaller than a grain of rice, smaller than a grain of barely or of millet, smaller than the germ closed within a grain of millet. This *ātman* which is in the heart is also bigger than the earth, bigger than the sky, and bigger than all these worlds put together." From these

→ the openings through which Vaiśvānara relates himself to the external world (eyes, nostrils, ears, mouth, genitals and anus), to which the sagittal suture (*brahmarandhra*) on the top of the skull must be added. The terminals of all minor *nāḍīs* are added so as to reach a total of 72,000 openings. He who has performed actions according to his *dharma*, has his soul exit through the eight 'mouths' above the navel; ***see*** *GP*, II.11.7-9. On the contrary, the soul of one who has performed negative *karman* exits from below; ***see*** *GP*, II.3.91. Interesting is the grotesque pantomime of the birth of the donkey during the holidays of Carnival and *Holī*. The soul of the dying sinner (or of the bear) is ejected through flatulences, which the licentious carnival masses trivially reproduce. It transmigrates and is immediately reborn as a donkey.

8. *BṛU*, IV.4.1-2. When the *prāṇa* exits from the body, the body falls as a cut down tree; ***see*** *GP*, II.31.28. "The *ātman* itself dwells within the heart. There reside one hundred and one *nadīs*. From each *nadī* another hundred *nadīs* depart. Indeed, each of the principal *nadīs* terminates with 72,000 secondary *nadīs*. In each *nadī* the *vāyu udāna* circulates. The *udāna* moves towards each of these *nadīs*, leading to the world of merit if meritorious actions were performed, to the world of demerit if non meritorious actions were performed, and to the world of men if both kind of actions were performed;" *PU*, IV.6-7.

9. "It [the *prāṇa*] withdraws in That which supports [it]; [this is inferred] by certain facts, as the coming close to it;" *BS*, IV.2.4.

Upaniṣadic quotes we can see how the dimensions of the internal 'Thumbalino' have been described in a much more imaginative way in Purāṇic myths.

Before going into the complex network of paths that Hinduism indicates as man's posthumous destiny, it is necessary to return to the most diffused beliefs concerning the make-up of the human being, even at the cost of being repetitious. Indeed, the 'fall' of the body[10] involves the problematic reorganization of the invisible part of man. This reorganization, from a theoretical point of view, reveals how the human being is not just an entity composed of two parts, that is, of spirit and matter, or of body and soul, as thought by the ordinary Westerner. For the Indians, human individuality is composite and multiple, as has been amply illustrated in this study. It is the living soul (*jīvātman*) that gives an appearance of unity to this multiplicity. The same is true regarding the body. The elements which make it up are taken from the outer environment. Water, which forms the highest percentage of our tissues, is borrowed from the outside when we drink. Thus, when a man dies, the water from his body is returned to the cosmic circulation of liquids. The earthly part of his body returns to ash upon his death, as do all other elements making up his gross body.

When the human being is alive, these elements are held together in an organic way by the *jīvātman*, reaching such a high degree of apparent unity, that every individual commonly identifies himself with his body. The same takes place for the diverse subtle powers making up the sheath of the living soul. Always repeating the same error of evaluation, man identifies

10. In India, the term designating death is *dehānta*, 'end of the body,' rather than *mṛtyu*. This latter term has a wider range of meaning and designates the disappearance of even the subtle bodies of the same being.

himself with his mind,[11] or with his emotions and sensations. From these we understand that it is the *ātman* that keeps them united, using them, but not identifying itself with them. When illness, old age, and death rob the body of sensations, the *jīvātman* continues to benefit from other powers. Similarly, the annulment of the individual will and the mind do not affect the existence of the living soul.

The vital breaths animating the body of the *jīvātman* represent the forces of connection between the gross matter and the psychic sphere. These then are the first parts of the integral human being to be disactivated after death. Some of these *prāṇa*s which participated in the prenatal nature of the *piṇḍa,* gather round the *jīvātman* to follow it in its posthumous pilgrimage. But most of the *prāṇa*s that the living being absorbed from the outer environment during his life are returned to the atmosphere, unable to follow the individual soul.

The corpse, no longer animated, maintains the form it had during life for some time. It conserves some organic powers that are apparently vital; the nails and hair continue growing for several hours. Certain particular movements, normal during life, occur by mechanical contraction. Macabre cases are known in which the deceased sits up. This is determined by *rigor mortis* and inflicts terror those watching him.[12]

Analogously, the *prāṇa*s remaining in the human environment keep an appearance of unity for a time. They dissolve

---

11. This position is typical of the Western world, so profoundly influenced by the Cartesian *cogito ergo sum.*

12. These phenomena occur more frequently during cremation and are produced by heat. While gathering data on the Maṇikarṇikā Ghāṭ of Varanasi, I saw an arm rising from a corpse burning on the pyre.

their ties with the body by means of decomposition.[13] In the same way in which the gross elements (*bhūtas*) return to nature, these subtle components are returned to the atmosphere. The body undergoes a liquefaction and a gaseous change. The psychic residues undergo the same fate although with a slower rate. These latter residues cause that ghostly phenomenon of decomposition known as *ignis fatuus*, the fatuous fire.[14] Because of the close relationship that they maintain with bodily elements, even these psychic residues are called *bhūtas*. Funeral rites are dedicated, for the most part, to the control, neutralization, and destruction of the *bhūtas*. Even cremation does not guarantee the total destruction of the psychic corpse. Every precaution is taken so that it cannot return to disturb the living. The *bhūtas*, although lacking consciousness, maintain the memory bank of the deceased. It is for this reason that the *bhūta* of a deceased never improvises new appearances, but repeats the same action, as in a faulty film, and emits the same sounds, as a broken record. When these pseudo beings infest a house they usually go back over the old layout, not heeding the modifications that have meanwhile taken place. They can be heard walking down corridors that have been restructured, or going up stairs that no longer exist. Their tendency is to move in a straight line, avoiding curves and bends that are insurmountable obstacles for their incapacity of adaptment.[15]

13. The decomposing of the five elements, that is, the death of the body, is variously described as 'becoming quintuple,' 'reaching five,' etc. (*Mbh*, XII.267.10). Because of the connection of *bhūtas* and *piśācas* with putrefaction, these have been defined as 'flesh eaters'; often leading to the distorted notion that they are 'cannibal' spirits.

14. *See* G.G. Filippi, *Alcune note, op. cit.*

15. On this issue, *see* G.G. Filippi, *Il culto del Meru a Bali, op. cit.*, pp. 173-74.

The *bhūta*s are kept away by sacred diagrams (*alpona-vrata maṇḍala*) that Indian women make with coloured powder on the threshold of their houses and on the outer walls. It is well-known that these sacred diagrams are believed to keep evil away. Certainly the correct performance of funeral rites is the best defence from returning ones. The danger they represent is of proportional duration and intensity to the degree of interest that the deceased's psyche had towards worldly things when he was alive. A wise and just man leaves behind a *bhūta* that is not too malicious, and of brief duration. Instead, one who had an egotistical interest in worldly things, thus augmenting his psychic characteristics, his will and attachments, leaves an aggressive *bhūta* behind him, reluctant to decompose.[16]

I have already mentioned cases of persons who underwent a violent death or who could not benefit from a complete funeral. In these cases it is not only the psychic 'shell' but also the living soul that will remain in torment as a *piśāca*, while waiting for his descendents to free him from ties with this world, thus consenting him to form a body of *preta*. If the *bhūta*s represent subtle forces dangerous for the living, but deprived of their individuality, the situation of the soul in torment is dangerous for itself and for others.[17] The *piśāca* is not precisely a deceased, since he is unable to go to the abode of the dead. For this reason, any magical interferences may dangerously

16. In most legends, avarice is the strongest attachment of the psychic corpse: he craves for what he had left behind in this world. The *bhūta* comes back in order to look after his treasure. In this case, *bhūta*s perform the functions of all *yakṣa*s and of their king Kubera. It is said that those who resist death, in their successive existence will undergo a constant experience of agony; *see ŚB*, X.4.3.9-10.
17. From the point of view of the living, the *bhūta* and the *piśāca* manifest exactly in the same way. The seemingly identical behaviour is responsible for the confusion between the two categories of ghosts.

modify his posthumous destiny. Of course, it is possible that a positive influence is exerted upon him; thanks to the interest of a holy man; in this case, the *piśāca* can better his state.[18]

To conclude with the *bhūta*s, whether dangerous or harmless, resistent or crumbling, they are destined to dissolution. As one corpse decomposes faster than another, so may *bhūta*s maintain their apparent individuality for a time before it dissolves.[19] In some cases in infestation, the phenomenon provoked by *bhūta*s lasted for centuries. In these cases an exorcist is called in, one who knows the techniques of disintegrating the psychic aggregate constituting the *bhūta*.

Some living beings as well as animals and plants, may be infested by *bhūta*s when they are in an imbalanced psychic condition. The blandest cases are those concerning people in a temporary state of psychic weakness. As previously seen, the most frequent possession on the part of *piśāca*s is that of the adolescent.[20] Because of his rapidly developing body, his psychic components are forced to adapt to the changes taking place, and his psyche undergoes continual alterations between depression and exaltation. During the phase of exaltation, the ego accentuates the individual's potential, with characteristic attitudes of aggressiveness, vitality, and egoism. When the youth is in this condition, he is able to oppose all attempts of psychic infiltration, as noted by those who have assisted at the

---

18. A brāhmaṇa saint or divine grace can help attain the condition of *pitṛ*; see *GP*, II.7.
19. In ancient times, the term *maṭmaṭa* referred to the fatuous fire produced by vegetable fermentation rather than by animal putrefaction, as is the case of *bhūtas*; see *AV*, VIII.6.15.
20. Often evil possession, by spirits or sorcerers, is called *manaspapman*, 'the evil of the mind.' By the term *nyāsa*, on the other hand, is meant the propitious ritual possession done by deities and living or deceased saints. The term *āveśya* may be used to define both evil and divine forms of possession.

session of hypnosis. In the depressive state, the adolescent is prostrated by a sense of self-pity, passivity, psychological suicide. In this 'void,' a *bhūta* may insinuate itself producing an evident case of possession.[21] A loose component, which in the past had been part of a *bhūta*, but is presently in an advanced state of dissolution, may intervene in the adolescent. The mildest and most short lived are those phenomena known with the French term of *déjā vu*: those unpleasant or surprising sensations felt when someone lives with an experiences as if he already had it in his memory bank. This experience usually takes place during growing period and it is due to the fact that a living being, in a moment of distraction or fatigue, is 'possessed,' for an instant, by a memory element of a *bhūta* in decomposition.

It is possible to enumerate diverse individuals who have the possiblity of becoming chronic receptacles of the psychic components left in this world by the deceased. They are insane, demented, imbalanced by pathologic or traumatic causes. This explains the attitude of respect and suspicion that Indian villagers reserve to such persons. In other cases, psychic derangement can be sought or even provoked in an artificial way, to obtain the power of communicating or fighting with the invisible, by mediums, oracles, shamans, exorcists. However, even this type of individual has some congenital anomaly such as sleep walking, epilepsy, homosexuality.

Even though they do not strictly enter into our field of studies, but because of a certain organic unity, mention must be made of some of the possession cases that have taken place by other living beings. The most noted example is also the most ordinary. It deals with the influence exerted by a grandfather,

21. Possession may also be caused by *yakṣa*s and living human beings, with positive or negative effects, as well as by *gandharva*s and gods with positive effects, especially of an oracular nature.

above all a paternal grandfather, upon the psychic formation of his grandchild. In certain cases this influence can be so strong as to give the impression that the grandfather lives again in his grandson. Westerners too hastily define this with the term reincarnation. But often this happens when the grandfather is still alive. The phenomenon produces itself naturally by biological means. It is noted that children resemble their grandparents even more than their parents, at least generally speaking. In India this phenomenon is ritually favoured, with the desire to transmit the grandfather's most positive characteristics to his descendents. There are a number of stories in which the powers of a magician, a sorcerer, a *yogin*, or a saint are said to be able to posses a living soul who is not fully conscious, or even to animate a corpse.

The most edifying story in this regard is that of Śaṁkarācārya, who took possession of a King's corpse in order to experience carnal love without breaking his vow of chastity. Causing a general fright, the King's body arose from the funeral pyre. Śaṁkarācārya, in the *rājā*'s clothing, immediately began to enjoy his hundred wives. Between one amorous appointment and another, he also dedicated himself to the administration of the government. The court's *purohita* quickly realized that the King behaved too intelligently and wisely, in respect to his wicked and pleasure loving past. Thus the founder of Advaita, unmasked, was induced to return to his ascetic body which had remained in a cataleptic wait.

Radically different are the stories in which weak individuals are magically possessed by witch doctors who use them without scruples, leading them to desperation and death.

The relationship of grandfather-grandson described above brings to mind the psychic continuity of the ancestors which perpetuates in the living individual. This concept is analogous to the Western conception of metempsychosis, and flanks in some ways what is known as metasomatosis. The idea of the perpetuity of the human seed is alive in the individual consciousness. The seed, although belonging to the father's body, is transmitted to the body of the son.[22] It is as if one seed alone is transmitted from generation to generation, always remaining the same. The idea of longevity, with which one conquers the earth, is related to this vision.

The feminine correspondent of longevity is the umbilical cord. This has united all individuals of the female sex for generations, going back to the first woman who, obviously, was without the umbilical scar.

In India, the concept of metempsychosis is utilized to define specific family characteristics. All members of a family are similar from a psychological as well as a somatic point of view. This is the most profound concept defining the *sapiṇḍa*s. In a wider sense the same rule holds true for more distant relatives, for clans, even extending to the entire caste. Thus, families group together because they are descendents of the same ancestor. The same can be said for the archetype governing a specific *gotra* and the principle defining caste. There are specific rituals (*sampradāna*) with which certain psychic components can be transmitted from a dying individual to a living one.[23]

---

22. "From the beginning the embryo has always resided in man, which is the same sperm and heat produced by all the body's limbs; in this way he carries the self in himself . . . .;" *AiU*, IV.1.
23. On this particular case of 'controlled metempsychosis,' *see* the long and detailed description furnished by *Kauṣitakī Upaniṣad*, II.15. Something similar happens when a teacher (*guru*) grants his disciple an equal status, passing on his own psychic potency. Techniques for transmitting spiritual power are well-known among Tibetan *ṭulku*s.

13

The Journey to the Kingdom of Yama

As we have already said, the *jīva*, the soul of the deceased, is painfully torn from his body by the *yamadūtas*, who use hooks to do this, after having suffocated him.[1] These *yamadūtas* are not particular beings at all, such as human beings, animals, or gods. In reality, they are the same *piśācas* who hang around new corpses, attempting to eat the *piṇḍa* offered to the deceased.[2] The human souls in torment continue to presecute the *preta* during the whole period consecrated to his transformation into *pitṛ*, in order to nourish themselves with bits of the *śrāddha* offered by the living relatives.[3] The situation is symbolic of a

1. *See GP*, II.2.43. Natural death always takes place through suffocation, as it is symbolized by the attribute *paśu* with which the living are designated. *Paśu* derives from *pāśa*, noose, which not only represents the state of beings 'on the leash of God,' but also the state of those who end their lives strangled from the slipknot of death. The other death, the violent one, be it positive, as in the case of a sacrifice, or negative, as in the case of an accident, is represented by the cutting off of the head; *see* G.G. Filippi, *On Some Features, op. cit*. It goes without saying that natural death and violent death are to be identified repectively with the 'good' and 'bad' death previously discussed.
2. *See GP*, II.2.43. They hinder the posthumous path of the dead stealing them the ritually offered food; *see GP*, II.20.7.
3. The *piśāca* could not become a *preta* precisely because no *sapiṇḍa* had performed funeral rites for him; *see GP*, II.9.47-49.

journey.[4] *Yamadūtas*, tormented souls, appear as if they were sent by Yama, of whom they have the same fierce features.[5] They lead the soul of the deceased and torment him, during the journey of one year necessary to reach his own posthumous destiny. Along the way, the *yamadūtas* consume the *piṇḍa* offerings that the eldest son donates in favour of his father who is in the condition of *preta*.[6]

And so it is, that on the thirteenth day after his death, the soul of the deceased, pulled along and mistreated, begins its journey towards the south, in the direction of the kingdom of Yama. The way is fatiguing and the path burns like red-hot copper.[7] Since the archaic times, the beginning of this way is watched over by the two dogs of Yama, Śyāma and Śabala, sons of Saramā.[8] They bite the *pretas*, but are diligent escorts for the just souls.[9] Along the way, the *jīva* passes through the cities

4. In other words, the *preta loka* is at the same time the *pretayāna*.
5. *See GP*, II.30.17. Yama himself must be viewed as the first dead among men; the one who explored the path of the hereafter and opened it for future generations.
6. The various tortures that the *yamadūtas* inflict on the *preta* correspond to the reiterated effort of depriving the *preta* of the positive effects of the *śrāddha*.
7. *GP*, II.33.4.
8. ***See*** *ṚV*, X.14.10-12. They are described as having tawny hair, four eyes, oblong muzzle, and as being panting and vigorous. The four eyes are a common Vedic symbol, expressing the simultaneous vision of the four directions; ***see*** P.E. Dumont, *L'aśvamedha. Déscription du sacrifice solennel du cheval dans le culte védique* (Louvain, 1927), p. 27. ***See also*** J. Gonda, *Eye and Gaze in the Veda* (Amsterdam, 1969), p. 71 n. 15. Nobody knows who was the first to say that the four eyes call to mind some special dog breeds, bearing eye-like spots above their eyebrows. In any case, practically all scholars — with few noticeable exceptions — cite this awkward interpretation when dealing with this issue.
9. ***See*** *ṚV*, X.14.11.

of Yāmya (of Yama), Sauripura (city of the sun), the fortress of Nāgendrabhavana (castle of the Lord of Serpents), the cities of Gandhamādana (Passion for Perfumes) — also called Gandharva — Krūrapura (cruel city), Krauñca (city of the curlews), and finally the castle called Vicitrabhavana or Citranagara, the reign of Vicitra, younger brother of Yama.[10] During each of these stops, the soul undergoes various vexations and tortures. At the same time, the *jīva* also finds a *piṇḍa* at every stop, sent to him ritually by his living relatives. These restore his forces so that he may continue his long journey.

Having passed the city of Vicitra, he reaches the banks of the Vaitaraṇī, the lurid river of blood, excrements, and pus. Here the souls of the just rid themselves of their sins, thus feeding the fetid current.[11] A boat takes the souls across the river. The Indian *khevaka* (Yamadūta) who guides the boat, requests a Vaitaraṇī cow[12] as a return for his services, and for all the rituals performed in the equinoxes, at sunsets, during eclipses, or in all the endings of the cycles that make up human life upon the earth.[13] Upon reaching the other bank, the *jīva* resumes his tragic journey, always mistreated by the *yamadūtas*. He still has to pass through the horrid cities of Bahvapāda (the servile foot), Duḥkhada (permanent pain), Nānākrandapura (city of every sort of lamentation), the palace of Sutaptabhavana (of the youngest son), and then the cities of Raudra (the Adverse), Payovarṣana (rain of milk), Sītādhya (the Profound), and Bahubhūti (of the thousand ghosts).

10. *See* *GP,* II.16.1-2.

11. *See* *GP,* II.30.43.

12. *See* *GP,* II.16.25-28. According to a Celtic tradition, still alive in Lancashire, he who makes the gift of a cow to the poor, after death will be taken to the country of the dead by the cow spirit, passing through the Milky Way; *see* E. & M.A., *Encyclopaedia of Superstitions* (Ch. Hole, 1961), p. 116.

13. *See* *GP,* II.47.22-23.

This journey lasts a whole year, during which the *preta* feeds itself on a *piṇḍa* found at every stop.[14] One easily understands that the sixteen *piṇḍas*, found in the sixteen cities the pilgrim soul has crossed, symbolize the *śrāddha* called *malina ṣoḍaśī*, or the sixteen impure, which is the minimum offering assuring the deceased to become *preta* and then *pitṛ*. Thus, we are now considering the least favourable destiny of those who have avoided the danger of remaining prisoners of the *vāyuja śarīra* as *piśācas*.

At the end of the year, the *preta* finally reaches Yamanagara.[15] Here the *preta* assumes a body composed of the essence of its merits, increased by the offering of the *śrāddha*.[16] Therefore, in this context, *Yama loka* and *pitṛ loka* seem to be identical. The transformation of *preta* into *pitṛ* is allegorically described as a journey, in place of that of the formation of a *piṇḍaja śarīra*.[17] Yamanagara is situated to the south-west, and it is inaccessible to *devas* and *asuras*.[18] The city is square, with four entries, and seven circles of walls. The palace of Yama is at the centre, decorated with gold, lapis-lazuli and pearls. Many banners fly on the roof. The sinner's soul is taken into Yama's presence. Yama is sitting on his throne, flanked by Kāla and Mṛtyu. The god of death has red eyes, a gloomy look, clenched jaws, appears threatening, and holds an iron rod in one fist and a noose in the other. Around these fierce characters, monstrous

14. In this journey towards Yama's kingdom, one's destiny depends on one's kārmic tajectory, while caste differences are all abolished after death; *see GP*, II.18.12-13.

15. *See GP*, II.5.81-154.

16. *See GP*, II.5.143.

17. The *piṇḍaja śarīra* is obtained when the *jīva* reaches the *Yama loka*, a year after his death; *see GP*, II.10.83.

18. Indeed, only human beings can have access to the *post mortem* of humans, be it in the *deva loka* or the *asura loka*; *see* chapter 1, n. 17.

ghosts of diseases wander about.[19] The sinner is sent immediately to the court of the guilty souls (*vicrabhū*). In fact, next to Yama's palace is the iron palace of Citragupta,[20] judge of the dead. It is decorated with allegorical painted murals. Next to this palace are the abodes of Fever, of Colic, of Cancer, of Kāla's noose, of Indigestion, of Lack of Appetite, of Cholera, of Headache, of Coma, of Dissentery, and of Intestinal Burning. Those condemned by Citragupta are brought here. The abodes of these diseases are hells (*naraka*).[21]

From this we gather that there is a first category of 'new-born' *pitṛ*s condemned by Citragupta. These go to hell and this same hell is in Yamanagara, that is, in the *pitṛ loka*. The abodes of the various diseases, located in the same Yamanagara, are considered to be underground[22] and, at the same time, below one another.[23] The principal hells are seven in number. The first, *raurava*, is a desert of burning coals upon which the souls run unceasingly, vainly looking for a cool shelter. The second is *mahāraurava*, still hotter; here the pain in the feet is so intense that it forces the souls to roll around seeking repose for the

19. *See GP*, II.5.147-149.
20. Lit. 'hidden portrait,' Yama's right hand, Citragupta symbolizes man's true nature which — at his stage of posthumous evolution — surfaces shamelessly, either betraying the hypocrite or emphasizing the hidden virtues of the humble. In medieval mythology, Citragupta is seen as an actual judge of the dead, weighing the actions performed by humans during their lives. Citragupta, as a true bureaucrat, is also identified with the scribe, patiently annotating all human actions in his immense account book. This latter one is certainly not a medieval innovation, Sufic or other, since it is certainly of archaic Indian origins. Indeed, *ŚB*, XI.2.7.33 mentions a scale on which all good and bad actions are weighed; *see* C. Della Casa, *op. cit.*, p. 43.
21. *See GP*, II.33.4-39.
22. *See GP*, II.3.55.
23. *See GP*, II.3.75.

feet, by distributing the burns all over the 'bodily' surface. Moreover, in this hell annoying insects torment and bite those parts of the 'body' that do not touch the ground. The third hell called *atiśīta* has opposite characteristics — very cold, dark, forcing the souls to drag around on the ice, while suffering from hunger and thirst. In the *niṣkṛntana* hell, the damned are laid upon a wheel made of blades, which cruelly cuts them to pieces incessantly. The *apratiṣṭha* hell, *pitṛ*s condemned here are tied to a water mill as if they were being dried, and forced to vomit blood due to the velocity of the infernal machine. In the *asipatravana* hell, the souls are forced to undergo constant climatic changes, passing suddenly from a red-hot heat to a polar cold, represented by the cutting leaves of an ice tree. Hordes of infernal dogs bite them without pause, impeding them to defend themselves from heat and cold. Finally there is the deepest of hells, *taptakumbha*, where the *pitṛ*s are torn to pieces by lurid vultures. When the victims are piteously reduced, the vultures catch them in their claws, and flying high in the sky, let them fall into vessels of boiling iron, where they atrociously regenerate.[24]

The *Garuḍa Purāṇa* lists another twenty-eight minor hells,[25] but it is not our intention to go into ulterior details of the numerous and discreet *naraka*s.[26] At this point we can better understand why, the *śrāddha* called 'the sixteen impure,' is also

24. *See GP*, II.3.10-48.

25. *See GP*, II.3.50-72.

26. *MDhŚ*, IV.88-90 lists twenty-one *naraka*s, while *MP*, XII lists only six. *AP*, 352.13 lists twenty-eight — each one being divided in one hundred and forty-four circles — while *BP*, IV.2.146-150 lists twenty-seven. These descriptions do not always agree and also the names of the various hells vary. This multiplicity of opinions mirrors the lack of a single theoretical framework within Indian mythology. It also indicates that each single case represents an individual hell, since every being creates his own hellish existence through action.

not sufficient to help him avoid *naraka*, although it permits the deceased to arrive at the *pitṛ loka*. Whoever as *preta* — in the course of his journey made up of sixteen stopovers towards Yama's kingdom — finds the offerings of the complete *śrāddha* and the gifts of lantern, bed, etc., will be able to remedy his faults, thus obtaining a more favourable judgement.

When the journey is concluded, and the *preta* becomes *pitṛ*, he arrives at the city of the King of the Dead. The city appears splendid to him, cheered by the songs and sounds of *gandharvas* and *apsaras*. Although it is Yamanagara, for this soul the city is Dharmarājapura, the city of the King of Justice.[27] Yama himself appears to him under a benevolent aspect, smiling and wearing jewels.[28] Here the *pitṛ* is sent before Citragupta, and stands in the presence of the positive and negative actions he performed during his lifetime.[29] Eight *śravaṇas* will testify in his favour: they are a sort of angel who untiredly goes through the three worlds registering the actions of the living.[30] The *pitṛ*, in this case, is sent to the town of Vivasvatapura,[31] identified with Dharmarājapura (and also called Yamanagara), where he experiments suffering or enjoyment corresponding to his own past actions and to the funeral offerings tributed to him.[32]

We can say that at the beginning of his new condition as *pitṛ* he experiences the *narakas*, to then experience the more heavenly

---

27. *See GP*, II.16.47.
28. *See GP*, II.5.151. The King of the Dead has seven names, depending on the category of deceased which approach him. These names are: Yama, Dharmarāja, Mṛtyu, Antaka, Vaivaśvata, Kāla, Sarvaprāṇahara; *see GP*, II.8.28-29.
29. *See GP*, II.19.2.
30. *See GP*, II.16.49-53.
31. *See GP*, II.19.4.
32. *See GP*, II.10.88-89.

atmosphere of *svarga*.[33] The *pretas* who have received complete funeral rites, after having passed the Vaitaraṇī river, will go directly to Dharmarājapura, by virtue of the relieving effects of *śrāddha* rites.[34]

The *preta* of virtuous persons, on the thirteenth day after death, and after the complete *śrāddha*, receive rather a different treatment from those described above. In place of the sinister *yamadūtas*, singing *gandharvas* and *apsarases* appear to him. Surrounded by music and perfumes, these *pretas* take their place on luminous flying carts (*vimāna*), that are the same as their splendid *piṇḍaja śarīra*, and in this manner they are taken to the more benign aspect of Yama.[35] The journey across the desolate regions of the south always takes a year, but in this case, it is a pleasant transfer, and the transformation into *pitṛ* takes place sweetly, at the conclusion. He does not have to appear at the court of Citragupta, but is sent directly to the *deva loka*, where the *pitṛs* conduct a blessed existence similar to that of the gods.[36] Also the *deva loka*, however, must be considered as a section of Yama's dominion. Analogous to the *narakas*, the different heavens of the divine world must also be understood as one on top of the other,[37] and all vertically on top of Hell.

---

33. *Svarga*, the sky, is 'made up' of the good actions which one has operated in life; *see GP*, II.48.39. ". . . . the 'ritual entities' create a world for the *pitṛs*, so that they may exist therein, so that it may become their form of existence;" J. Gonda, *Loka, op. cit.*, p. 65. "Man is born in the *loka* which he himself has created;" *ŚB*, V.2.2.27.

34. *See GP*, II.5.81-154.

35. *See GP*, II.3.88.

36. *See GP*, II.6.137-140.

37. The *deva loka* is made up of a series of planes laid one upon the other, giving it the appearance of a mountain. For this reason it is also known as Meru, like the mythical cosmic mountain. The highest of all skies is the *vaikuṇṭha* sky, located on top of the Meru; *see GP*, II.22.76-77. Meru's top touches the firmament, that is, the bottom →

One can say that the joys of the *pitṛ*s inhabiting the *deva loka* is imperfect, as under them they can see the abyss of the *naraka*s, and this vision veils their happiness with fear and sadness.[38] Similarly, hell is rendered more painful for the same reason, since even the damned, looking up, have vision of the beatitudes to which they have no access.[39] Once again, the non-schematic attitude of Indian mythology imposes itself. Indeed, on whatever level one finds himself, be it *naraka* or *svarga*, one is in hell in respect to superior conditions, and in heaven in respect to inferior conditions.[40]

In such an elastic perspective, the tri-division, as described above, is nevertheless maintained: there are *pitṛ*s who are condemned to the *naraka*s; those who enjoy pleasure or suffer torture and those who live in heaven like the gods. Indeed, it is clearly stated that the *preta*, after the annual *sapiṇḍīkaraṇa* in which he becomes a *pitṛ*, obtains divinity, humanity, or animality.[41] This corresponds to the doctrine of the three worlds, *svarga*, *pṛthivī*, and *pātāla*, according to the three-fold division operated by the *guṇa*s.[42] The *Garuḍa Purāṇa* calls these

→ of that which is known as the Northern Ocean. Curiously, some scholars have thus stated that the *vaikuṇṭha* is either situated on top of the Meru or the bottom of the ocean.

38. *See GP*, II.32.75-76.

39. *See GP*, II.32.74.

40. It is precisely for this reason that there are as many skies as hells; *see GP*, II.3.76-77. *Atharvaveda*, XVIII.4.64 identifies *svarga* with the *pitṛ loka*.

41. *See GP*, II.10.1. If he becomes a *deva* the *śrāddha* for him is *amṛta*; if a man, cereal; if an animal, grass. Moreover, since the destinies of all beings are both unique and manifold, the text goes on enumerating other different cases: if he becomes a *gandharva*, the *śrāddha* for him is orgasm; if a cobra, air; if a bird, fruit; and so on; *see GP*, II.10.4-7.

42. The *deva loka* of Yama's kingdom must not be confused with the *svarga* of the three-fold cosmic partition. Indeed, the abode of men, →

three categories of *pitṛ*s with the ritual names of *agnisvātta*, *barhiṣada*, and *somapa*.[43] The souls remain in the different sections of the *pitṛ loka* for an extremely long time, that can even last until the *mahāpralaya*,[44] the extreme unsurpassable limit for living and dead beings in this world. Then they transmigrate to a different condition of existence. The damned will remanifest themselves as unconscious objects, animals or, if humans, as deformed, demented, or outcasts.[45] On the other hand, those who have expiated their guilt and acquired virtues in the *pitṛ loka* may manifest in the four castes. Holy souls are reborn as *devas*.[46] But that is another story.

One may ask, at this point, how we are to understand the southern direction by which one arrives at the *Yama loka*. *Dakṣiṇa* is the term used to define the south as a cardinal direction, and indeed all texts indicate the orientation of the kingdom of Yama as 'Dakṣiṇapati.' Literally, *dakṣiṇa* means 'right.' The cardinal direction selected by Hinduism to orient itself, however, is the east — direction of the rising sun. One addresses himself for prayers, temples are oriented and altars are erected in the same direction, i.e. east.[47] Along the equinoctial

→ be they alive or dead, is entirely included within the *manuṣya loka* (or *pṛthivī*). The celestial abode of ancestors called *deva loka*, on analogy with the happy abode of the gods, corresponds to the blissful section of the *pitṛ loka*. On these issues, *see* chapter 1, n. 17 and chapter 2, n. 8.

43. The *agnisvātta, somya* and *barhiṣada* of *ṚV*, X.15 and *MDhŚ*, III.195-199.

44. *See GP*, II.34.88-89.

45. *See GP*, II.3.80-84.

46. *See GP*, II.3.85-90.

47. The sun moves opposite to man, as time moves opposite to the development of becoming, and as death moves opposite to life. Indeed, in Indian mythology the sun (*vivasvat*), time (*kāla*) and death (*mṛtyu*) are all viewed as forms of Yama. The death of →

axis, along the west-east direction, the earthly humanity proceeds. The right side for one who directs himself along this way falls to the south, whereas the left side faces north (*uttara*). *Uttara*, anyhow, means 'superior,' 'more elevated' and although indicating the left direction it does not mean 'left' (*vāma*) as one would infer. Instead the south is sometimes defined *adhara*, reflecting the sense of 'inferior,' 'lower.'[48] It has been said that the equinoctial axis represents the world of men indicated by the apparent movement of the sun in the sky. This movement occurs in the celestial sphere determining the ecliptic plane that divides the sky into northern and southern hemisphers. In Vedic terminology these two hemisphers are called northern ocean and southern ocean. From this we deduce that the *preta*s move towards the south in order to reach the sky of the antipodes, seat of the deceased. For this reason the *Garuḍa Purāṇa* — though describing the path of *preta*s as a wandering towards southern lands — states that the *yamadūta*s conduct the souls of the deceased in the southern sky in order to reach the non-terrestrial city of Yāmya on the eighteenth day.[49]

When one describes the Kingdom of Yama as 'underworld' we must understand it as located in the southern sky (or ocean), under the planet earth, and not, as is often erroneously thought, to be under the ground.[50] That the *pitṛ loka* was located

→ animals symbolized by moving contrariwise — such as the crab (Cancer) and and other abyssal creatures — is noteworthy.

48. *Uttara* also means 'future,' 'following.' Thus, *dakṣiṇa* could analogously be interpreted as meaning 'past,' 'anterior.' This would agree with the symbolism of gods and *pitṛ*s (or the *asura*s, to whom the *pitṛ*s correspond in a cosmic perspective), representing the future and past generations respectively.

49. *See GP*, II.16.1-2.

50. The southern and northern hemispheres are always to be understood as part of the human world. They correspond to the skies of the gods and the abyssal oceans (*pātāla*) of the *asura*s, →

in the sky (heaven) and not in the bowels of the earth had already been established in the Vedas.[51]

It is interesting to note that there are two zodiacal constellations lying on the ecliptic plane: *jyeṣṭhā*, 'the oldest,' and *mūla*, 'the root.'[52] The ruling deity of *jyeṣṭhā* is Indra, the Lord of *svarga*, while the *pitṛ*s are the collective entity ruling *mūla*. This latter is formed by two stars that are significantly called *śyāma* and *śabala*.[53] We must add that *jyeṣṭhā* and *mūla* are nowadays the most southern constellations of the zodiac,[54]

→ although they are not to be identified with these. One may thus easily understand why the *asura*s are defined as anti-gods (*a-sura*). Indeed, every single *asura* and *deva* represents only a half of the whole celestial sphere. "The round orb of the earth, made up of the five elements, dwells in space at the centre of the starry sphere, just like a piece of iron situated among magnets. The earth is covered everywhere by trees, mountains, cities, forests, rivers, oceans and other things. At the earth's centre is the Sumeru, the abode of the gods. Below it are the *asura*s. The gods view the condition of *asura*s like that of a man whose reflection in water shows him face downwards. And the *asura*s, on the other hand, think of the gods as dwelling below them. In space, just above the Meru, is located one of the poles; the other pole is just below, always situated in space. Fixed to the poles, the starry sphere rotates, thanks to the *pravaha* wind;" Thibaut (ed.), *Pañcasiddhaāntikā* (2nd edn. 1968), 69.

51. ***See*** *Ṛ̥V*, I.35.6; *ŚB*, XII.8.1.19.

52. Both constellations, according to Western zodiac, are part of Scorpio, a deadly autumal constellation related to the celebrations in honour of the deceased, Halloween, and *pitṛ pakṣa*. On these issues, see the fine research of one of our students, Marco Tomat, *Devayāna e Pitṛyāna: i due cammini postumi e le loro figurazioni celesti* (Venice, 1986; unpublished thesis), pp.135-40.

53. ***See*** Kalinath Mukherji, *Popular Hindu Astronomy* (Calcutta, 1905), p. 39.

54. This is the present situation of the celestial sphere with respect to the earth, taking into consideration the procession of equinoxes; ***see*** M. Tomat, *Devayāna e Pitṛyāna*, *op. cit.*, pp. 149-53.

situated in the crossing between the ecliptic path and the Milky Way.[55] It is precisely here that the door of Yama's domain is located. The *preta*, after his equinoctial wandering, presents himself here in order to undertake the journey southward along the Milky Way.[56] In India as well as among a great number of peoples, the Milky Way is considered to be the path undertaken by the shadows of the deceased (*chāyāpatha*).[57] The Milky Way is called either lunar current (*somadhārā*) or solar path (*suryapatha*) depending on whether it leads to celestial abodes or to hells: "Path of the Sun God, it was called *devapatha*, but it was also used by the *pitṛgaṇa*s (the multitude of ancestors)."[58] It will be our commitment to return to this subject in a future research, dedicated to the posthumous destinies of the human being in Hindu thought and myth.

---

55. One of the names of the Milky Way is Mandākinī, designating the southern celestial Gaṅgā, sacred to the *pitṛ*s; *MP*, 121.4-5.
56. The souls of the deceased descend southward, along the so-called *ajavīthī*, 'the path of the goat.' They are attracted by the star Agastya (Canopus), which marks the point where the heavy bodies fall according to the direction of *tamas*. Agastya, the founder of the *ekoddiṣṭa*, had opened himself a way towards the south, passing through dense forests. He had then persuaded the mountains to remain without vegetation until the time of his return. But Agastya never came back, and thus the path connecting the north with the south remained open. This story calls to mind the myth of Yama, who opened the path to the hereafter on which the souls of the deceased could pass. Even within the cosmological framework of Dante's *Divina Commedia*, Lucifer, King of the Dead, coincides with the point of gravitational attraction.The difference is that while Lucifer and the Christian Hell are situated at the centre of the earth, Yama-Agastya and their domain are situated in the southern celestial sphere.
57. *See* Giorgio de Santillana-Herta von Dechend, *Il mulino di Amleto Saggio sul mito e sulla struttura del tempo* (Milano: Adelphi, 1983; 1st English edn. 1969), p. 296.
58. K. Mukherji, *op. cit.*, p. 16.

Glossary

ācārya: Teacher of Sacred Texts.

acit: Unconscious beings, numerals.

adhara (or *dakṣina*): South.

adharma: The disorder, an irreligious situation.

adhidaiva: The Macrocosm.

adhideha: **See** *vāyuja śarīra*.

adhvaryu : Yajurvedic priest supervising the oblations and the erection of the altar.

adhyātma: The Microcosm.

Aditi: "The Boundless," Goddess, Mother of the Gods.

Āditya: Goddess Aditi's sons, the Suns.

Advaita: Non-dualistic doctrine of Śaṁkara.

Agastya: (1) *Ṛṣi Anārya*, personification of *tamas* as force of gravity. (2) Canopus, the star attracting the fall of bodies.

aghorī: *Yogin* member of a śāktic school holding to the *kāpālika* stream. The *aghorīs* dedicate to sexual and necrophagical worships.

Agni: The God Fire; "Subtle" husband of the unmarried maidens.

agnidagdha: The people whose corpses are burnt on the pyre.

agnihotra: Daily oblation to the fire of milk, oil, oatmeal.

agnihotṛ: Priest dedicated to the Fire Sacrifice (*agnihotra*).

Agni Purāṇa (*AP*): One of the great (Mahā)Purāṇas dealing with the Traditional Sciences.

agnisvātta: One of the three category of the *pitṛ*s who enjoys the fire.

ahaṁkāra: The self-consciousness, source of the individuality.

āhavanīya: The sacrificial fire of the Sky.

ahitāgni: *Brahman* who preserves the sacred fire for the Solemn Sacrifices.

Aitareya Brāhmaṇa (*AiB*): Ritual Text belonging to the collection of the *Ṛgveda*.

Aitareya Upaniṣad (*AiU*): Upaniṣad belonging to the collection of the *Ṛgveda*.

ajavīthī: "Goat track," path leading the dead men's Souls toward the south.

ākāśa: The element ether.

akṣaya vaṭa: A celebrated banyan tree of Allahabad.

alpona (or *vrata maṇḍala*): Labyrinthic drawings that the Indian Ladies paint on the ground or the walls of their houses.

amṛta: The Immortality Beverage or the Immortality itself.

anagnidagdha: "Who is not given to Fire" : People whose corpses are not burnt, but buried or delivered to streams or to the air.

anahitāgni: The *Brahman* who preserves only a Sacrificial Fire.

ānanda: Bliss.

ānandamaya: Consisting of Bliss.

anārya: Not *ārya*, not member of the three highest castes.

aṇḍaja: The beings born from an egg, the oviparous.

aṅga: The principal limb of the body.

añjali-mudrā: Hands joined in position of greeting.

anna: Food.

annamaya: "Consisting of Food," denomination referred to the gross body.

annaprāśana: *Saṁskāra* celebrating the first solid meal of the child.

Annapūrṇā: "The Primordial Food," name of the Goddess of the Food and of the Conceiving.

Antaka: "Leading to the End,"· *Yama*.

antaḥkaraṇa: The internal sense consisting of *buddhi*, *ahaṁkāra* and *manas*.

antardhāna: Invisibility; *see brahmalīna*.

antarikṣa: Region between sky and earth, the atmosphere.

antyeṣṭi: The "last sacrifice," the Funeral.

anumati: Night of new Moon, propitious for the dead men.

anustaraṇī: Cow sacrificed, in ancient times, during the funeral of the *ahitāgni*.

anvāhāryapacana: The Sacrificial Fire of the Atmosphere.

anyavāpa: "Settled among the outsiders," the cuckoo.

apamārga: *Achyranthes Aspera*.

apāna: The inhaled *prāṇa*.

āpas: The element water.

apratiṣṭha: "Unstable," name of a hell.

apsaras: Water Nymph; the Nymphs are the mythic lover of the *gandharva*s.

āpyāyani: The umbilical cord.

araṇi: Two wooden steaks used for the ritual lighting of the Fire.

Āraṇyaka: Vedic texts describing the internal rites.

Arāyī: The *rākṣasī* who provokes abortions.

ariṣṭa: Condition of mental isolation in the dying man.

ārṣa: A class of marriage.

artavan: The female "seed," the blood.

Arundhatī: (1) *Alcor*, small star pertaining to the *Ursa Major*, wife of the *ṛṣi* Vasiṣṭha (2) Sometimes the Pole Star.

arūpaka: Informal, without form.

ārya: "Noble," a member of the three highest castes.

Aryaman: One of the twelve Suns, God who makes safe the trails and the routes.

as: Verbal root of the verb "to be."

aśauca: Funeral impurity, mourning.

asipattra (or *asipatravana*): "Tree with cutting leafs," woodland hell where the slaughtermen of animals and plants are condemned.

āśrama: (1) The *guru*'s house, and in the wider sense, the initiation school. (2) The four life stages of the *dvija*.

asthi sañcayana: The gathering of the bones after the cremation.

asu: A being, human or not.

asura: (1) An anti-God, a Titan; (*vivāha*). (2) A class of marriage; (*loka*). (3) World of the *asuras*, **see** *pātāla*.

Aśvin: Horse-headed Twins, Gods of Medicine.

Āśvin: Lunar month corresponding to September-October.

Āśvalāyana Gṛhya-Sūtra (*AGS*): A Text of daily ritual.

atala: One of the seven *pātāla*s.

Atharva Saṁhita (*AS*): The *Atharvaveda*'s Hymns.

Atharvaveda (*AV*): One of the four collections of the Śruti.

atiśīta: "The freezing," name of a hell.

ativaha sthāna: Situation beyond the body or after the fall of the body.

ativarṇāśramī: The human being who surpasses the conditions of caste and *āśrama*.

ātman: The Self, the real principle of every beings, identified with the *Brahman* of Vedānta.

ātura saṁnyāsa: *Saṁnyāsa* taken on death's door.

aughar: ***See*** *aghorī*.

avatāra: Bodily manifestation of God Viṣṇu on the earth.

āveśya: Possession of the body by an alien entity.

āyur: The well balanced life, the health.

Āyurveda: The health science, the Medicine.

āyuṣya: (1) Second stage of the *saṁskāra* of the birth (*jātakarma*). (2) Longevity (or *cirajīvan*).

Ayyapam: Popular name of Aiyanār, form of the God Śiva (or his son). Guardian of the fields, he is particularly worshipped in the Dravidian Country.

Bahubhūti: The town of the "Thousand Ghosts."

Bahvāpada: The town of the "Servile Foot."

bājarā: Vegetables containing their seeds in ears or pods.

bālagraha: Nightmares troubling the children.

bālya: (1) Childhood. (2) Heroism. (3) Condition of concentration of the *saṁnyāsin*.

banyan: ***Ficus bengalensis***, *nyagrodha*.

Bardo Tödol: Tibetan Book of the Death.

barhisoda (or *barhiṣad*): Category of *pitṛs*, enjoying the celestial light.

Baudhāyana Pitṛmedha-Sūtra (*BPS*): Text of Funeral Ritual.

Bhagavad-Gītā (*BG*): Celebrated section of the *Mbh*, in form of dialogue.

Bhāgavata Purāṇa (*BhāP*): One of the great Purāṇas dealing with the feats of Kṛṣṇa.

bhāṣya: (1) Traditional Commentary of some Sacred Text. (2) Language.

bhīmarathī: The dreadful night from which one wakes up older-looking.

Bhīṣma: The strongest and fair hero of the *Mbh.*

bhū: The earth, "our" world.

bhūta: (1) Every gross element — ether, air, fire, water, earth. (2) A phantom caused by the decomposition, an *ignis fatuus* or will-o'-the-wisp.

bīja: The germ contained in the seed.

bījaka: "Germinal."

Brahmā: ***See** Brahman.*

brāhma(vivāha): A kind of marriage.

Brahmā (m. subst.): The God presiding over the development of the Manifestation. Along with Viṣṇu and Śiva, he constitutes the Trimūrti. Sometimes he is got into the personal God *Īśvara*.

brahmacārin: The boy who is spending his first *āśrama* of the *dvija* life, the Student.

brahmacarya: The first stage or *āśrama* of the *dvija*-life.

brahmalīna: Dissolution of the corpse, extraordinary vanishing of the body after the death.

brahmamedha: Burial of a *saṁnyāsin*.

Brahman (or *Brahmā* n. subst.): The Supreme Principle, unconditioned and not dual.

brahman (or *brāhmaṇ, brāhmaṇa*): (1) Priest, member of the highest caste (2) The knower of the *Brahman.*

Brāhmaṇa: Ritual Texts of the Veda.

brahmāṇḍa: (1) The egg of *Brahmā*. Seven skies and seven earths are contained in it. (2) The egg from where the human world has been manifested.

Brahmāṇḍa Purāṇa (*BP*): One of the great Purāṇas.

brahmarandhra: The opening of the head, the fontanel or aperture in the skull.

brahmarṣi: Seers of sacerdotal caste.

Brahma-Sūtra (or *Vedānta-Sūtra*) (*BS*): Collection of synthetic aphorisms attributed to Bādarāyaṇa, commented by the most important *ācārya* of the Vedānta.

brahmavid: *Brahman* whose family descends from the *Atharvans* or from the *Āṅgirasas*. He dedicates to Fire-worship.

Bṛhadāraṇyaka Upaniṣad (*BṛU*): Ancient Upaniṣad of the white *Yajurveda.*

Bṛhaspati: The Priest of the Gods.

Bṛhat Saṁhitā (*BS*): The encyclopaedic work of Varāhamihira (sixth century AD).

budbuda: "Bubble," the first stage in the Embryo development.

buddhi: Contemplative intellect.

cakravartin: Universal King.

cakṣus: Eye, the faculty of sight.

Caraka Saṁhita (*CS*): Text of *Āyurveda* attributed to Caraka.

caraṇāmṛta: "Nectar of the Feet," water used for washing a divine image.

caru: Oblation of rice offered to the deceased, the *piṇḍa*.

catuspād: The quadrupeds.

Caitanya: Founder of a famous Vaiṣṇava school (fifteenth-sixteenth century AD).

cetanadhātu: The conscious element of the individual Soul.

chāga: Billy goat, sacrificial animal.

Chāndogya Upaniṣad (*ChU*): Ancient Upaniṣad of the *Sāmaveda*.

chāyāpatha: "Shades trail," a name of the Milky Way.

cirajīvan: The longevity.

cit: (1) The Universal or the individual Consciousness. (2) The conscious beings, human, animals and plants.

Citragupta: The Judge of the afterlife.

citta: The rational consciousness, faculty of *manas*.

cūḍākaraṇa: *Saṁskāra* of the tonsure.

cuḍail (cuḍel): Soul of a women who died during childbirth? They have the feet turned backwards.

daitya: A class of Anti-gods or Titans.

ḍākinī (*ḍāken*): A kind of Fairy, sometimes a Witch.

Dakṣa: (1) A Celestial Priest. (2) One of the six Āditya. (3) Father of Aditi (mother of Ādityas).

dakṣiṇa: (1) Right side. (2) South.

dakṣiṇā. Priest's fee for the performance of the sacrifices.

Dakṣiṇāpati: "Lord of the South," *Yama*.

dānava: A class of Anti-gods or Titans.

darbha (or *kuśa*): Herb consecrated to Viṣṇu (*desmostachya bipinnata*?) (also see *dūrvā*).

dāsa: Denomination for the deceased śūdra when he reaches the *pitṛ loka*.

Dattātreya: *Ṛṣi* worshipped until today as a human manifestation of Brahmā, Śivạ and Viṣṇu together.

dehānta: "The end of the body," Sanskrit term to express the concept of the bodily death. Less definitive term than *mṛtyu*.

deva: "The Bright Ones," the Gods.

deva loka: The "locus" of the Gods. The *pitṛ*s who get the salvation go to this place. Some time confused with the *svarga*.

devapatha: Path leading to *deva loka*. Do not mistake with *devayāna* that leads beyond the *deva loka*.

devayāna: The path of the Gods. Journey leading to the *Brahmaloka* through the *deva loka*. It is the posthumous way for a special category of *yogins* destined to reach the Deferred Liberation *Krama Mukti*, not examined in this study.

dhanañjaya vāyu: "The breath that provides treasures," the *prāṇa* lingering in the corpse. Wizards and *aghorīs* may use it for their purposes.

dharma: (1) The Universal Law. (2) The religious duties. (3) The Hinduism.

Dharmarāja: "King of Justice;" propitious name of *Yama*.

Dharmarājapura: "King of Justice Town." So *Yamanagara* is perceived by one who get the salvation.

Dharma-Sūtra: Sacred Books enumerating the Hindu Religious Duties.

Dhātar (or *Dhātṛ*): Divinity presiding at the procreation. Some time identified with Brahmā.

dhātu: An element, a limb, a substantial component.

dīkṣā: (1) Initiation. (2) Consecration of the patron of a solemn sacrifice.

dīkṣanīyeṣṭi: The ritual of initiation or consecration.

Diti: Mother of the Titans or Anti-Gods (*daitya*).

div: The "Bright one," the sky.

Ḍom: Clan of an untouchable Tribe, dwelling in Varanasi from many centuries. They attend to every practical aspects of the cremations on the *ghāṭs*.

Duḥkhada: The Town "Perpetual Sorrow."

Durnaman: "Bloody flow," *rākṣasa* provoking abortions.

dūrvā: Sacred Herb (***cynodon dactylon***).

Dvaita: The duality.

Dvāpara yuga: The third *yuga*, the Bronze Age.

Dvārakā: The Capital of the Kingdom of Kṛṣṇa.

dvija: Twice-born. Every member of the three highest castes having got the sacred cordon.

dvipād: The bipeds.

ekādaśa: "Eleven," so it is called the *śrāddha* offered during the eleventh day after the cremation.

ekoddiṣṭa: All the *śrāddhas* performed after the cremation, in order to lead the *preta* to the *pitṛ loka*.

eṣanā: Attraction, desire.

gaṇa: (1) Multitude. (2) In later age, dwarf *yakṣa*.

Gaṇapati (or *Gaṇeśa*): Lord of the *gaṇas*, elephant-headed God.

gandha: *Tanmātra* of the olfaction. Perfume.

Gandhamādana (or *Gandharva*): The town of the *gandharvas*.

Gāndhārī: Daughter of the King Subala of Gāndhāra.

gandharva: Class of Demigods. Subtle beings.

gandharvagraha: Hysteria.

gandharvagṛhīta: Possession by a *gandharva*. Hysteria.

gandharvanagara: "The town of the *gandharvas*," that is to say the mirage.

Gaṅgā: (1) The Ganges, female divinity identified with Goddess Pārvatī. (2) Another name for the Milky Way.

garbha: (1) Foetus, sometimes embryo. (2) Abbreviation of *garbhāśaya*, meaning matrix, womb.

garbhādhāna: *Saṁskāra* performed before the conception.

garbhagṛha: The "abode of the embryo," the ***sanctum*** of the Hindu Temple.

garbhāśaya: The "receptacle of the embryo," the womb.

Garbha Upaniṣad (*GU*): Minor Upaniṣad of the *Atharvaveda*.

gārhapatya: The sacrificial earthen Fire.

garma: The heat.

Garuḍa Purāṇa (*GP*): One of the great Purāṇas.

Gauḍapāda: Author of the *Kārikās* included in the *MāU*.

Gautama Buddha: (1) Founder of the Buddhism. (2) In late Hinduism the ninth *avatāra* of Viṣṇu.

Gautama Gṛhya-Sūtra: Ritual Text ascribed to the Ṛṣi Gautama Śaradvat.

gāyatrī (or *sāvitrī*): The most sacred Hymn of the *Ṛk* collection dedicated to the Sun.

ghaṭa kumbha: (1) A terracotta pot used to collect the bone remains after the cremation. (2) Retention of the breaths during the controlled respiration.

ghrāṇa: The sense of smell.

ghṛta (or *ghī*): The clarified butter.

Ghṛtāci: *Apsaras* who distracted the mind of Ṛṣi Viśvāmitra from asceticism.

godāna: The ritual gift of cow.

Gorakṣa Nātha (or *Gorakh Nāth*): A Nāth, founder of the school of the Kānphaṭa *Yogins*.

gotra: Clan formed by all the descendants of the same caste and from the same mythic ancestor.

graha: (1) The "Grasping," the "Constricting." Category of *incubi*, nightmares obsessing the women. (2) Planet.

grahī: *Succubi*, nightmare obsessing the men.

gṛhasthin: *Dvija* in the life stage of *gṛhasthya*.

gṛhasthya: Second stage of the life of the *dvija*, stage of householder.

Gṛhya-Sūtra: Texts describing the obligatory rituals for the *gṛhasthins*.

guhya (or *guhyaka*): "Cave dwellers," invisible spirits.

guhyaloka: The world of the *guhya* where the heroes killed in battle go.

guṇa: (1) Chord, bowstring. (2) Term of the Sāṁkhya defining the three tendencies of the primordial substance *prakṛti*.

Gupta: Denomination for the deceased vaiśya when he reaches the *pitṛ loka*.

guru: Master, teacher, especially in the initiation context.

haviryajñīyanivāpa: Scattering in the wind the ashes of a deceased.

Hiraṇyagarbha: The golden embryo enclosed in the *brahmāṇḍa*.

Holī: A carnival holiday of Spring, in honour of Kṛṣṇa.

homa: Sacrifice with a liquid oblation offered in the Fire.

iḍā: The edible remains of the sacrifice, personified by the Goddess of the same name.

iḍāpātra: ***See*** *kapāla*.

Ikṣvāku: Vedic King founder of the Solar Dynasty.

Indha: The "Kindler," *Indra*.

Indra: The King of the Gods.

indriya: The ten faculties of sense and action plus the mind.

Īśvara: The "Lord," the personal God, Maker of the Universe.

Īśvarakṛṣṇa: The Author of the *Sāṁkhyakārikā*s.

Itihāsa: The epic poems *Mahābhārata* and *Rāmāyaṇa*.

jāgarta sthāna: Conscious state while one is awake.

janman: Birth, synonym of *jātakarma*.

Jarā: "Old age," name of the killer of Kṛṣṇa.

Jaratkāru: "Who leads to the old age," a *ṛṣi* who saw his own ancestors hanging from a rope that a mouse was gnawing. He hastened to have a son in order to deliver the forefathers through the *ekoddiṣṭa*.

jarāyu: (1) Snake's caste-off skin. (2) Chorion covering the embryo of the superior animals.

jātakarma: *Saṁskāra* performed on the moment of the birth.

jātavedas: "Well-known by the human beings," an attribute of Agni.

jāti: (1) Birth. (2) Familiar position. (3) Caste.

jīva (or *jīvan*): (1) Life. (2) Living beings. (3) Living Soul.

jīvan mukti: Liberation obtained during the bodily life.

jīvātman (or *jīva*): The living soul, the individual psyche.

jñāna-kāṇḍa: The Gnosis, the doctrinal part of the Hinduism.

jñānendriya: The sense faculties, the five senses.

jvara: Fever, name of a daughter of the Śiva's ire.

jyeṣṭha: The "Oldest," a constellation.

Ka: "Who?," Interrogative pronoun used to define an aspect of Prajāpati.

Kabīr: Famous *sant* of the devotional way (*Bhakti mārga*).

kāla: (1) The Time. (2) The Death. (3) The God of the death. (4) The black colour.

kāladūta: "Premonition."

kāla mukha: The "Death Mouth" monstrous mascaron of the Hindu Iconography. Some time called *kīrti mukha*, "Face of Glory."

kalila: "Mixed," the just fertilized ovum.

Kali yuga: The last and present dark age, the Iron Age.

kalpa: A cosmic cycle, a day of Brahmā.

Kalpa-Sūtra: Ritual Texts of smṛti including the Śrauta, the Gṛhya and the Dharma-Sūtra.

kāma: (1) The desire, the passionate love. (2) The God of Love, *see* Kāmadeva.

Kāmadeva: The God of Love.

kamaṇḍalu: Wooden bowl used by the Indian ascetics.

Kaṁsa: Usurper of the throne of Mathurā, maternal uncle of Kṛṣṇa.

kāṇḍa: Section, part.

kaṇva: Devils provoking abortions.

kapāla: (1) Skull. (2) The bowl put on the face of the deceased ritualist (also *iḍāpātra*).

kapāla kriyā: The ritual of the breaking skull of the corpse laying on the pyre.

kāpālika: Follower of a śāktic sect dealing with macabre ritual objects and sexual techniques of asceticism.

kapota: Spotted pigeon, bird of ill-omen.

kārikā: "Celebration Verses," short doctrinal poems. The most celebrated are the *kārikā*s of Gauḍapāda and Īśvarakṛṣṇa.

karma-kāṇḍa: The ritual part of the Hinduism.

karmakāṇḍin: The ritualist priests.

karman: (1) Deed, action. (2) Rite.

karmendriya: The five faculties of action.

karṇavedha: *Saṁskāra* of the perforation of the earlobes.

Karurāma: A founder of the *aghorī* School of Varanasi.

kaṭapūtana: The *piśāca* produced by a kṣatriya.

Kāṭhaka Gṛhya-Sūtra: A ritual Text.

Kathā-Sarit-Sāgara: Celebrated book of short tales written by Somadeva (eleventh cent.)

Kauṣitakī Brāhmaṇa: A *Brāhmaṇa* included in the *Ṛgveda*.

Kauṣitakī Upaniṣad (*KU*): Middle Upaniṣad of the *Ṛgveda*.

kāya sādhanā: Practice of martial Arts leading to longevity.

keśānta: The *saṁskāra* of the first shaving of the beard.

keśin: Lion's mane nightmares provoking abortions.

khaṇḍa: A chapter, an ensemble of paragraphs.

kinnara: Half man and half horse Spirits, similar to the *gandharva*s and to the *kiṁpuruṣa*s.

kīrti mukha: ***See*** *kāla mukha*.

kośa: Envelop (of *ātman*).

krama mukti: Delayed Liberation, that one gets as result of the *devayāna*.

Krauñca: The town of the curlews.

kravyāda (or *kravyd*): "Meat eater." Epithet of the fire (Agni) of the funeral pyre. The *bhūta*s are called so far their function of distructors of corpses (used also for the *piśāca*s).

Kṛṣṇa: The eighth and most important *avatāra* of Viṣṇu.

Kṛṣṇājina: The skin of the black antelope, used as a carpet for rituals and meditation.

kṛta yuga: *See satya yuga*.

Krūrapura: "the cruel town."

kṣaṇa: An instant, the quantity of time passed in a twinkling of an eye.

kṣatriya: The members of the second caste, the warriors.

kṣudrabrahmāṇḍa: Small egg of Brahmā, microcosm, *piṇḍa*.

kubera: God of the wealth and leader of many groups of spirits.

kūdī: Faggots of sticks or twigs.

kuṇḍalinī: The power (*śakti*) snake-shaped, coiled in the lower part of the sacral plexus.

kuśa: ***See*** *dūrvā*.

laḍḍū: Sweet balls liked by Gaṇapati.

laukikāgni: "Worldly Fire." With this one lights the fire of the pyre for the people who do not maintain the sacrificial fire.

liṅga śarīra: Subtle body.

loka: A world.

loṣṭaciti: "Altar of bricks;" synonym of *stūpa*.

mada: (1) Madness, mental confusion similar to the condition of a furious buffalo. (2) Erotic frenzy. (3) Perfumed secretion screened by the temples of the rutted elephants.

mahābrāhmaṇa (or *mahāpaṇḍita*): Honorary title for the ritualist brāhmaṇa recognized as authorities in the *karma-kāṇḍa*.

Mahābhārata (*Mbh*): Epic poem.

mahāpralaya: The dissolution of a *kalpa*.

mahārājā: Great King.

mahāraurava: "The very terrible," name of a hell.

mahat: ***See** buddhi*.

mahātala: One of the seven *pātāla*s.

Mahāvīra: The founder of the Jainism.

Maitrāyaṇī Saṁhitā (*MS*): Collection of Hymns of the black *Yajurveda*.

Maitrāyaṇī Upaniṣad (*MU*): Ancient Upaniṣad of the black *Yajurveda*.

malina ṣoḍaśī: "The sixteen impure;" name of the imperfect *śrāddha* that limits to the oblation of just the first sixteen *piṇḍa*s.

manas: The mind, the reason.

manaspāpman: Obsession.

Mānava Dharma-Śāstra (*MDhŚ*): The book of the Laws of Manu.

Mandākinī: A name of the Milky Way.

maṇḍala: (1) Circular drawing. (2) Magic ring.

maṇḍapa: Pavilion, vestibule.

maṇḍūka: Frog.

Māṇḍūkya Upaniṣad (*MāU*): An Upaniṣad of the *Atharvaveda*.

manomaya: "Consisting of mind."

mantram: (1) Vedic verses. (2) Syllable or word with an vibrating effect, right for offering a support for the spiritual realization.

Manu: The genius of the human species, law-maker of the present humanity and twin of Yama.

Manu-Smṛti: ***See*** *Mānava Dharma-Śāstra*.

manuṣya: Human being.

manuṣyaloka: The world that the human beings may test during the bodily life.

manvantara: The historical cycle of a humanity.

Mārkaṇḍeya Purāṇa (*MP*): One of the great Purāṇas.

Martāṇḍa: "Died egg," abortive son of Aditi.

Marut: Demigods of the atmosphere, corresponding in the microcosm to the *prāṇa*s of the deceased ones.

mastiṣka: Brain, the mind organ.

maṭmaṭa: ***Ignis fatuus***, fire produced by the fermentation of the vegetables.

maṭha: School for *bramacārins*, under the guidance of an *ācārya*.

Mātṛkā: Seven Goddesses of the Tantrism.

Matsya Purāṇa: One of the great Purāṇas.

medhājanana: First rite performed during the *jātakarma*.

Meru: The cosmic mountain, the *axis mundi*.

Mīrābāī: Princess and famous poet of *bhakti* (sixteenth century).

mokṣa: The Liberation from every bondage, supreme aim of the man. Synonym of *mukti* and *nirvāṇa*.

mṛga: Deer.

mṛtyu: Death, the God of death.

mūla: (1) Root, a name for the Universal Substance. (2) The name of a constellation.

muni: "Who is plunged in the silence," the ascetic enjoying the spiritual loneliness.

nāḍī: Canal, subtle vein.

nāḍīsūtra: "Cord canal," the umbilical cord.

nāga: (1) Snake, cobra, dragon. (2) A Category of Titans.

nāgarāja: King cobra, chief of the *nāgas*.

Nāgendrabhavana: The castle of the King *nāga*.

nakṣatra: Constellation.

nāmakaraṇa: *Saṁskāra* of the giving of the name.

nāman: "Name;" Along with *rūpa*, the "form," is the binomial building up the individuality (***see*** *nāmarūpa*).

nāmarūpa: ***See*** *nāman*.

Namuci: *Dānava* slaughtered by Indra.

Nānākrandapura: The town "Full of groans."

Nanda: The adoptive father of Kṛṣṇa.

nāndi śrāddha: Rite performed in the course of the delivery, in honour of the ancestors.

naraka: Hell, lowest part of the *pitṛ loka*.

nātha: School of Tāntric *yogin*.

Nidrā Devī: The sleep, sister of Mṛtyu.

Nighaṇṭu: Work of Yāska.

nimba (or *nīm*): ***Azadirachta Indica***, a tree with very bitter leafs.

Nimi: Son of Ikṣvāku, the sole case of mummification known in India.

Nirṛti: Personification of the disorder.

Nirukta: Vedic science, explaining the meaning of the words through the assonance, considered by the Western scholars as pseudo-etymologies. Title of the Commentary of the *Nighaṇṭu* of Yāska.

niṣkarmaṇa: The first ritual going out of the new-born.

niṣkṛntana: "The chopper of men," a hell.

nyāsa: Possession of a human being by a God, or by an alive or dead holy man.

oṁ (*auṁ*): The supreme monosyllabic *mantram*.

pāda: (1) The faculty of deambulation. (2) A foot. (3) A fourth (1/4).

Paddhati: Mediaeval Texts on the *saṁskāra*s often consulted up to the present-day.

padma āsana: The lotus position, used by the *yogin* for the meditation.

Padma Purāṇa (*PP*): One of the eighteen great Purāṇas.

pakṣa: Half lunation, or period of fifteen days.

pañcabhūta: The five elements.

pañcakośavāda: The doctrine of the "five envelops of *ātman*," described in the *Taittirīya Upaniṣad*.

pañcakṛta: "Consisting of five [elements]." The gross body or *sthūla śarīra*.

Pañcasiddhāntikā: A Treatise on Astronomy recovering five lost works of Varāhamihira.

pañca śrāddha: *Śrāddha* offered with the purpose of shortening to the dead man the period of *preta*.

Pancaviṁśa Brāhmaṇa (*PB*): Text of ritual music of the *Sāmaveda*.

Pāṇḍava: The son of Pāṇḍu. One of the five brothers, heroes of the *Mbh*.

pāṇḍityam: To be *paṇḍita*, the function of teacher.

Pāṇḍu: The father of the Pāṇḍavas.

pani: The faculty of prehension.

Parameṣṭhin: (1) Disciple of Brahmā or of Prajāpati, representing the cosmic potentiality (the cow). (2) Some time synonym of Virāj.

paramparā: Tradition, transmission of the initiation from *guru* to disciple.

Pāraskara Gṛhya-Sūtra: A text of *gṛhya* ritual.

Parivrājaka: Perfect and realized *Brahman*.

Pārvatī: *Śakti* of Śiva.

pāśa: "Leash, noose."

paśu: The domestic animals.

pātāla: (1) The underground abysses, realm of several hierarchies of *asura*. (2) Name of the deepest of the hells.

pathika: "The traveller;" In this way is called the corpse during the transfer to the cremation ground.

pāyu: The faculty of excretion.

Payovarṣaṇa: The town "Milky rain."

peśī: "Ball of flesh," the embryo since the fifteenth day after the conception.

piṇḍa: (1) Seed, seminal being, microcosm (called also *kṣudra brahmāṇḍa*, small *brahmāṇḍa*. (2) Sweet ball offered to the *pitṛ*s or Gods in several rites, especially during the funeral ceremonies (or *pūraka*).

piṇḍa dāna: The *piṇḍa*s offered with the purpose of reuniting the recent dead persons with their *pitṛ*. One performs in the case there is some doubt on the efficacy of the funeral rites.

piṇḍaja śarīra: The "body produced by the *piṇḍas*;" When to the *vāyuja śarīra* one adds the *piṇḍaja śarīra* formed by the offerings of *piṇḍas*, the deceased person gets the body called *yātanā śarīra* (see).

piṇḍa pitṛ yajña: *Śrauta* term defining the *śrāddha*.

pippala: ***Ficus religiosa***.

piśāca: A soul in torment, dead man unable to become neither *preta*, not *pitṛ*.

piśācamocana: Exorcism for the possession by the *piśācas*.

piśācī: Female soul in torment.

pīṭha: Shrines of pilgrimage dealing with the Durgā cult.

pitṛ: Ancestor. Favourable or unfavourable state of the deceased people waiting for the rebirth.

pitṛgaṇa: The multitude of the ancestors.

pitṛloka: Abode of the *pitṛ*, often identified with the *Yamaloka*. In that abode the saved souls dwell in the *svargas*, and the damned ones in the *narakas*, waiting for the rebirth.

pitṛmedha: Funeral Rites for Universal Kings.

pitṛ pakṣa: Dark fortnight of the Moon in the Āśvina month (September-October) consecrated to the ancestors.

pitṛyāna: The trail of the ancestors. It is covered by the people who reach the Moon, without dwelling upon the *pitṛloka*. This posthumous destiny, reserved to a special category of *yogins*, is not examined in this study.

pītu: The disciples regarding the food control.

Pracetas: "The Wise one," attribute of Agni.

pradakṣiṇā: Ritual deambulation to right hand, following the apparent movement of the Sun.

Prajāpati: "Lord of the subject beings," aspect of Brahmā as author of a *loka*.

prājāpatya (*vivāha*): A kind of marriage.

prājña: Third *pāda* of *ātman* in the *Māṇḍūkya Upaniṣad*.

prakṛti: Universal Substance, material Causes of the Cosmos.

pralaya: The dissolution of a *manvantara*.

prāṇa: The respirable air, the breath of life, the psychic energies. The first *vāyu*.

prāṇamaya: Consisting of *prāṇa*.

praṇava: The monosyllable *Oṁ*.

prāṇāyāma: The disciplines regarding the birth control.

prasāda: Grace, bliss. It spreads out through the food, the remains from the sacrifices dedicated to the Gods.

prasavya: Ritual deambulation to left hand, opposed to the apparent movement of the Sun.

Praśna Upaniṣad (*PU*): Middle Upaniṣad of the *Atharvaveda*.

pratyaṅga: The secondary limbs of the body.

pravāha: Wind provoking the rotation of the stars around the Pole Star.

preta: The "voyager," the dead man travelling towards the world of the *pitṛ*s.

pretaloka: The abode of the *preta*s.

Preta Mañjarī (or *Preta Kāṇḍa*): Section of the *Garuḍa Purāṇa* describing the man's posthumous destiny.

pretayāna: The path towards the town of Yama.

pṛthivī: The element earth. The world as abode of the human beings.

pūjā: A rite focused on the images worship.

puṁsavana: *Saṁskāra* of the quickening of the male child.

pūraka: See *piṇḍa*.

Purāṇa: "Ancient Books," Collections of Myths and Traditional

Sciences, Dynastic Stories. Among them one divides eighteen great (Mahā)Purāṇas and eighteen minor (Upa)Purāṇas.

pūrṇāvatāra: Full *avatāra*.

purohita: The *brāhmaṇa* playing the role of Court "chaplain."

Purūravas: Founder of the Lunar Dynasty and husband of Urvaśī.

puruṣa: The Spirit. The essence (correlated with *prakṛti*). The human being. The man.

Pūṣaṇ: God of food and fertility similar to *Annapūrṇa*, leading to the right ways.

put: "The clutching," name of a hell.

putra: Son.

Raghuvaṁśa: Poem of Kālidāsa on the feats of Rāma.

rahasya: Mystery, secret meaning.

rājā: King.

rājarṣi: Seers of royal caste.

rajas: *Guṇa* of the spread. Passion. "Female seed."

rākṣasa: (1) Night Devils. (2) Kind of marriage.

rakṣasī: Female of *rākṣasa*.

Rāma: Seventh *avatāra* of Viṣṇu.

Rāmāyaṇa: Epic poem on the feats of Rāma.

rasa: (1) The *tanmātra* of the sapidity. (2) Essence, saliva, lymph.

rasana: The taste.

rasātala: One of the seven *pātāla*s.

rasāyana: Indian Alchemy.

Rati: (1) Personification of the pleasure. (2) Wife of Kāma.

Raudra: The town "Hostile."

rourava: "The terrible," name of a hell.

Ṛbhu: Human craftsmen, the *Ṛbhus* were raised to the dignity of Gods in recognition of their skill.

Ṛk Saṁhitā (*ṚS*): The Hymns of the *Ṛgveda*.

Ṛgveda (*ṚV*): One of the collections of the Veda.

rocana: The sky.

roṭī: Round bread.

ṛṣi: Vedic seer.

ṛta: The order, the ritual rule.

ṛtukāla: The right moment. The moment when the individual destiny falls on the cosmic situation.

ṛtvij: The priest who supervises the sacrifices.

ṛtviya: Ritual purity that the family regains coming out of mourning.

Rudra: Vedic name for Śiva. Synonym of *marut*.

rūpa: (1) The "form;" Along with *nāman*, the 'name,' it is the binomial making the individual manifestation. (2) The *tanmātra* of the visibility.

Śabala: (1) "Spotted," one of the two dogs of Yama. (2) Name of the star *Scorpionis*.

śabda: The *tanmātra* of the sonorousness.

sādhana: The way of spiritual realization followed by the *sādhu*.

sādhu: (1) Synonym of *saṁnyāsin*. (2) Religious mendicant about to become a *saṁnyāsin*.

Sādhya: Demigods of the retinue of Brahmā. They were the sacrificers before the men.

Śakti: (1) The power of manifestation of the Supreme Divinity. (2) The wife of a God.

śalagrāma: Fossil ammonites. They are considered the terrene manifestation of the *cakra*, the wheel weapon of Viṣṇu.

samādhi: (1) Direct contemplation. (2) A way to express the death of the *saṁnyāsins*. (3) Funeral monument for a *saṁnyāsin*.

samāna: The air, the wind (*vāyu*) presiding at the assimilation and the digestion.

samāvartana: The *saṁskāra* of leaving the *guru*.

Saṁhitā: The Vedic Hymn.

śamī: ***Mimosa suma***.

saṁjñā: The knowledge of the external world.

Śaṁkara: The greatest *ācārya* of Advaita Vedānta (eighth century).

Sāṁkhya: One of the six *darśanas* of the Hinduism.

Sāṁkhyakārikā: The oldest text of Sāṁkhya, attributed to Īśvarakṛṣṇa.

saṁnyāsa: Fourth stage of the *dvija*-life.

saṁnyāsin: The *dvija* embracing the fourth stage of life.

sampradana: Rite performed in order to transmit psychic elements to another individual.

sampradāya: Initiation Organization.

saṁskāra: (1) Rites celebrating the development of the life from birth to death. (2) Kārmic links.

saṁyojana śrāddha: Rite that joins up the *preta* and its *pitṛ*s.

saṁdhyā: Daily Rites performed at dawn and sunset.

śaṁkha: The shell, symbol of Viṣṇu.

santa: A category of ascetics.

sapiṇḍa: "Having the seed in common," the relatives until the fifth degree of kindred.

sapiṇḍīkaraṇa: Rite that introduces the *preta* in the condition or in the world of *pitṛ*.

saptāṅga: The seven parts of the world or of the human body.

Sarasvatī: Ancient river now dried up, personified by the homonymous Goddess of the Wisdom, wife of Brahmā.

Saramā: She-dog, mother of the two dogs of Yama.

śarīra: Body.

Śarmā: Name for the died brāhmaṇa dwelling the *pitṛ loka*.

Sarvaprāṇahara: "The remover of all the Soul," Yama.

sat: The real being.

Śatapatha Brāhmaṇa (*ŚB*): *Brāhmaṇa* of the white *Yajurveda*.

satī: The widow sacrifice on the husband pyre.

sati kāla: Votive stele in memory of the widow cremated on the husband pyre.

sattva: The *guṇa* expressing the upward tendency.

satya: Reality, Truth.

Satya Yuga: The first *yuga*, the Golden Age.

Sauripura: The town of the Sun.

śava: Corpse.

savitar: A name of the Sun.

sevā: Sacred service.

siddha: Category of *yogins* pursuing the control of the eight supernatural powers (*sides*).

śikhā: (1) Crown. (2) Hairs lock that the brāhmaṇas wear on the top of the shaved head.

sīmantonnayana: *Saṁskāra* of parting the hair at the centre.

Sinīvālī: Goddess of the new Moon acting as a liquids repellent; Among other things, she provokes the deliveries.

Sītādhya: The "Deep" town.

Śiva: God of the Trimūrti, personifying the death and the transformation.

śmaśāna: Cremation ground. In origin "burial."

śmaśāna sādhanā: Meditation performed on the cremation ground.

Smṛti: "Memory," Sacred Texts founded on the oral Tradition and, for this reason, less authoritative then the Śruti's Texts.

snātaka: The *brahmacārin* who took leave of the *guru*.

Soma: (1) Ritual God representing the liquids. (2) "Subtle husband" of the unmarried maids. (3) Sacrificial beverage offered to the Gods. (4) The Moon.

Somadeva: Author of the celebrated collection of short tales *Kathā-Sarit-Sāgara*.

somadhārā: "Stream of Soma," other name of the Milky Way.

somapa (or *somya*): A category of *pitṛ*s enjoying the Moon light.

śonita: Female blood.

sparśa: The *tanmātra* of the tangibility.

śraddhā: (1) The intention of the sacrifice. (2) The faith. (3) The confidence.

śrāddha: Offering of *piṇḍa*s leading the *preta* to the *pitṛ loka*.

Śrauta-Sūtra: The solemn ritual texts sung or heard in certain Brahmaṇic Families.

śravaṇa: Messengers of the Gods, controllers of the human deeds.

śrotra: The sense of hearing.

sṛṣṭi: The production of *sthiti*.

Śruti : "Listening," the Vedic Texts.

sthūla śarīra: The gross body, composed of the five elements or *bhūta*s.

sthiti: The Cosmos, the Universal Manifestation.

stūpa (or *thūpa*): Tumulus, Funeral Monument erected in memory of Kings and *Cakravartins*.

śūdra: The fourth caste, the *anāryas*.

śukra: Masculine seed, sperm.

sūkṣma śarīra: The subtle body composed by the *tanmātras*.

Sumeru: **See** *Meru*.

sura: The Gods.

sūryapatha: "Solar course," another name for the Milky Way.

Suśruta Saṁhitā (*SS*): Text of *Āyurveda* attributed to Suśruta.

suṣumnā: (1) Subtle vien piercing the spinal column. (2) Used as synonym of umbilical cord.

suṣupta sthāna: State of the conscience in deep sleep without dreams.

sutala: One of the seven *pātālas*.

Sutaptabhavana: The palace "of the youngest son."

Sūtra: Texts of the *smṛti*.

svadhā: Libation in honour of the Ancestors.

svadharma: Individual duty towards the Cosmos and the human Society.

svapna sthāna: State of the conscience in dream.

svarga: Heaven, abode of the Gods.

svastika: Symbol of the rotation around a centre.

svedaja: The beings born from the warm moisture, that is to say from the sweat.

Svetāśvatara Upaniṣad (*ŚU*): Middle Upaniṣad of the black *Yajurveda*.

Śyāma: (1) "The Dark one," one of the two dogs of Yama. (2) Name of the star *Scorpionis*.

taijasa: The subtle manifestation.

Taittirīya Saṁhitā (*TS*): Hymns collection of the black *Yajurveda.*

Taittirīya Upaniṣad (*TU*): Ancient Upaniṣad of the black *Yajurveda.*

talātala: One of the seven *pātāla.*

tamas: The *guṇa* of the attraction downward.

tanmātra: Subtle principles of the gross elements.

Tanūnapāt: A name of Agni.

tapas: The heat produced by the asceticism.

taptakuṁbha: "Red-hot Cauldron," name of a hell.

tarati: "To surpass a narrowing in the road," to cross.

tārpya: Priest's dress worn only in peculiar celebrations and representing the celestial vault.

tattva: Every production (*vikāra*) of *prakṛti.*

tejas: (1) The element fire. (2) The vital warmth.

tīrtha: (1) Ford. (2) Places of pilgrimage close to a river, a lake, a sea.

Tīrthaṁkara: "Who leads across the ford;" title for the Englightened ones of the Jainism.

Tretā yuga: The second *yuga*, the Silver Age.

triguṇa: The three *guṇas*.

trikāla: The triple Time, past, present and future.

triloka: The three worlds constituting the Universe.

trimūrti: The triple aspect of the Unique God.

Tṛṣṇā: "Thirst," mythic daughter of Love and Pleasure.

tulasī: The Indian basil, sacred to Viṣṇu.

ṭulku: Tibetan term (Skt. *nirmāṇakāya*, body of transformation) defining the individual who was born as a receptacle of spiritual influences and who manifests some psychic elements in common with his predecessor.

turīya: "The fourth." Fourth *pāda* of *ātman*. This supreme State cannot be expressed with a name.

tvac: The sense of touch.

Tvaṣṭar: The Divine Craftsman, the modelling of the embryo.

ucchiṣṭa: The food remains of the sacrifice.

udakakarman: Ritual ablution.

udāna: The expiration.

udbhija: The beings born from seeds, the germiniparous.

udumbara: ***Ficus glomerata***.

ulūka: Little owl, bird of ill-omen.

ulva: Amnion, the envelop protecting the embryo.

upanayana: *Saṁskāra* of the entrance in the caste.

Upaniṣad: Doctrinal Texts of the Veda.

upastha: Faculty of the procreation.

upoṣaṇa: Cremation.

uragraha: Nightmares.

Urvaśī: *Apsarā,* wife of King Purūravas.

utkrānti: ***See*** Vaitaraṇī.

uttara: North, Superior, Subsequent.

uttarāyaṇa: The northwards journey of the Sun.

vāc: The faculty of speech.

vaikuṇṭha (or *Indraloka*): Domain of Viṣṇu on the top of the Meru.

Vaiśvānara: Name of Agni in the form of Macranthrope.

vaiśya: Merchants and landowners, members of the third caste.

Vaitaraṇī (or *utkrānti*): (1) Cow whose presence is necessary in the funeral rites. (2) River dividing the world of living beings from the hell.

Vaivasvata: "Son of Vivasvat," patronymic of the twins Yama and Manu.

Vājasaneyi Saṁhitā: Hymns of the white *Yajurveda*.

vāma: Left side.

vāmana: (1) A dwarf. (2) Fifth *avatāra* of Viṣṇu.

vānaprastha: "The forest-dweller," third stage in the life of the *dvija*.

vānaprasthin: The *dvija* in the stage of *vānaprastha*.

vāpyāyaṇī: "Water pipe," the umbilical cord.

Varāhamihira: Author of the *Bṛhat Saṁhitā* (sixth century).

Varmā: Name of the deceased kṣatriya staying in the *pitṛ loka*.

Varuṇa: The God of the celestial waters.

Vasu: Gods of the Dawn, carrying on the atmospheric waters.

Vasubandhu: Celebrated Buddhist philosopher (fourth-fifth century).

Vasudeva: Father of Kṛṣṇa.

vāyu: (1) The element air. (2) Synonym of *prāṇa*. (3) The Wind God. (4) Vedic Gods sometimes identified with the *rudras* or the *maruts*. (5) The plant of a building.

vāyuja śarīra (or *adhideha*): "Body of air," condition of the deceased man after the gross body's loss and before the assumption of the state of *preta*. In this condition it can be locked up and become a *piśāca*.

vāyu-maṇḍala: The atmosphere, domain of the winds.

Veda: The most important Sacred Books of the Brāhmaṇic Tradition.

Vedāṅga: "The limbs of the Veda," the six sciences of Vedic origin.

Vedānta: "The end of the Veda," the Brāhmaṇic Metaphysics.

vedārambha: *Saṁskāra* introducing the *brahmacārin* to the study of the Veda.

vedī: The Vedic altar.

vetāla: Spirits possessing the corpses.

Vetālapañcaviṁśati: "Twenty-five tales of the *vetāla*," popular story belonging to the *Kathā-Sarit-Sāgara* of Somadeva.

Vicitra: Younger brother of Yama, sometimes confused with Citragupta.

Vicitrabhavana (or *Citranagara*): The castle of Vicitra.

vicrabhū: The chair or the Tribunal of Citragupta.

vidyā (or *vijñāna*): Science, analytic knowledge, wisdon.

vidyārambha: Educative *saṁskāra* of learning of the Sanskrit Alphabet.

vijñāna: **See** *vidyā*.

vijñānamaya: "Consisting of discrimination."

vikāra: Product, effect.

vilakṣaṇā: Bed.

vimāna: Celestial blazing chariot, symbol of *taijasa* (*piṇḍaja śarīra*).

Virāj: The ruler of the human world in its gross modality.

Vīramitrodaya Saṁskāra Prakāśa: Medieval Treatise on the *saṁskāra*s.

vīra kala: Stele in memory of heroes killed in battle.

virāṭ: Bounded, individual.

Viṣṇu: God of the Trimūrti, personification of the stability.

Viṣṇudharmottara Purāṇa: Encyclopaedic epitome of *Garuḍa Purāṇa*.

Viṣṇu Purāṇa (*VP*): One of the great Purāṇas.

viśva: Universal.

viśva-virāṭ: "Universal and particular at the same time," name of the cosmic manifestation of Kṛṣṇa.

Viśvadeva: Hierarchy of minor Gods of vaiśya caste.

Viśvāmitra: Celebrated *muni* and *ṛṣi*.

Viśvāvasu: King of the *gandharva* and "subtle" husband of the unmarried maidens.

vitala: One of the seven *pātālas*.

vivāha: Marriage.

vivarta: Unreal appearances. "To mistake a rope for a snake."

Vivasvān: ***See*** *Vivasvat*.

Vivasvat: The Sun, father of Manu and Yama.

Vivasvatapura: ***See*** *Dharmarājapura*.

Vraja (or *Braj*): Region on the banks of the Yamunā, where Kṛṣṇa spent his childhood.

vrata: The ascetic vow.

vṛṣa kāṣṭha: Column put up as memorial for an ancestor.

vṛṣotsarga: Rite consisting in the release of two bullocks.

vyāna: Inhaled air setting the bodily humours in motion.

vyāhṛti: The utterance of the *mantram "bhū bhūvar svar,"* "earth, atmosphere, sky."

Vyāsa-Smṛti: Minor Texts on the *dharma*.

vyoman: Sky.

yajña: Sacrifice.

Yājñavalkya Smṛti: Text belonging to the Dharma-Sūtras.

yajñopavīta: Brāhmaṇic cordon. It is given to the *dvija* during the *upanayanu*.

Yajurveda: One of the four Vedas.

yakṣa: A subtle being, like an elf.

Yama: The first dead man, brother of Manu, and King of the next world.

yamadūta: The messengers of Yama, the Angels of the Death.

Yamaloka: The world of Yama, the next world.

Yamanagara: The town of Yama.

Yama Sūkta (or *Yama Gāthā*): Hymn of the *ṚV*, X.14.

Yamunā: (1) One of the sacred rivers of India. (2) In the Mythology, sister of Yama and Manu.

Yāmya: ***See*** Yamanagara.

Yaśodā: Adoptive Mother of Kṛṣṇa.

Yāska: Author of the *Nighaṇṭu*.

yātanā śarīra: "Body of suffering," composed by the *vāyuja* and the *piṇḍaja śarīra*. It is the subtle body of *preta* and *pitṛ*.

yātu (*jādū*): Witchcraft.

yātudhāna: Wizard, black magicians.

yava: Barley.

Yayāti: Mythic founder of some solemn rites.

yoga: Union (*mokṣa*). A way to reach *mokṣa*. The *darśana* theorized by Patañjali.

yogin: (1) The human being having realized the union with the *Brahman*. (2) In a wider sense all those practising *yoga*.

yoni: Matrix, womb, female reproductive organ.

yonija: The beings born from a womb, the viviparous.

yuga: Four Ages in the history of a humanity.

yūpa: Sacrificial post of the Vedic rites.

Bibliography

Sanskrit

Atharvaveda Saṁhitā, ed. by Śrīpāda Damodara Satavalekar, Svādhyāya Maṇḍala, Pāradī, Bombay, 1957.

Gayā Śrāddha Paddhati, Ācārya Paṇḍita Śrīśivadatta Mitra Śāstrī, Kailāśa Pustakalaya, Gayā, 1981.

Īsādidasopaniṣadaḥa, Śāṁkarabhāṣyayutāḥa, Śrī Govinda Śāstrinā Tippanībhiḥa Samalaṁkṛtāḥa, Motīlāla Banārsīdāsa, Dillī, 1964.

Kātyāyana Śrauta-Sūtra, ed. by H.G. Ranade, Ranade Publication Series, Poona s.d.

Mahābhārata, ed. by R.N. Dandekar, 5 vols., Bhandarkar Oriental Research Institute, Poona, 1971.

Preta Mañjarī, Sampādaka Sv. P. Vāyunandan Miśra, Ṭīkā Sv. P. Agnināráyaṇa, Saṁskṛt Pustakālaya, Vārāṇasī, 2044.

Ṛgveda Saṁhitā, ed. by Ś.D. Satavalekar, Svādhyāya Maṇḍala, Pāradī, Bombay, 1957.

Sanatsujātīyadarśanam, Dr. Pārasanātha Dvivedī, Vārāṇaseya Saṁskṛta Saṁsthāna, Vārāṇasī, 1985.

Śrautakośaḥā, by B.N. Dandekar, Vaidika Samsodhana Mandala, Poona, 1973.

Taittirīya Saṁhitā, ed. by Ś.D. Satavalekar, Svādhyāya Maṇḍala, Pāradī, Bombay, 1957.

Upaniṣad Saṃgraha, Sa Cāyam Bhāgadvayopetah Paṇḍit Jagadīśa Śāstriṇā, Motilāla Banārsīdāsa, Dillī, 1970.

Yajur Veda Saṁhitā, ed. by Ś.D. Satavalekar, Svādhyāya Maṇḍala Pāradī, Bombay, 1957.

Other Languages*

Abbott, Justin E. & Godbole, Pandit N.R., *Stories of Indian Saints*, 2nd edn., Motilal Banarsidass, Delhi, 1982.

Agni Purāṇam, ed. by Manmatha Nath Dutt Shastri, 2 vols. Chowkhamba Sanskrit Series Off., Varanasi, 1967.

Aguilar, H., *The Sacrifice in the Ṛgveda*, Bharatiya Vidya Prakashan, Delhi, 1976.

The Aitareya Āraṇyaka, ed. by A.B. Keith, 2nd edn., Master Publs., New Delhi, 1981.

Altekar, A.S., *Education in Ancient India*, Benares, 1934.

Arce, Javier, *Fumus Imperatorum*, Alianza ed., Madrid, 1988.

Ariès, Philippe, *Storia della morte in Occidente* BUR I Ital. ed., Milano, 1978.

Ariès, Ph., *L'Uomo e la Morte dal Medioevo a oggi*, I It. ed. Laterza, Bari, 1985.

Arora, Udai Prakash, *Motifs in Indian Mythology — Their Greek and other Parallels*, Munshiram Manoharlal Pbs., New Delhi, 1981.

Atharvaveda, a cura di Ch. Orlandi e S. Sani, U.T.E.T., Torino, 1992.

*Atre, Shubhangana "Many seeds apple: the fruit of fertility," in *Bulletin of the Deccan College*, XLV, Pune, 1986.

Auboyer, Jeannine, *La vie quotidienne dans l'Inde ancienne*, éd. Hachette, Paris, 1961.

Sri Aurobindo, *The Problem of Rebirth*, Sri Aurobindo Ashram, Pondicherry, 1952.

Avalon, Arthur, *Il Potere del Serpente*, ed. Mediterranee, Roma, 1968.

*Baldissera, Fabrizia, "Le grandi Madri che uccidono," in *ACME*, Un. degli Studi di Milano, 1989.

Barber, Paul, *Vampiri, sepoltura e morte*, Pratiche Ed. (1st edn., *Vampires, burial and death*, Yale Un. Press, London 1988), Parma, 1994.

Basu, S.P., *The Concept of Brahmā*, Sundeep Prakashan, Delhi, 1986.

The Bhagavad Gītā with the Commentary of Sri Samkaracharya, ed. by A.M. Sastry, Samata Books, Madras, 1979.

Bhattacharya, Narendra Nath, *Indian Puberty Rites*, Indian Studies, Calcutta, 1968.

Bhattacharyya N.N., *Ancient Indian Rituals and their Social Contents*, Manohar Book Service, Delhi, 1975.

Bhattacharyya, N.N., *A Glossary of Indian Religious Terms and Concepts*, Manohar, Delhi, 1990.

Bloomfield, Maurice, *A Vedic Concordance*, 3rd edn., Low Price Publications, 1990.

Borman, William A., *The Other Side of Death: Upaniṣadic Eschatology*, India Book Centre, Delhi, 1990.

Bose, D.N. & Hiralal Haldar, *Tantras: Their Philosophy and Occult Secrets*, Oriental Publishing Co., enlarged 3rd edn.,, Calcutta, 1956.

Bose, Sir Jagdis Chunder, *Réactions de la Mati ere Vivante et non Vivante*, I Fr. éd. Gauthier-Villars et C. (1st edn., London, 1902), Paris, 1926.

Briggs, George Weston, *Gorakhnāth and the Kānphaṭa Yogīs*, 2nd edn., Motilal Banarsidass (1st edn., 1938), Delhi, 1973.

Brennand, W., *Hindu Astronomy*, 2nd edn., Caxton Publications India (1st edn., 1896), Delhi, 1988.

van Buitenen, J.A.B., *The Pravargya: An Ancient Indian Iconic Ritual: Described & Annotated*, Deccan College Publ., Pune, 1968.

Caland, W., *Die altindische Todten-und Bestattungsgebräuche*, Amsterdam, 1896.

Calmet, Abbé Augustin, *Dissertazioni sopra le apparizioni de' spiriti, e sopra i vampiri, o i redivivi d'Ungheria, di Moravia ec.*, ed. Arktos, Carmagnola, 1986.

Caraka Sa]mhitā, ed. by P. Sharma, 3 vols., Chaukambha, Varanasi, 1981.

Castrairs, G.M., *Death of a Witch*, Hutchinson, London-Melbourne-Sydney-Auckland-Johannesburg, 1983.

Cenkner, William, *A Tradition of Teachers: Sankara and the Jagadgurus today*, Motilal Banarsidass, Delhi, 1983.

Comba, Antonella, *La medicina indiana* (*Ayurveda*), Promolibri, Torino, 1990.

*Coomaraswamy, Ananda Kentish, "Swayamatrnna: Janua coeli," in *Zalmoxis*, II, Bucarest, 1939.

Coomaraswamy, A.K., *Yakṣas*, Washington, 1928-31.

*Coomaraswamy, A.K., "Angel and Titan: An Essay in Vedic Ontology," in *JAOS*, LV.

Covarrubias, Miguel, *Island of Bali*, 2nd edn., KPI, London, 1946.

Crooke, William, *The Popular Religion and Folklore of Northern India*, 2 vols., 4th edn., Munshiram Manoharlal, New Delhi, 1978.

Daniélou, Alain, *Le polythéisme Hindou*, Buchet-Chastel, Paris, 1960.

Das, Veena, *Structure and Cognition: Aspects of Hindu Caste and Ritual*, Delhi, 1977.

Dash, Vaidya Bhagwan, *Āyurveda for Mother & Child*, Delhi Diary Pbls., New Delhi, 1975.

Death and Afterlife, ed. by Stephen T. Davis, Macmillan Press Ltd., London, 1989.

Death and Eastern Thought, ed. by F.H. Holck, Abingdon Press, Nashville & New York, 1974.

Della Casa, Carlo e Pier Angelo Carozzi, *L'aldil a nella fede dei popoli*, Unicopoli, Milano, 1985.

*Demieville, Paul, "Sur la mémoire des existences antérieures," in *Bulletin de l'École Française d'Extrème Orient*, XXVII, 1926.

De Santillana, Giorgio e Herta von Dechend, *Il Mulino di Amleto, saggio sul Mito e sulla struttura del Tempo*, I Ital. ed. Adelphi (I ed. *Hamlet's Mill*, 1969), Milano, 1983.

*Dolcini, Donatella, "Il segno della vera conoscenza di *Gorakhnāth*," in *Annali di Ca' Foscari*, S.O., XIX, 3, 1980.

Drury, Naama, *The Sacrifical Ritual in the Śatapatha Brāhmaṇa*, Motilal Banarsidass, Delhi, 1981.

Dumézil, George, *Mariages indo-européens*, Payot, Paris, 1979.

*Dumézil, G., "Viṣṇu et les Marúts à travers la reforme zoroastrienne," in *Journal Asiatique*, CCXLI, 1953.

Dumont, P.E., *L'Aśvamedha, Description du sacrifice solennel du cheval dans le culte védique d'aprés les textes du Yajurveda blanc*, Paris, Paul Geuthner, Louvain, 1927.

E. & M.A., *Encyclopaedia of Supersititions*, ed. Ch. Hole, 1961.

*Edgerton, Franklin, "The Hour of Death: Its Importance for Man's Future Fate in Hindu and Western Religions," in *Annals of the Bhandarkar Oriental Research Institute*, VIII, 1926.

Eichinger Ferro-Luzzi, G., *The Self-milking Cow and the Bleeding Lingam*, Otto Harrassowitz, Wiesbaden, 1987.

Filippi, Gian Giuseppe, *Tantrismo e Arte*, Arch e, Milano, 1978.

*———, *Mort et Libération d'apr es Sha]mkarācārya*, Arch e, Milano, 1978.

*———, "Il culto del Meru a Bali," in *Annali di Ca'Foscari*, SO, XXIX, 3, 1990.

*———, "*Cakravartin:* Mythic and historical Simbols," in *Annali di Ca' Foscari*, SO, XXX, 3, 1991.

*———, "The Secret of the Embryo according to the *Garbha Upaniṣad*," in *Annali di Ca' Foscari*, S.O. XXXI, 3, 1992.

*———, "Sacrifical meaning of the Mahiṣamardinī," in *Annali di Ca' Foscari*, SO, XXXII, 3, 1993.

*———, "Alcune considerazioni sui *bhūta* come composti corporei," in *Atti del Settimo Convegno Nazionale di Studi Sanscriti*, Torino, 1996.

*———, "On some aspects of *Bhūta*s in the Birth-Death passage," in *Prakr̥ti, the Integral Vision*, vol. V, ed. by K. Vatsyayana, D.K. Printworld (P) Ltd., New Delhi, 1995.

Filliozat, Jean, *The Classical Doctrine of Indian Medicine*, 2nd. edn., Munshiram Mahoharlal Pbls., Delhi, 1964.

*Filliozat, J., "Temples et tombeaux de l'Inde et du Cambodge," in *Académie des Inscriptions & Belles-Letters*, Comptes rendus Jan.-Mar., 1979.

*———, "La vie historique et actuelle du Veda," in *Académie des Inscriptions & Belles-Letters*, Comptes rendus Jul.-Oct. 1980.

Filliozat, J., *Religion — Philosophy — Yoga*, 2nd edn., Motilal Banarsidass, Delhi, 1991.

Fonterose, Joseph, *Python*, University of California Press, Berkeley-Los Angeles-London, 1980.

Frawley, David, *Gods, Sages and Kings: Vedic Secrets of Ancient Civilization*, 2nd edn., Motilal Banarsidass, Delhi, 1993.

*Freed, S.A. & R.S. Freed, "Spirit Possession as Illness in a North Indian Village," in *Ethnology*, III, 1964.

Gaignebet, Claude, *Le carnaval: Essais de mythologie populaire*, ed. Payot, Paris, 1974.

van Ganepp, Arnold, *Les rites de passage*, Paris, 1909.

Ghosh, Ekendranath, *Studies on Rigvedic Deities*, 2nd edn., Cosmos Publs., New Delhi, 1983.

Ghosh, Shyam, *Hindu Concept of Life and Death*, Munshiram Manoharlal Pbls., New Delhi, 1989.

*Gnoli, Gherardo, "Le 'fravaŝi' e l'immortalit à," in *La mort, les morts dans les sociétés anciennes*, ed. by G. Gnoli et J.P. Vernant, Cambridge University Press, Cambridge, 1982.

*Gnoli, Raniero, "Merte e sopravvivenza nello Śivaismo kashmiro," in *Rivista degli Studi Orientali*, XLII, 1967.

Gonda, Jan, *Loka — World and Heaven in the Veda*, Noord-Hollandische Vitgevers Maatschappij, Amsterdam, 1966.

Gonda, J., *Eye and Gaze in the Veda*, Amsterdam, 1969.

Gonda, J., *Le Religioni dell'India*, 2 vols., 2nd edn., Jaca Book (1st edn., W. Kohlhammer, Stuttgart 1960), Milano, 1978.

Gopal, Ram, *India of Vedic Kalpasūtras*, 2nd edn., Motilal Banarsidass, Delhi, 1983.

Granet, Marcel, *La religion des Chinois*, P.U.F., Paris, 1951.

Griffith, Ralph T.H., *Hymns of the Ṛgveda*, 2 vols., 2nd edn., Munshiram Manoharlal Pbls. (1st edn., 1889), Delhi, 1987.

Griffith, R.T.H., *Hymns of the Sāmaveda*, 1st edn., Munshiram Manoharlal Pbls. (1st edn., 1895-96), New Delhi, 1936.

Guénon, René, *L'Erreur Spirite*, Riviere, Paris, 1921.

Guénon, R., *L'homme et son Devenir selon le Védûanta*, Boissard, Paris, 1925.

Guiart, Jean (ed.), *Les hommes et la mort: Rituals funéraires a travers le monde*, Musée National d'Histoire Naturelle, Paris, 1979.

Gualtieri, Antonio R., *The Vulture and the Bull. Religious Responses to Death*, University Press of America, Boston, 1984.

Guidieri, Remo, *La route des morts*, éd. du Seuil, Paris, 1980.

Gupta, Beni, *Magical beliefs and Superstitions*, Sundeep Prakashan, Delhi, 1979.

Gupta, S.P., *Disposal of the Dead and Physical Types in Ancient India*, Delhi, 1972.

*Halim, M.A., "Les practiques funéraires a Harappa," in *Les Cités Oubliées de l'Indus*, éd. Musée Guimet, Paris, 1988.

Harf-Lancner, L., *Morgana e Melusina*, 2nd edn., Einaudi (1st edn., Champion, Paris 1984), Torino, 1989.

Hazra, R.C., *Studies in the Puranic Records on Hindu Rites and Customs*, 2nd edn., Motilal Banarsidass, Delhi, 1975.

Hertz, Robert, *Sulla rappresentazione collettiva della morte*, 2nd edn., Savelli, Roma, 1978.

Hillenbrandt, Alfred, *Vedic Mythology*, 2 vols., 2nd edn., Motilal Banarsidass (1st edn., *Vedische Mythologie*, Breslau, 1891), Delhi, 1980.

*———, *Vedische Mythologie*, 2 vols., 2nd edn., Breslau, 1927.

*———, "Death and Disposal of the Dead (Hindu)," in *Encyclopaedia of Religion and Ethics*, IV.

Hoffman, F.J., *Rationality and Mind in Early Buddhism*, 2nd edn., Motilal Banarsidass (1st edn., 1987), Delhi, 1992.

Hopkins, E. Washburn, *Epic Mythology*, Verlag von Karl J. Trubner, Strassburg, 1915.

M. Hulin, *La face cachée du temps*, éd. Fayard, Paris, 1985.

Hutton, J.H., *Les Castes de l'Inde*, Payot, Paris 1949.

*Irwin, John, "The Stūpa and the Cosmic Axis: The Archaeological Evidence," in *South Asian Archaeology*, Naples, 1977.

Īśvarakṛṣṇa, *Le strofe del Sāṁkhya*, a cura di Corrado Pensa, ed. Boringhieri, Torino, 1960.

*Jacobi, H., "Death and Disposal of the Dead (Indian, non-Aryan)," in *ERE*, IV.

Jayadeva, *Gītagovinda*, a cura di G. Boccali, Adelphi ed., Milano, 1982.

Joshi, J.R., *Some Minor Divinities in Veidc Mythology and Ritual*, Deccan College Postg. & Res. Inst., Pune, 1977.

Joshi, Rasik Vihari, *Le ritual del la dévotion Kṛṣṇaite*, Institut Français d'Indologie, Pondichéry, 1959.

*Kaelber, Walter O., "Tapas, Birth, and Spiritual Rebirth in the Vedas," in *History of Religions*, XV, 1976.

Kaelber, W.O., *Tapta Mārga — Asceticism and Initiation in Vedic India*, State University of New York Press, New York, 1989.

Kakar, Sudhir, *Sciamani, mistici e dottori*, Pratiche Ed. (1st edn., *Shamans, Mystics and Doctors*, Knopf, New York, 1982), Parma, 1993.

Kapur, Sohaila, *Witchcraft in Western India,* Sangam Books, Bombay, 1983.

Keith, Arthur Berriedale, *The Religion and Philosophy of the Veda and Upanishad,* 2 vols., 3rd edn., Motilal Banarsidass (1st edn., 1925), Delhi, 1989.

———, *Rigveda Brāhmaṇas,* 2nd edn., Motilal Banarsidass (1st edn., 1920), Delhi, 1971.

———, *The Veda of the Black Yajus School Entitled Taittirīya Saṁhitā,* 1st edn., Motilal Banarsidass (1st edn., 1914), Delhi, 1967.

*Kinsley, David, "The Taming of Shrew (Kālī)," in *Studies of Religion,* I. 1972.

*Kinsley, D., "Freedom from Death in the Worship of Kālī," in *Numen,* XXII, III, 1975.

*Kinsley, D., "The Death that Conquers Death: Dying to the World in Medieval Hinduism," in *Religious Encounters with Death. Insights from the History and Anthropology of Religions,* ed. by E. Reinolds & E.H. Waugh, Pennsylvania State Un. Press, 1977.

Knipe, D.M., *In Image of Fire: The Vedic Experience of Heat,* Motilal Banarsidass, Delhi, 1975.

Kramrisch, Stella, *The Hindu Temple,* 2nd edn., Motilal Banarsidass (1st edn., Calcutta 1946), Delhi, 1976.

*Lazzeroni, Romano, "Il nettare e l'ambrosia: su alcune rappresentazioni indoeuropee della morte," in *Studi e Saggi Linguistici,* suppl. di *L'Italia dialettale,* vol. LI (N.S. XXVIII), 1988.

Law, B.C., *Heaven and Hell in Buddhist Perspective,* 2nd edn., Bhartiya Publ. House (1st edn., Calcutta 1924), Varanasi, 1973.

*Levin, Mary, "Mummification and Cremation in India" in *Man*, XXX, 1930.

*Long, Bruce, "Life Out of Death: A Structural Analysis of the Myth of the Churning of the Ocean of Milk," in *Hinduism: New Essays in the History of Religions*, ed. by Bardwell L. Smith, Leiden, 1975.

Lorenzen, David, N., *The Kāpālikas and Kālāmukhas*, Thomson Press, New Delhi, 1972.

The Laws of Manu, tr. by G. Bühler, 2nd edn., Motilal Banarsidass, Delhi, 1964.

Macdonell, A.A. and A.B. Keith, *Vedic Index of Names and Subjects*, 2 vols., 3rd edn., Motilal Banarsidass (1st edn., London 1912), Delhi, 1982.

Macdonell, A.A., *Vedic Mythology*, 2nd edn., Motilal Banarsidass (1st edn., Strassburg 1898), Delhi, 1974.

*Magnone, Paolo, "The Development of Tejas from the Vedas to the Purāṇas," in *VIII World Sanskrit Conference*, Wien 1990.

*———, "Vāmana. L'avatāra del Nano," in *Abstracta*, n. 48, 1990.

The Mahābhārata, ed. by J.A.B. van Buitenen, Un. of Chicago Press, Chicago, 1973.

*Malamoud, Charles, "Les morts sans visage," in *La mort, les morts dans les sociétées anciennes*, ed. by G. Gnoli et J.P. Vernant, Cambridge University Press, Cambridge, 1982.

*Mandle, P.B., "Symbolic Death and Spiritual Renaissance," in *Annual Folklore Fellows of India Conference*, Mysore, 1978.

Mani, Vettam, *Purāṇic Encyclopaedia*, Motilal Banarsidass, Delhi, 1975.

Mārkaṇḍeya Purāṇa, ed. by F.E. Pargiter, Asiatic Society Publ., Calcutta, 1904.

Martino, Ernesto de, *Morte e pianto rituale*, 3rd edn., it. U.S. Boringhieri, Torino, 1983.

Mastromattei, Romano, *La Terra Reale. D ei, spiriti, uomini del Nepal*, V. Levi ed., Roma, 1988.

The Matsya Purāṇam, ed. by Jamna Das Akhtar, Oriental Publs., Delhi, 1972.

Meyer, Johann Jakob, *Sexual Life in Ancient India*, 2nd edn., Motilal Banarsidass, Delhi, 1989.

Meulenbeld, G.J., *The Madhavanidana and its Chief Commentary*, E.J. Brill, Leiden, 1974.

The Minor Law-books, tr. by J. Jolly, 2nd edn., Motilal Banarsidass, Delhi, 1965.

Mishra, Laxman Prasad, *Mistici Indiani Medievali*, U.T.E.T., Tornino, 1971.

Mishra, Ratan Lal, *The Mortuary Monuments in Ancient and Medieval India*, B.R. Publ. Corp., Delhi, 1991.

Misra, Sadal, *Un Mito Indiano: Nasiketa ovvero la storia del nato dal naso*, a cura di D. Dolcini, Pagus ed., Treviso, 1988.

Mookerjee, A., *Kundalini: The Arousal of the inner Energy*, Thames and Hudson, London, 1982.

Mukherji, Kalinath, *Popular Hindu Astronomy*, Sree Saraswaty Press Ltd., Calcutta, 1905.

Mukhopadhyaya, G., *Studies in the Upaniṣad*, Calcutta Sanskrit College Research Series, n. IX, Sanskrit College, Calcutta, 1960.

Muir, J., *Original Sanskrit Texts*, Oriental Publs., 5 parts, vol. IV (2nd edn., The Sacred Books of the Aryan Series, Calcutta), Delhi, 1972.

Myths of Creation, ed. by S.S. Dange, G.M. Rajarshi, University of Bombay, Bombay, 1987.

Norbu, Namkhai, *Dzog-Chen, lo stato di Autoperfezione*, Ubaldini, Roma, 1986.

*O'Flaherty, Wendy Doniger, "The Submarine Mare in the Mythology of Śiva," in *JRAS*, n. 1, 1971.

———, *Asceticism and Eroticism in the Mythology of Śiva*, London New York Toronto, 1973.

*———, *The Origins of Evil in Hindu Mythology*, Motilal Banarsidass, Delhi, 1976.

*———, *Women, Androgynes and other Mythical Beasts*, Un. of Chicago Press, Chicago, 1980.

*———, "Karma and Rebirth in the Vedas and Purāṇas," in *Karma and Rebirth in Classical Indian Traditions*, W.D. O'Flaherty ed., 2nd edn., Motilal Banarsidass, Delhi, 1983.

*Oguibenine, B.L., "Sur le Symbolisme du type chamanique dans le Ṛgveda," in *Ucenyje Zapiski Tartuskogo Gosuclarstennoge*, vol. CCI, Tartu, 1968.

Oldenberg, H., *Die Religion des Veda*, Berlin, 1923.

———, (tr.) *The Grihya-Sūtras*, 2nd edn., Motilal Banarsidass, Delhi, 1964.

*Orlandi, Chatia, "Le vie di comunicazione nell'India antica," in *Pubblicazioni del Dipartimento di Linguistica*, Un. di Pisa, Pisa, 1990.

Pañcasiddhantika, ed. by Thibaut, 2nd edn., Motilal Banarsidass, Delhi, 1968.

Pandey, Raj Nali, *Hindu Saṁskāras*, 2nd edn., Motilal Banarsidass (1st edn., 1948), Delhi, 1969.

Pargiter, F.E., *Ancient Indian Traditions*, Cosmo Publs., New Delhi, 1979.

Parpola, Asko, *The Sky-Garment*, ed. Finnish Oriental Society, Helsinki, 1985.

*Parry, Jonathan, "Death and Cosmogony in Kashi," in *Contribution to Indian Sociology*, XV, 1 & 2, 1981.

*Parry, J.P., "Sacrificial Death and the Necrophagous Ascetics," ed. by M. Bloch and J. Parry, In *Death and Regeneration of Life*, Cambridge University Press, Cambridge, 1982.

*———, "The Aghori Ascetics of Benares," in *Indian Religion*, ed. by R. Burghart & A. Cantlie, Curzon Press Ltd., London, 1985.

*———, "Death and Digestion: The Symbolism of Food and Eating in North Indian Mortuary Rites," in *Man*, XX, 1985.

*———, "The End of the Body," in *Fragments to a History of the Human Body*, ed. by M. Femer Urzone Inc., New York, 1989.

———, *Death in Banaras*, Cambridge Un. Press, Cambridge, 1994.

Pascal, Carlo, *L'Oltretomba dei Pagani*, 2nd edn., Alkaest, Genova, 1981.

Pathak, V.S., *Smarta Religious Tradition*, Kusumanjali Prakashan, Meerut, 1987.

Prasad, Swami Muni Narayana, *Karma and Reincarnation*, D.K. Printworld (P) Ltd., New Delhi, 1994.

Prasad, Rajendra, *Karma Causation and Retributive Morality*, Munshiram Manoharlal, New Delhi, 1989.

Pratimālakṣana of the Viṣṇudharmottara, ed. by D.C. Bhattacharya, Harman Publishing House, New Delhi, 1991.

Der Pretakalpa des Garuḍa-Purāṇa, von Emil Abegg, Vereinigung wissenschaftlicher Verleger, Berlin unt Leipzig, 1921.

Preta Mañjari, ed. by Mannilal Abhimanyu, Bombay Pustak Bhandar, Varanasi, 2032 V.S.

Pedraza, Filar, *La Bella, enigma y pesadilla (Esfinge, Medusa, Pantera . . . .)*, Almudin, Valencia, 1983.

Piggott, Stewart, *Prehistoric India to 1000 BC*, Penguin Books Ltd., Harmondsworth, 1964.

*Przyluski, Jean, "La Princess a l'odeur de poisson et la Nāgī dans les traditions de l'Asie Orientale," in *Études Asiatiques*, 1925.

Ranke, Kurt, *Indogermanische Totenverebrung*, F.F. Communication no. 140, Helsinki, 1951.

*Rau, Shanta Rama, "Banaras, India's City of Light," in *National Geographic* 169, 1986.

Raveri, Massimo, *Il Corpo e il Paradiso — Esperienze Ascetiche in Asia Orientale*, Marsilio ed., Venezia, 1992.

Renfrew, Colin, *Archaeology and Language: The Puzzle of Indo-European Origins*, Jonathan Cape Ltd., London, 1987.

Rénou, Louis et Jéan Filliozat, *L'Inde classique*, Payot, Paris, 1947.

*Rigopoulos, Antonio, "The Genealogy of Dattatreya," in *Annali di Ca' Foscari*, SO, XXXII, 3, 1993.

Ṛgveda Saṁhitā, ed. by H.H. Wilson, VI vols., Nag Publs., Delhi, 1977.

*Roth, R., "On the Morality of the Veda," *JAOS*, III.

Roux, Jean-Paul, *La mort chez les peuples altaṅques anciens et médiévaux*, Adrien-Maisonneuve, Paris, 1963.

Saletore, R.N., *Indian Witchcraft*, Abhinav Publ., Delhi, 1981.

Salute Malattia Morte: India ed Europa a confronto, a cura di G.G. Filippi, I.p.L., Milano, 1991.

Śaṅkarācārya, *Vedānta-Sūtras*, tr. by G. Thibaut, 2nd edn., Motilal Banarsidass, Delhi, 1962.

*Sannino Pellegrini, Agata, "Āpas in Īśā Upaniṣad," in *Annali dell'Istituto Orientale di Napoli*, vol. 34, N.S. XXIV, 1974.

*———, "Osservazioni sul significato del termine *tapas* nel *ṛgveda*," in *Atti del terzo Convegno Nazionale di Studi Sanscriti*, Torino, 1986.

*———, "Sulla connessione del desiderio con l'azione nel pensiero indiano: presupposti e sviluppi," in *Lo sguardo da lontano* (Atti del IX Congresso internazionale di studi antropologici, 1988.

*———, "Sull'interpretazione del termine *sat*," in *Miscellanea in onore del Prof. Giusto Monaco*, 1988.

Saraswati, Baidyanath, *Kashi, Myth and Reality of a Classical Cultural Tradition*, Indian Institute of Advanced Study, Simla, 1975.

———, *Brahmanic Ritual Traditions: In the Crucible of Time*, Indian Inst. of Adv. Study, Simla, 1977.

*———, "Untouchability in Hindu Society: An interpretation," in *Journal of Sociel Research*, vol. XXX, n. I & II, 1987.

Sarup, Lakshman, *The Nighantu and the Nirukta*, 2nd edn., Motilal Banarsidass, Delhi, 1967.

The Śatapatha-Brāhmaṇa, ed. by J. Eggeling, 5 vols., 2nd edn., Motilal Banarsidass, Delhi, 1963.

Sati: Historical and Phenomenological Essays, ed. by Arvind Sharma, Motilal Banarsidass, Delhi, 1988.

*Scheffler, H., "Ancestor Worship in Anthropology," in *L'Homme*, VI, 1966.

Sharma, Dakshina Rajan, *Origin and Development of the Rituals of*

1. Vārāṇasī, Maṇikarṇikā Ghāṭ, one among the five *śmaśāna* of Kāśī.

2. Vārāṇasī, the preparation of the *piṇḍa*s.

3. Vārāṇasī, the eldest son shaves the hairs before his father's cremation.

4. Vārāṇasī, the corpse is lifted from the stretcher and put on the pyre.

5. Vārāṇasī, the *piṇḍa*s are offered to the ground *Gnius*.

6. Gayā, collective *piṇḍadāna* on the shore of Phalgu.

7. Vārāṇasī, the eternal fire of the Ḍoms.

8. Vārāṇasī, Ṭiku, an *aghorī*, shows its *kapāla*.

Ancestor Worship in India, Bookland Private Ltd., Calcutta, Allahabad, Patna, 1963.

*Sharma, Om Prakash, "The Law of Karma and Rebirth," in *Bulletin of the Mithila Institute*, III, n. 2, 1967.

*———, "The Ashram of Baba Kina Ram Ji Aghori in Varanasi: A Study of its Historical and Spiritual Aspects," in *Assembly of the World's Religions*, New Jersey, 1985.

*Shastri, D.N., "Cult and Images of the Pitṛs," in *JISOA*, VII, Calcutta.

*Shulman, David, "The Serpent and the Sacrifice: An Anthill Myth from Tiruvarur," in *History of Religions*, XVIII, 2.

Singh, Balbir, *Karma and Reincarnation*, Arnold Publs., New Delhi, 1989.

Singh, Karan, *Essays on Hinduism*, Ratna Sagar, New Delhi, 1987.

Singh, Purushottam, *Burial Practices in Ancient India*, Prithivi Prakashan, Varanasi, 1970.

Sinha, Surajit & Saraswati, Baidyanath, *Ascetics of Kashi*, N.K. Bose Memorial Foundation, Varanasi, 1978.

Staal, F., *Agni*, 2 vols., Asian Umanitas Press, Berkeley, 1983.

Stevenson, Sinclair, *The Rites of the Twice Born*, 2nd edn., Munshiram Manoharlal (1st edn., London, 1920), New Delhi, 1971.

*Stietencron, Heinrich von, "Bhairava," in *Zeitschrift der Deutschen Morgenländischen Gesellschaft*, suppl. I, Teil 3 F. Steiner Verlag GMBH, Wiesbaden, 1969.

*———, "Die Göttin Durgā Mahiṣāsuramardinī," in *Visible Religion, Annual for Religious Iconography*, vol. II, E.J. Brill, Leiden, 1983.

Sudhi, Padma, *Aesthetic Theories of India*, 3 vols., Intellectual Publ. House, New Delhi s.d.

Suśruta Saṁhitā, 3, vols. ed. by K.L. Bhishagratna, Chowkhamba Sans. S., Varanasi, 1991.

Svoboda, Robert, E., *Aghora, at the Left Hand of God*, Brotherhood of Life, Inc., Albuquerque, 1986.

———, *Aghora II: Kundalini*, Rupa & Co. (1st edn., Albuquerque 1993), New Delhi, 1994.

———, *Ayurveda*, Annenia (1st edn., Albuquerque 1992), Milano, 1994.

Tawney, C.H., *The Kathā Sarit Sāgara, or Ocean of the Streams of Story*, 2nd edn., Munshiram Manoharlal, New Delhi, 1992.

Thomas, Louis-Vincent, *La Mort, Que sais-je?*, P.U.F., Paris, 1988.

Thomas, P., *Secrets of Sorcery, Spells and Pleasure Cults of India*, D.B. Taraporevala sons & Co. (P.) Ltd., Bombay, 1983.

Tibon, Gutierre, *La triade prenatal* (*Cordón, placenta, amnios*), FCE, Mexico, 1981.

Tiwari, Jagdish Narain, *Disposal of the Dead in the Mahābhārata*, Kishor Vidhya Niketan, Varanasi, 1979.

*Toffin, Gérard, "Les rites funéraires des hautes castes hindouistes néwar (Népal)," in *Les Hommes et la Mort; rituels funériraes a travers le monde*, Le Sycomore, Objects at Mondes, Paris, 1979.

Tomat, Marco, *Devayāna e Pitṛyāna: i due cammini postumi e le loro figurazioni celesti* (Tesi di Laurea inedita) Venezia, 1986.

Tripathi, Bansi Dhar, *Sadhus of India*, Bombay, Popular Prakashan, Bombay, 1978.

Tull, Herman W., *The Vedic Origins of Karma — Cosmos as Man in Ancient Indian Myth and Ritual*, 2nd edn., Sri Satguru Publs., Delhi, 1990.

*Ucko, P.J., "Ethnography and Archaeological Interpretation of Funerary Remains," in *World Archaeology*, vol. 1, n. 2, ott, 1969.

Varāhamihira's *Bṛhat Saṁhitā*, ed. by M. Ramakrishna Bhat, 2 vols., Motilal Banarsidass, Delhi, 1981.

*Varenne, Jean, "Le Judgement des morts dans l'Inde," In *Le Judgement des morts*, ed. du Seuil, Paris, 1961.

The Vedānta-Sūtras of Bādarāyaṇa with the Commentary of Baladeva, tr. by R.B.S.Ch. Vasu, 2nd edn., Munshiram Manoharlal, New Delhi, 1979.

Vedānta-Sūtras with the Commentary by Śaṅkarācārya, ed. by George Thibaut, 2 vols., 1st Indian edn., Motilal Banarsidass (1st edn., 1904), Delhi, 1962.

Vermeule, Emily, *Aspects of Death in Early Greek Art and Poetry*, Un. of California Press, Berkeley, 1979.

Vesci, Uma Marina, *Death & Sacrifice in the Vedas*, 1st edn., Motilal Banarsidass, Delhi, 1985.

Vidyarnava, Rai B.S. Chandra, *The Daily Practice of the Hindus, Containing the Morning and Midday Duties*, Munshiram Manoharlal, New Delhi, 1979.

Vidyarthi, L.P., B.N. Saraswati & Makhan Jha, *The Sacred Complex of Kashi*, Concept Publishing Company, Delhi, 1979.

Viennot, Odette, *Le culte de l'arbre dans l'Inde ancienne*, P.U.F., Paris, 1954.

*Visuvalingam, Elizabeth-Chalier, "Bhairava: Kotwāl of Vārānasī," in *Varanasi Through the Ages*, Bharatiya Itihas Sankalan Samiti, Varanasi, 1986.

Wilson, H.H., *The Vishnu Purāṇa*, Punthi Pustak, 4th edn. (1st edn., 1840), Calcutta, 1972.

Wolff, Carlo Felice, *I Monti Pallidi*, 14th edn., Cappelli, Bologna, 1982.

Index

Acit beings, 28

Action,
- facility of, 27
- principle of, 8

Activation, principle of, 86

Aeschylus, 34n

Agni, 179

Agnisvātta ritual, 204

Ahaṁkāra, 17, 20, 22, 26, 28, 32, 36, 38-39, 53, 57-58, 66, 70, 76, 86, 88, 94-95, 125

Ahitāgni, 113, 171

Air (*vāyu*), 18, 61

Ākāśa (ether), 18, 60, 180

Altekar, A.S., 71n-72n

Anahitāgni, 171

Ānandamaya-kośa, 85, 93

Ancestor, transformation of deceased into, 149-69

Annamaya-kośa, 86-87

Annaprāśana saṁskāra, 67-68

Antaḥkaraṇa (internal organ), 89

Antarikṣa (atmospheric environment), 115

Antyeṣṭi, 129

Anustaraṇī, 113-14, 134, 140

Apāna (inspiration), 61, 89

Apparent death, 184

Apratiṣṭha hell, 200

Apsarās, 83, 90, 201-02

Arce, Javier, 172n

Arora, U.P., 25n, 42n, 104n

Ārṣa vivāha, 79

Āraṇyakas, 116

Arūpaka (super individual) being, 94

Aśauca (impurity), 127, 132, 147, 163

Asipatravana hell, 200

Āśrama (stage of life), 106, 179

Asura marriage, 79

Asuras, 35

Atharvaveda, 76

Atiśīta hell, 200

Ātman, 59, 85*n*, 185-86, 188
- *pādas* of, 87, 93, 97-98

Ātura saṁnyāsa, 109

Auboyer, Jeannine, 145n

Aurobindo, Sri, 135n

Avalon, Arthur, 38n
Āveśya, 184
Āyuṣya-cirajīvan (longevity), 102

Bājarās, 111
Barhiṣada ritual, 204
Basu, S.P., 100n
Bhagavad-Gītā, 31-32, 98, 117
Bhattacharyya, N.N., 70n
Bhūtas, 43-44, 46, 87, 117, 128, 180-82, 189-92
Birth (*jāti*), 5, 14
  from conception to, 37-61
  moment of, 22-23, 25
Bodily life, end of, 99-117
Body,
  offering of, 131-47
  potencies of, 9
Bose, D.N., 154n
Brahma, 33
Brahma vivāha, 79
Brahmacārin, 74-76, 178
Brahmāṇḍa, 17, 91
Brahma-Sūtras, 186
Buddhi, 38, 76, 85-86, 89, 94
Buddhism, 2, 84
Buitenen, J.A.B. van, 113

Cakṣus (sight), 21, 27
Caland, W., 142n, 150n
Carozzi, P.A., 11n, 139n-40n, 144n, 147n
Carstairs, G.M., 116n, 159n, 168n
Cenkner, William, 74n-75n
Chāndogya Upaniṣad, 175, 185-86
Chāyāpatha, 207
Cit beings, 28
Citragupta, 201-02
Citta, 88
Cognition, principle of, 86
Comba, Antonella, 44n, 49n-50n, 58n, 61n
Consciousness, 38, 59, 92, 95, 153-54
Coomaraswamy, A.K., 7n, 24n, 35n, 77n, 83n, 93
Cosmic cycle (*kalpa*), 37
Covarrubias, M., 133n, 135n
Cremation,
  funerals without, 171-82
  rites, 171
Cūḍākaraṇa saṁskāra, 68-70
Cūḍākaraṇa rite, 126

Daiva vivāha, 79
Dakṣiṇa 204
Dange, S.S., 17n
Daniélou, Alain, 12n
Dante, 207
Das, Veena, 42n
Dash, Vaidya Bhagwan, 58n
De Vries, Jan, 172n
Death (*mr̥tyu*),
  agony and its rites, 119-29
  conception of, 3, 5
  fantasy, 124

last sacrifice, 131-47
moment of, 22
myths, 124
phenomenon of, 1-2
process of, 119-29
science of, 125
Westerners approach to, 1-2
Deceased, transformation of ancestor into, 149-69
Dechand, Herta von, 32n, 207n
Deep sleep state, 123-24, 184
Della Casa, C., 11n 122n, 139n-40n, 144n, 147n, 199n
Demons, 91, 115
Deva loka, 95, 202-03
Devapatha, 207
Devas, 204
Dhanañjaya vāyu, 143
Disincarnate human beings, 93
Dolcini, D., 25n
Dream state (*svapna sthāna*), 89, 116, 123
Dumezil, Georges, 79n, 172n
Dumont, P.E., 196n

Earth (*pṛthivī*), 19, 32, 60
Ekādaśa, 161
Ether (*ākāśa*), 18, 60
Excretion (*pāyu*), 22, 60

Femer, M., 52n
Ferro-Luzzi, G.Eichinger, 174n
Filippi, G.G., 7n, 33n, 43n, 45n, 48n, 51n, 61n, 87n, 104n, 115n, 120n, 124n, 176n-77n, 181n-82n, 189n, 195n
Filliozat J., 33n, 55n-56n
Fire (*tejas*), 19
Five sheaths, doctrine of, 85
Fonterose, J., 13n
Frawley, David, 40n
Freed, R.S., 158n
Freed, S.A., 158n
Funerals,
customs, 173
rites, 131
without cremation, 171-82

Gaṇa, 90
Gāndharva vivāha, 79
Gāndharvas, 81-84, 87, 90, 152, 201-02
Garbhādhāna rite, 39-40, 78, 81, 161
Gārhapatya, 131
Garuḍa Purāṇa, 147, 200, 203, 205
Germinparous (*udbhija*) beings, 25
Glaser, B.G., 109n
Gnoli, G., 111n
Godāna (gift of cow), 112-13
Gonda, J., 11n, 42n, 72n, 77n, 137n-38n, 140n, 155n, 161n, 171n-72n, 174n, 179n, 196n, 202n
Gotra, 194

Granet, Marcel, 115n
Grasping (*pāṇi*), 22
Greek Roman mythology, 34
Gṛhastha stage of life, 75
Gṛhasthin, 85, 101, 179
Gṛhasthya, 106
Ghṛta, 131
Gṛhya-Sūtras, 39, 41, 114, 131
Griffith, R.T.H., 55n
Grimm, J., 96n
Grimm, W., 96n
Guhya, 90
Guṇas (attributes), 31-36, 203
Gupta, Beni, 96n
Gupta, S.P., 173n

Haldar, Hiralal, 154n
Halim, M.A., 145n
Harding, Esther, 83n
Harf-Lancner, L., 96n
Hearing (*śrotra*), 21, 60
Hells (*narakas*), 199-200
Henry, V., 56n
Hillerbrandt, A., 5n, 83n, 116n, 138n, 150n, 171n, 174n
Hinduism, 2, 12
Hiraṇyagarbha, 91-93
Hoffman, F.J., 84n
Human being (*manuṣya*)
  capacities, 9
  other beings and, 5-16
  potencies, 9
  structure of, 79-98
Human body,
  saptāṅga (seven parts) of, 88
Human life,
  from birth to marriage, 63-78
  from conception to, 37-61
Hutton, J.H., 149n

Immature death, 104
Individual beings,
  categories of, 24-25
  development of, 29-30
  five elements, 18-20
  indriyas, 20-22, 28
  nature of, 17-30
  potentialities, 35-36
Individual consciousness, 21
Individuation, principle of, 14, 28, 32, 86
Indriyas, 20, 38, 51-52, 57, 59-60, 66, 89, 97, 120, 122
  jnanendriyas, 20-21, 61
  karmendriyas, 20-22, 61
Indus valley civilization, 2
Irwin, John, 178n

Jacobi, H., 158n
Jāgaṛta sthāna, 53-54, 63, 89
Jainism, 2
Jātakarma (*Janman*), 59-61
Jati (birth), 5, 14
Jha, Makhan, 109n
Jinn, 91
Jīva, 43-44, 49-50, 59, 84, 93, 133, 167, 184, 195-97

Jīvan (life), 5, 14

Jīvātman, 125, 187-88

Jñānendriyas, 20-21, 61, 64

Joshi, J.R., 83n-84n

Jyeṣṭhā constellation, 206

Kāla (becoming), 8

Kali yuga, 103

Kalpa (cosmic cycle), 37, 44

Kalpa (duration of world), 99-100

Kāma (pleasure), 64, 121

Kāma eṣaṇā (desire or attraction), 81

Kapāla kriyā, 143

Karman doctrine, 55, 95

Karmendriyas, 20-22, 61, 68

Karṇavedha saṁskāra, 70

Keith, A.B., 40n, 74n, 86n, 172n

Keśānta saṁskāra, 77

Kinnara, 90

Knipe, D.M., 19N

Kramrisch, Stella, 18n

La Bella, 80n

Laḍḍū, 111

Laukikāgni, 172

Lazzeroni, R., 5n-6n, 101

Life (*jīvan*), 5, 14
  stages in, 75-76

Liṅga śarīra, 153

Living soul,
  new conditions of, 183-94
  Purāṇic myths about, 185-87

Loṣṭaciti, 177

Macabre cases, 188

Macdonell, A.A., 40n, 74n, 86n

Macrocosm (*adhyadaiva*), 87, 91

Mahāpralaya, 204

Mahāraurava hell, 199

Maitrāyaṇī Upaniṣad, 33-34

Malamoud, Charles, 111n, 129n, 143n, 166n, 176n, 181n

Malina ṣoḍaśī, 160-61, 198

Manas (mind), 20-21, 27-28, 52-54, 66, 88, 107, 122-23, 185

Māṇḍūkya Upaniṣad, 39, 93-94, 97-98

Manomaya-kośa, 86, 93

Manu, 79

Manuṣya, see, Human being (*manuṣya*)

Manuṣya loka (world of humans), 11-13, 15, 34, 36-37, 88, 96

Manvantaras (geological cycles), 99

Marriage (*vivāhu*), 78
  types of, 79-80

Marut, 90

Medhājanana, 59

Metempsychosis, 194

Meulenbeld, G.J., 63

Meyer, Jacob, 46n

Microcosm (*ādhyātma*), 87, 91

Minerals, life of, 26

Misra, Sadal, 25n

Mittal, K. Rai, 184n

Mortals, 13

Mṛtyu, see, Death (*mṛtyu*)

Muir, J., 100n

Mukherji, Kalinath, 206n-07n

Mukhopadhyaya, G., 14n

Mūla constellation, 206

Nāgas, 178

Nāmakaraṇa saṁskāra, 64

Nāndī śrāddha, 60

Nature, evolutionary components of, 31-36

Nietzsche, F., 100n

Niṣkarmaṇa saṁskāra, 65

Niṣkṛntana hell, 200

Norbu, Namkhai, 181

O'Flaherty, Wendy Doniger, 18n, 41n, 65n, 81n

Odour (*ghrāṇa*), 21

Ogre-Yama, 185

Old age, signs of, 119-20

Oldenberg, H., 56n, 137n

Olympic gods, 34

Oṁ, 131, 146

Other beings, 5-16, 23
  human beings and, 5-16

Oviparous (*aṇḍaja*) beings, 25

Paddhatis, 73

Paiśāca marriage, 79

Pañca śraddhā, 161

Pañcabhūta (five elements), 18-20

Pañca-kośavāda, 85, 93

Pañcakṛta (five elements), 91

Pandey, R.B., 39n, 57n, 59n-60n, 64n, 67n, 71n, 74n, 80n, 108n, 111n, 114n-15n, 117n, 131n, 133n-34n, 136n, 139n, 141n, 144n, 146n, 149n, 152n-53n, 156n, 172n, 176n-79n

Parpola, Asko, 134n

Parry, Jonathan, 52n-53n, 102n-03n, 109n, 123n, 158n, 179n

Pascal, Carlo, 172n

Pātāla (inferior worlds), 11-12, 32, 203

Pāyu (excretion), 22, 60, 87

Pedraza, Pilar, 80n

Piggott, Stewart, 133n

Piṇḍa dāna, 168

Piṇḍaja śarīra, 198, 202

Piṇḍas, concept of, 37-39, 41-43, 45-51, 84-85, 87, 91-93, 135, 156, 160-65, 167, 188, 195-96, 198

Piśācas, 115, 128, 158-59, 168-69, 179, 182, 190-91, 195, 198

Pitṛ, 93, 139, 163-68*r*, 195, 198, 200-04, 206

Pitṛ loka, 163, 166, 198-99, 201, 204-05

Pitṛ medha, 177

Pitṛgaṇa, 207
Poltergeist, 169
Pradakṣiṇā, 132
Prajāpati, 66
Prājāpatya vivāha, 79
Prajñā, 94-95, 153, 159
Prakṛti, attributes (*guṇas*) of, 31-36
Prāṇamaya-kośa, 86-87, 93
Prāṇas, 89, 123-24, 143, 152, 175, 185-86, 188
Prasavya, 139
Premature death, 104-05, 180
Preta, 160-65, 167-68, 190, 196, 198, 201-03, 205, 207
Preta Mañjarī, 147
Pṛthivī, 203
Przyluski, Jean, 25n
Puṁsavana rite, 55-57, 132
Pūraka, 135, 156, 161
Purification, doctrine of, 8
Pūrṇāvatāra principle, 98

Rajas guṇa, 31-33
Rākṣasa, 90
Rākṣasa marriage, 79
Ram Gopal, 56n, 76n
Rāmāyaṇa, 117
Rasana (sense of smell), 67
Raurava hell, 199
Renou, L., 33n
Ṛgveda, 78, 141-43, 173
Ritual *karman*, 175
Roth, R., 128

Śabala, 206
Sacred diagrams (*alpona-vrata maṇḍala*), 190
Sādhus, 106, 175
Śālagrāma, 180
Saletore, R.N., 57n
Samādhi, 177-78
Samāna (digestion/assimilation), 89
Samāvartana saṁskāra, 77
Saṁdhyā rite, 163
Śaṁkarācārya, 193
Saṁnyāsa, 106, 109
Saṁnyāsin, 75, 177
Saṁnyāsins burial, 175-79
Sampradāna rituals, 106, 194
Saṁskāras, 9, 36, 55, 57-59, 101, 129, 179
Saṁyojana śrāddha, 164-65
Santillana, Giorgio de, 32n, 207n
Sapiṇḍas, 127, 149-50, 156, 194
Sapiṇḍīkaraṇa, 164-65, 203
Saraswati, B.N., 109n
Śarīra, 59
Śatapatha Brāhmaṇa, 174
Satī, 142
Sattva guṇa, 31-33
Sensation, faculties of, 27
Separation, principle of, 14

Sharma, Arvind, 142n
Shastri, D.N., 150, 163
Sight (*cakṣus*), 21, 27
Sīmantonnayana rite, 57-58
Singh, P., 115n, 134n, 145n
Singh, Vibhuti Narain, 160n
Śiva, 33
Śmaśāna, 138, 156, 177
Smell (*gandha*), 18
Somadhara, 207
Sound (*śabda*), 18
Speech (*vāk*), 22
Śrāddha, 41-42, 86, 111, 147, 155, 158, 160-61, 167, 179, 195, 198, 200-02
Śrauta tradition, 131
Sṛṣti (manifestation), 34
Staal, F., 81n
Stevenson, Sinclair, 105n, 107n, 127n
Sthūla śarīra (gross body), 133, 153
Strauss, A.L., 109n
Stūpa, 177-78
Sudhi, Padma, 19n
Supreme Divinity, 185-86
Sūryapatha, 207
Suṣupta sthāna (dreamless sleep/ dream state), 53-54, 89-90, 92-95, 116, 123-24
Svarga (superior worlds), 11-12, 32, 202-03, 206
Svoboda, R.E., 44n, 52n, 84n, 102n
Śyāma, 206

Taddei, M., 178n
Taijasa, 89, 91, 93, 97
Taittirīya Saṁhitā, 42
Taittirīya Upaniṣad, 85, 87, 93
Tamas guṇa, 31-34
Tāmasika state, 95
Tanmātras, 44, 86, 92, 124-25
Taptakumbha hell, 200
Taste (*rasa*), 18
Tejas (vital heat), 124-25, 152, 158, 185
Thibaut, 206n
Thieme, 7n
Tibon, Gutierre, 60n
Tiwari, J.N., 145n, 171n, 174n, 178n
Tomat, Marco, 206n
Touch (*sparśa/tvac*), 18, 21
Transmigration, doctrine of, 8
Triguṇa, description of, 31-36
Trikāla (three-fold time), 34
Trilokas, 32
Trimūrti, 33

Ucko, P.J., 172n
Udakakarman water, offering of, 149
Udāna (expiration), 89
Upadhyaya, Pandit Vaikunthnath, 183

Upanayana saṁskāra, 71-73, 76
Upoṣaṇa (cremation), 113
Uragrahas (nightmares), 115

Vāc (speech), 185
Vaiśvānara, 87-89, 91, 98
Vaitaraṇī, 111-12, 114, 162, 197, 202
Vānaprastha stage, of life, 75
Vāṇaprasthins, 75, 106, 175, 179
Varāhamihira, 23n
Varenne, J., 5n
Vatsyayan, K., 45n
Vāyīya śarīra, 198
Vāyu (air), 18, 61, 89, 152
Vedārambha saṁskāra, 73-76
Vermeule, Emily, 172n
Vernant, J.P., 111n
Vesci, Uma Marina, 89
Vetālas (vampires), 115, 128
Vico, G.B., 100n
Vidyārambha saṁskāra, 71
Vidyarthi, L.P., 109n
Viennot, Odette, 49, 116n
Vijñānamaya, 93
Vijñānamaya-kośa, 86
Violent death, 180
Virāj, 91
Virāṭ being, 87
Vision (*rūpa*), 18
Viṣṇu, 33
Viśva being, 87
Viśvavirāṭa svarūpa, 98
Viviparous (*yonija*) beings, 24-25
Vṛsotsarga rite, 162
Vyāna (liquids), 89
Vyāsa-Smṛti, 73

Waking state, 123
Walking (*pāda*), 22, 27
Water (*āpas*), 19
Water burial, 175
Wilson, H.H., 12n
Wolff, Carlo Felice, 96n

Yajñopavīta, 149
Yajurveda, 161
Yakṣas, 49-50, 90-91, 100, 128, 178
Yama, 107, 110, 112, 115, 156, 163, 167, 183-85
Yama Gāthā, 146
Yama kingdom, journey to, 195-207
Yama loka, 198, 204
Yama-Sūkta, 138
Yamadūtas, 183-84, 195-96, 202, 205
Yātanā śarīra, 154
Yātudhāna, 128
Yugas, 100, 128